A Paddler's Guide to the Delaware River

A Paddler's Guide to the Delaware River

Kayaking, Canoeing, Rafting, Tubing

THIRD EDITION

Gary Letcher

Rivergate Books

An imprint of Rutgers University Press

NEW BRUNSWICK, NEW JERSEY, AND LONDON

Library of Congress Cataloging-in-Publication Data
Letcher, Gary, 1952–
A paddler's guide to the Delaware river : kayaking, canoeing, rafting, tubing /
Gary Letcher. — 3rd ed.
    p.   cm.
Rev. ed. of: Canoeing the Delaware River, c 1997.
Includes bibliographical references and index.
ISBN 978-0-8135-5161-6 (pbk. : alk. paper)
    1. Canoes and canoeing—Delaware River (N.Y.-Del. and N.J.)—
Guidebooks. 2. Delaware River (N.Y.-Del. and N.J.)—Guidebooks.
3. Canoes and canoeing—Pennsylvania—Guidebooks. 4. Pennsylvania—
Guidebooks.   I. Letcher, Gary, 1952– Canoeing the Delaware River.
II. Title.
GV776.D34L47 2012
797.1'2209749—dc22   2011010863

A British Cataloging-in-Publication record for this book is available from the
British Library.

Visit our Web site: http://rutgerspress.rutgers.edu

Manufactured in the United States of America

Contents

Foreword

Maya K. van Rossum, the Delaware Riverkeeper

The Delaware River is the last major free-flowing river east of the Mississippi, its entire length unimpeded by man-made structures. Its free-flowing nature is one of the most touted and respected aspects of the Delaware.

Such freedom for the river brings freedom for those who use it. Paddlers (whether in canoes, kayaks, or other small craft) are able to put in at any point along its length and enjoy as much of the river as they choose. No dams or blockades disrupt the joy one feels when floating along its cool, clean waters or taking on the challenges of its rapids.

The joy of paddling this free-flowing river is magnified by the knowledge, and reality, that it includes the longest stretch (197 miles) of river anywhere in the United States that is so clean, and for that reason it is given special legal protections from degradation. Stops to swim, fish, and watch birds and wildlife can be fully and safely enjoyed.

The rich ecological history of the region is still evidenced today as one paddles down the Delaware's length. Unique cliff formations overlooking the river, rapids, islands, and a remarkably well-established green riparian buffer provide important habitat, beautiful views, and an incredible, glorious distraction from the intense activity of our day-to-day lives.

The Delaware River is unique in both its present-day beauty and its past history. We all know the Delaware as the site of many of the historic events that formed and shaped our nation. The remnants of this history are often evident, for those in the know, as one paddles down the river's waters.

A Paddler's Guide to the Delaware River makes all of this nature, beauty, and history accessible. It tells you about those special spots, where to put in and where to take out, the secret stories and locations to look for, where to find the quiet waters and the fast-flowing rapids. My copy of the earlier edition is dog-eared, water-spattered, and worn with repeated use—and yet I never head out onto the river without it.

As beautiful as the Delaware is—and as important as it is to the more than 15 million people who drink its waters, as well as to the many millions who eat its fish, work its shores, and benefit from its very existence—the river is fragile and at our mercy. So we must take it upon ourselves to preserve the freedom and health of the river from those who would seek to profit from it and thereby do it harm. Only by protecting the river are we able to protect ourselves. *A Paddler's Guide to the Delaware River* ensures that we will have the access, appreciation, and firsthand experiences with this beautiful treasure that give us the knowledge and commitment to ensure its health today and for all future generations.

Author's Notes on This Revised Edition

Such a difference a decade makes! This work was first published in 1985, with a revised edition in 1997. Since then, there have been so many changes in recreation on the Delaware that prior versions are obsolete and a complete overhaul is necessary.

The most obvious change is right on the front cover. The previous edition was titled *Canoeing the Delaware River*. Today, although plenty of people still favor a canoe, other kinds of boats are popular too. Modern plastic kayaks outsell canoes six-to-one nationwide. Some Delaware River outfitters report that rafts account for half their business, the rest divided among canoes, kayaks, and tubes. On some sections of the river inflatable tubes outnumber all other boats combined. The diversification of watercraft allows more people to enjoy the river, opening opportunities for those who might not feel skilled enough to handle a canoe or kayak. And so this revised edition and its title embrace the practitioners of all paddle sports on the Delaware.

Other changes involve the management of recreation on the river. Almost all of the river from Hancock, New York, to Trenton, New Jersey, has now been designated as part of the National Wild and Scenic River system, subject to special protections. The Delaware River Greenway Partnership, in cooperation with the National Park Service and the Delaware River Basin Commission, has sponsored establishment of the Delaware River Water Trail to foster opportunities for recreation on the river. A Tidal Delaware River Water Trail has also been designated by the Pennsylvania Environmental Council, in recognition of the increasing recreational use of the Delaware River estuary. Every year scores of paddlers join the Delaware River Sojourn on a voyage to promote awareness of the river, and the Lenape Nation sponsors a quadrennial "Rivers Rising" marathon all the way to Cape May.

New resources have allowed us to delve more deeply into some of the natural, historical, and cultural aspects of the Delaware. Many new books about people and places in the Delaware valley have been published. In 2006 the Delaware River Basin Commission updated its set of comprehensive recreation maps, which may serve as a companion to this book. In addition, some old works have been digitally indexed and made newly available. For example, surveys, diaries, and articles that long languished in university and government libraries have been brought to light, allowing us to attach a historical name to virtually every rift, eddy, and island along the course of the river.

As may be expected, there have also been many changes in features and services along the Delaware. Some access areas have closed, while new ones have opened. There are some new river outfitters, and some old ones have gone away. Severe flooding in 2004, 2005, and 2006 wreaked havoc along the river, especially within the Delaware Water Gap National Recreation Area: most of the primitive campsites on river islands were obliterated and have not been reopened; the Kittatinny Point Visitor Center was destroyed, but is now rebuilt.

Readers familiar with prior editions will also find structural and stylistic changes. Discussion of "features" is much more to the point, serving only to whet the reader's appetite, whereas the "river guide" includes more detail about people and events. The maps have been completely redrawn, and most of the photographs are new.

Paddling on the beautiful Delaware River—in a canoe, kayak, raft, or tube—is as much fun as ever. The scenery is magnificent, the water cool and clean, the rapids exciting, and the company convivial. I'll see you there, in my aqua-blue canoe and with a big smile.

Acknowledgments

The following people were helpful in preparing this revised edition, and I truly appreciate their effort and contributions:

Carol Collier, executive director, Delaware River Basin Commission (DRBC); Katherine O'Hara, communications assistant, DRBC; Karen Reavy, GIS specialist, DRBC; Eric Sildorff, aquatic biologist, DRBC; Dorothy Moon, cultural resource program manager, Upper Delaware Scenic and Recreational River (UDSRR); Loren Goering, chief of interpretation, UDSRR; Superintendent John Donahue, Delaware Water Gap National Recreation Area; Rick and Lisa Lander, Landers River Trips; Laura Ramie, Upper Delaware Council; Jessica Anderson, Pennsylvania Environmental Council; Maya K. van Rossum, the Delaware Riverkeeper; Elizabeth Jacques, Fort Delaware Museum visitor services; Greg Crance, the "Famous River Hot Dog Man"; Stu Gillard, National Canoe Safety Patrol; Micheal Brodhead, historian, U.S. Army Corps of Engineers; Joe Donnelly, Deputy Executive Director of Communications, Delaware River Joint Toll Bridge Commission; Paul Weamer, author of *Fly Fishing the Upper Delaware*; John Motzer, archivist, Delaware & Hudson Canal Society; Sara Berg, Delaware Canal State Park; Thomas Stoneback, executive director, National Canal Museum; Damon Tvaryanas, Trenton Historical Society; Andy Smith, David Soete, and Courtenay Kling, photographers; Penn Glendinning for patient expertise in preparing updated maps and illustrations; and Gretchen Oberfranc, hard-working copyeditor.

Last but not least, my wife, Shirley Letcher, and my mother, Sherrie Letcher, helped update riverside features, and my friends Courtenay Kling and David Griffin joined me in once again canoeing the beautiful Delaware.

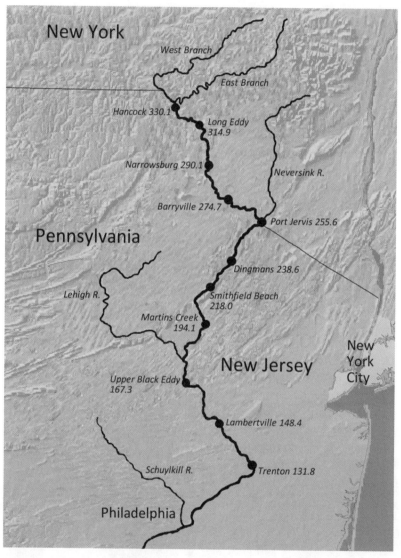

The Delaware River, showing sections and mileage as described in this book.

The Plan of This Book

This book is a guide to those who wish to experience the Delaware River in a canoe, kayak, raft, tube, or other unpowered craft. It describes the river from the confluence of the East and West Branches at Hancock, New York, to tidewater at Trenton, New Jersey, 200 miles downstream. No attempt is made to cover tributaries to the Delaware or the tidal Delaware estuary from Trenton to Cape May.

The overview discusses matters of interest to recreational river users. The chapters, or "river guides," provide a mile-by-mile account of rapids, villages, access points, natural features, and historic sites along the way. Each chapter describes one of the ten sections that can be paddled in one day (about 20 miles), beginning and ending at a public access point. Features in the chapters briefly introduce the reader to local people, events, natural history, and communities.

The river guides and maps in this book report mileage from the mouth of the Delaware River at Cape May, and are matched to recreational maps published by the Delaware River Basin Commission (DRBC). The DRBC maps may be used as a companion to this guidebook.

A Paddler's Guide to the Delaware River

Overview

The Pleasantest River in the World

On any summer day many thousands of canoeists, kayakers, and other boaters can be found plunging through the rapids or lazing along the eddies of the Delaware River. Some segments of the river offer a near-wilderness experience, yet are within easy reach of the cities and suburbs of the Mid-Atlantic states. The water is cool and clean, the scenery magnificent, and the rapids challenging. By all accounts, the Delaware is among the most popular rivers for recreational boating in the United States.

Canoeing on the Delaware River

In 1609 explorer Henry Hudson guided his ship *Half-Moon* into what he called the South River. He was so taken by its beauty that he declared it "one of the finest, best, and pleasantest in the world." And as Hudson looked over what would later be known as the Delaware, he saw the very activity we see today: people in canoes!

The Lenape Indians—also called "Delaware"—used canoes for transportation, fishing, commerce, and, we have to believe, just plain fun on the river. Canoes were as essential to their culture as automobiles are to ours. The Lenape made canoes out of hollowed poplar logs. Look at the tall, straight poplar trees that line the riverbanks and rise from the river islands, and imagine carving and burning out the pulp to make a fine canoe. Indeed, the Lenape word for poplar was *mux-hul-hem-en-shi*, "the tree from which canoes are made." An authentic Lenape canoe, discovered in the mud in the 1860s, is on display at the New Jersey State Museum in Trenton. It measures fourteen feet long, one and one-half feet wide, and one foot deep—about the same as the solo canoes we paddle today.

Canoeing waned as the Lenape were pushed from the valley and as the Delaware became a river of industry. Timber rafts from the north, Durham boats

Lenape Indians in dugout canoes met explorer Henry Hudson as he sailed into Delaware Bay and, pictured here, the Hudson River in 1609. Hudson called the Delaware "one of the finest, best, and pleasantest rivers in the world." (Image from *Harpers Encyclopedia of United States History*, 1912)

for iron and grain, canal barges full of coal, and scow ferries for personal and commercial crossings were the dominant craft on the Delaware for 200 years. Except for a handful of homemade boats for fishing or local transport, there were few canoes on the river.

Then, just before the turn of the twentieth century, those agile craft that hadn't been seen since the days of the Lenape began to return. The river, once again mostly free of industrial use, became popular for recreation. Fast trains from New York and Philadelphia brought well-heeled tourists to grand hotels at the Delaware Water Gap and other scenic locations along the river. The resorts promoted canoeing for their guests and kept a flotilla of boats available. The canoes of the day were made of wooden ribs covered with a lacquered canvas shell. They were surprisingly tough, easy to repair, and handled well enough in the water. In 1892, J. Wallace Hoff and his friends paddled all the way from Hancock, New York, to Trenton, then wrote of the adventure in *Two Hundred Miles on the Delaware River* (1893), one of the earliest accounts of recreational canoeing on the river.

The end of World War II brought a revolution to canoeing everywhere. The Grumman Aircraft company, which made the Hellcat Fighter and other warplanes, was left with warehouses of aluminum. A company executive, portaging his heavy canoe in New York's Adirondack Mountains, had a brainstorm: could a canoe be made of lightweight aluminum? Over the next few decades, Grumman and other manufacturers mass-produced aluminum canoes for the recreational market. These versatile, sturdy, and relatively cheap boats made the rental and livery business possible, bringing the opportunity to canoe the Delaware to the masses. Countless people, including your author, had their very first canoeing experience in a rented aluminum canoe on the Delaware River.

Today, the Delaware is more accessible than ever before. In 2008 the Delaware River Greenway Partnership and other sponsors worked cooperatively to develop the Delaware River Water Trail, stretching from Hancock to Trenton. Most of that length has been designated by the U.S. Congress as a National Scenic and Recreational River, subject to special protections. The National Park Service, state authorities, and volunteers from the National Canoe Safety Patrol keep an eye on river safety. River flow is controlled by dams on the major tributaries to assure sufficient water levels for recreational use. Thanks to modern pollution regulations and controls, the water is much cleaner than it once was. There are more public access points, more places to stay overnight in hotels or camps, and more ways to enjoy the river. A score of outfitters offer canoes, kayaks, rubber rafts, and tubes for rent, and most also provide shuttle service. It is easier than ever to experience the thrill of the rapids, the serenity of the eddies, and the magnificence of the valley of what is still one of the "finest, best, and pleasantest rivers in the world."

The Delaware River Watershed

The Delaware is the longest free-flowing river east of the Mississippi. The river begins at the confluence of the East and West Branches at Hancock, New York, and from there flows 330 miles to the Atlantic Ocean at Cape May. Tides surge as far upstream as Trenton, 133 miles from the mouth. The Delaware ranks seventeenth in length among the nation's rivers. Its watershed covers 13,000 square miles, about one percent of the continental United States.

The slope of the river averages 4.5 feet per mile over its course, generally dropping less steeply (and consequently with fewer rapids) the farther downstream one travels. At the gaging station in Milford, Pennsylvania, the river flows at an average 2.5 million gallons per minute; at Trenton, 5 million gallons per minute.

There are five major tributaries to the Delaware above Trenton: the East and West Branches, and the Lackawaxen, Neversink, and Lehigh Rivers. Each is controlled by dams that impound water in great reservoirs for the use of down-stream cities. In addition, several secondary tributaries—Mongaup, Bushkill, Brodhead, Paulinskill, Pequest, Musconetcong, Tohickon—and scores of minor streams contribute their waters to the Delaware.

Canoes, Kayaks, Rafts, and Tubes

Canoes have been the craft of choice for recreation on the Delaware since the days of the Lenape. A canoe is highly maneuverable, can make speedy progress, offers a steady platform for fishing, can be loaded with gear for an extended trip, requires only basic skill, is easy to carry on land, and is relatively inexpensive.

A canoe is an open-hulled boat typically intended for two or three occupants who use single-bladed paddles. The canoeists kneel on the bottom or sit on elevated seats. There are many kinds of special-purpose canoes: short solo boats, sleek racing hulls, banana-shaped ("rockered") white-water canoes, keeled excursion craft, even "war canoes" that can carry five or more people. A high-performance white-water canoe might be great in the rapids, but hard to keep straight in the slow sections of the Delaware or in a wind; on the other hand, a keeled excursion boat good on the slow pools would likely founder in the rapids. For general use on the Delaware, a plastic or composite flat-bottom canoe—the kind offered by most river outfitters—is preferred.

Kayaks are the Eskimo cousins of canoes. Kayaks are closed-hull boats built for one or two people, propelled by double-bladed paddles. The Eskimos constructed their kayaks of seal skin stretched over a wood frame; the modern versions are typically made of tough plastic or composite. Kayakers sit in a seat fixed to the hull, stretching their legs straight out, with their upper bodies often surrounded by a waterproof skirt. Kayaks come in several flavors, from long-hulled sea kayaks to compact white-water sport boats.

In recent years kayaks have become more popular on the Delaware, and most outfitters offer them for rent. A white-water sport kayak is great fun when playing in the rapids at Skinners Falls, Mongaup Rift, and Wells Falls. However, white-water kayaks require considerable skill, can carry only minimal gear, and are not well suited to the long, slow sections of the Delaware. On the other hand, sea kayaks, built for one or two occupants, are favored on the estuary below Trenton, but may not fare well in the upriver rapids. Recreational kayaks fall between these extremes and are good for most sections of the Delaware River. Some outfitters also offer sit-on-top kayaks, or "duckies," fun but not practical for long-distance travel on the river.

Rafts and tubes. Many river outfitters have added inflatable rafts and tubes

Canoeists and tubers approach Skinners Falls. Kayaks, canoes, rafts, and tubes are available for rent and shuttle at many river outfitters. (Photo by the author)

to their offerings. A raft can hold from four to eight people. They are ideal for beginners to go through rapids or when the water is running high. To be sure, six people sharing a raft is a more social experience than a solo run in a kayak. Rafts, however, are not well suited for an extended trip; they are cumbersome to maneuver, difficult to carry on land, and cannot make fast progress on the river.

Inflatable tubes have become extremely popular on some sections of the river. On a hot day a tube can be great fun for a short float with friends. A tube is easy to carry, unsinkable, and requires no skill. Indeed, some outfitters would rather rent tubes than canoes: more tubes can be carried on a truck, and they are cheaper to replace if lost or damaged. On the downside, tubes move only as fast as the current, cannot be controlled much, and cannot carry anything. Even when the air is warm, the water will feel cold after dragging your posterior in it for hours. And tubes are not a good choice in the more severe rapids.

Powered boats are not considered in this book. Use of powerboats, including "personal watercraft" (Jet Skis), is limited on the river upstream from the Delaware Water Gap, with exceptions only for low-powered fishing motors in some places. Powerboats are popular in some of the slow-moving segments of the river downstream from the Water Gap, and paddlers must take care to avoid collisions or swamping in their wake.

Canoe Safety

The river is more powerful than you. Respect it.

Most people who paddle the Delaware are novices, and a trip on the Delaware is their very first river experience. Many beginners do not want to admit —or are not aware—that they don't know how to handle their craft in all situations. They do foolish things and take unnecessary chances. Novices should take a look at expert paddlers. Experts *always* wear PFDs in white water, scout their route before going through, load their craft properly, and are prepared for emergencies. Most experts have learned the hard way. They have been swept downstream by the overpowering flow of rapids, wrestled swamped canoes off slippery rocks, and shivered with hypothermia in cold water. Many have had to rescue, or attempt to rescue, novices who did not know better. The expert paddler's pride has been washed away by close calls. She has learned to respect the river and is careful. Beginners must be even more careful.

Fifty-eight people have drowned on the upper Delaware since 1980, and many more on the sections below. *None* of the victims was wearing a properly fitted PFD, or life jacket. In other words, *no one* who wore a PFD drowned. The law requires that every watercraft—including canoes, kayaks, rafts, and tubes —have a PFD on board for each occupant. Where the river is under National Park Service jurisdiction (Hancock to the Delaware Water Gap), every child 12 years old and younger must wear a PFD at all times. All persons paddling the upper Delaware must wear a PFD when the river stage is above six feet on the Barryville gage. Call the Park Service river hotline at 845-252-7100 for a report of river conditions.

Know what do to when your craft capsizes or swamps—a very common event in the rapids. First, don't panic. There is no rapids on the Delaware so long that it cannot be ridden out by a capsized canoeist in a PFD. Hang onto the boat, it will continue to float. Get to the upstream side of it; when filled with water, a canoe becomes a one-ton mass to pin you against a rock. Point your feet downstream to kick away from obstructions. Do not try to stand in a rapids—your feet can get wedged in a crevice, with the current forcing you face-first into the water.

Authorities advise that all paddlers take the following safety precautions:

- Wear your PFD, especially in fast, high, or cold water. Do not tie your PFD into the boat. On the upper Delaware it is *required* that all persons *wear* a PFD when the river stage is above six feet on the Barryville gage, and that children 12 years old and under wear a PFD at all times when on the river.

It is common for paddlers to go for an unexpected swim. Wear your PFD! (Photo by Courtenay Kling)

- Wear river shoes—water shoes or leaky sneakers—for traction and to protect your feet.
- Swim only at designated areas and never alone. Do not try to swim across the river. Wear a PFD while swimming. Many drownings have happened when boaters stopped to swim.
- Hypothermia can kill you. Be prepared for cold water and cold air. Wear clothing suited to the weather and carry a change of warm clothes in a dry bag.
- Guard against sunburn. The sun comes at you not only from above; it is also reflected off the water. Wear a hat and protective clothing. Slather on the sunblock.
- Beware the nasty plants (poison ivy and sumac, stinging nettles) and insects (wasps, ticks, mosquitoes, and so on) on the riverbanks and islands.
- Bring enough drinking water. Never drink untreated river or stream water.
- Bring a first aid kit. Also a whistle, flashlight, throw rope, and pocket knife.
- Let someone know your starting and end points, and when you will return. Don't go alone. Get off the river before dark.
- Do not drink alcohol on the river. Alcohol and boating are a killer combination.
- Wear your PFD. Have we mentioned that?

It is easy to get your boat onto and off the river the entire length from Hancock to Trenton. There are more than 40 public access points and dozens of private launch areas operated by river outfitters. The rules vary, however, depending on the agency or outfitter that runs the access, and paddlers might be subject to a fine for violating the rules. Never trespass on private land to launch or land your boat.

Private Outfitters

Many people experience the Delaware via a river outfitter. The outfitter will provide the craft of your choice—canoe, kayak, raft, or tube—along with paddles, personal flotation devices (PFDs), and basic instruction, and then launch you from one of its river bases. At the end of the trip, you'll land at another of that outfitter's bases, and you will be shuttled back to the beginning.

There are dozens of public access points along the Delaware, this one at Lackawaxen, Pennsylvania. All boats launched or landed at sites maintained by the Pennsylvania Fish and Boat Commission must bear a valid registration or launch permit. (Photo by Courtenay Kling)

Some outfitters have campgrounds along the way for overnight trips. Most will allow you to launch and will shuttle your private boat for a fee, but will not allow you to launch or land a competitor's boat.

Public Access

The federal, state, and local governments, as well as some private landowners, offer public access to the river. The rules vary.

Delaware Water Gap National Recreation Area. Most of the access areas between Port Jervis and the Delaware Water Gap are operated by the National Park Service. There is a fee to enter some of these areas (as of this writing, $7/vehicle weekdays, $10/vehicle weekends), but no special registration or permit is required to launch canoes or kayaks. Private outfitters are authorized to use some of these areas under a permit from the National Park Service.

New Jersey and New York. Most public access points in New York are operated by the state Department of Environmental Conservation, and in New Jersey by the State Park Service or Division of Fish and Wildlife. No fee or permit is required to launch or land unpowered boats at most of these points. Be aware of parking restrictions.

Pennsylvania. Some access points are owned and maintained by municipal or county park agencies, and some by private businesses (power companies, for example). Generally, no fee or permit is required to launch or land an unpowered boat from these points.

Other access points in Pennsylvania are maintained by the Pennsylvania Fish and Boat Commission (PFBC). *A boat registration or launch permit is required to launch or land any boat, including canoes and kayaks, from PFBC access points.* Boat registration (as of this writing, $18 for two years) and launch permits ($10 for one year) must be obtained from PFBC. The best option for canoeists and kayakers may be instant online purchase of a boat launch permit.

River Stages and Floods

The difficulty and duration of a river trip varies with the river level, or "stage." When the river is low, plan on extra time to reach your destination. When the river is high, the trip will be faster but may be more difficult and dangerous. And don't even think about going out when the river is flooding.

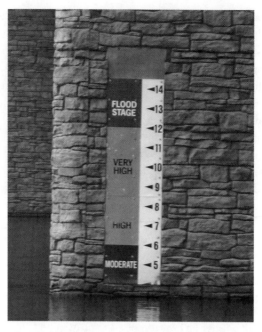

The "stage" of the river is shown on this staff gage at the Barryville-Shohola Bridge. River stage above "moderate" makes for dangerous boating. Call the National Park Service River Hotline, 845-252-7100, for a report of river conditions on the upper Delaware. (Photo by the author)

The stage of the river is *not* the same as its depth. *Stage* is the elevation of the river surface above a fixed point, whereas the *depth* of the river varies dramatically with drop-offs, holes, shallows, and reefs. River stage is monitored by the U.S. Geological Survey, which maintains gages at many points along the Delaware. Boaters will often see the squat little sheds that house the gages perched on the riverbank. In addition, a "staff gage" (essentially, a big ruler) may be affixed to or painted on bridge piers or other structures, an easy reference to river level.

Predictions of river stage on the Delaware are issued by the Middle Atlantic River Forecast Center, a unit of the National Weather Service. Its interactive website gives a graphic representation of river stage and forecasts; a green indicator on the River Forecast Center's map shows that the river is not flooding at a particular station along the river. Note, however, that the river may be too high for recreational boating even if not up to flood stage.

The National Park Service uses the river stage at Barryville, New York, as its reference for boating on the upper Delaware. Call the river information hotline (845-252-7100) for a recorded report of river stage and other conditions. River stage of "average"—2½ to 4 feet on the Barryville gage—is considered the best level for safe boating. A complete table of river stages is listed in the appendix.

The flow of the Delaware changes with the seasons, weather, and releases from dams on the river's tributaries. The river typically runs high with snowmelt and April showers, then ebbs with the coming of summer. Less rain, increased evaporation, and reservoir draw-down often combine to produce extremely low flows by August. The Delaware swells somewhat in the autumn, then freezes over by January. However, a dry spell can drop the river level as early as May, and summer storms can bring floods in August (the greatest of all recorded floods on parts of the Delaware occurred in August 1955).

Periodically the Delaware is subject to severe flooding, resulting in destruction of property and loss of life. The "Bridges Fresh" of 1841 destroyed almost all of the bridges that spanned the river at that time. Again, in October 1903 the Delaware rose to destructive heights, forever remembered as the "Pumpkin Flood" for the hundreds of pumpkins that littered the riverbanks. In August 1955 Hurricanes Connie and Diane combined to raise the Delaware to a record height, causing scores of deaths and many millions of dollars of damage. Recent years have seen a spate of severe flooding along the Delaware, including March 1996 (ice dams, snowmelt, heavy rain), September 2004 (remnant of Tropical Storm Ivan), April 2005 (ice dams, snowmelt, heavy rain), and June 2006 (a stalled cold front with heavy rain produced the greatest flood of record on parts of the upper Delaware).

Running the Rapids

For many people, the rapids are the best parts of the Delaware. The very names —Skinners Falls, Foul Rift, and Mongaup Rift—quicken the pulse of whitewater paddlers. Dozens of lesser rapids challenge the abilities of novices, bringing them back to the river for more.

Some of the most exciting rapids are found between Callicoon and Port Jervis on the upper Delaware. Here the pitch of the river is steepest, tumbling over shale ledges or through boulder fields to keep the best paddlers at the top of their game. Farther downstream, long, slow stretches are punctuated by sudden and often tricky plunges that can catch even accomplished paddlers off guard. Wells Falls, at Lambertville, is the most severe of all, the only rapids on the Delaware rated above Class II.

It's a wild ride through the rapids, here at Mongaup Rift. There are dozens of rapids on the Delaware rated up to Class II+. (Photo by Courtenay Kling)

The difficulty of rapids is graded on the International Scale of River Difficulty, from Class I (easy) to Class VI (virtually impossible).[1] A rapids designated Class II on a river in Switzerland would be roughly as difficult as a Class II rapids on the Delaware. These designations are used on the Delaware River Basin Commission's recreational maps and in this book:

Class I: Moving water with a few riffles and small waves. Few or no obstructions.
Class II: Easy rapids with waves up to three feet and wide, clear channels that are obvious without scouting. Some maneuvering required.
Class III: Rapids with high, irregular waves capable of swamping an open canoe. Narrow passages that often require complex maneuvering. May require scouting from shore.

There are no rapids on the Delaware ordinarily greater than Class III. Under normal conditions, only Wells Falls is rated Class II+. The complete scale is found in the appendix.

The descriptions of rapids in this book are based on average flow typical of late spring and early summer. Higher or lower flow might dramatically alter the characteristics of rapids, and this contingency is noted to the extent possible. During the high, cold flows of April and May most Delaware rapids should be regarded as one class higher than listed. When flooding occurs, the river is too dangerous to paddle regardless of the time of year.

Timber Rafting

In the nineteenth century, rafting on the Delaware meant huge log rafts floated by the thousands every spring from the uppermost reaches of the river down to Easton, Trenton, and Philadelphia, their very structures made of timber for market. The practice began in 1764, when Cochecton pioneer Daniel Skinner built a raft of logs to carry his farm goods downriver to Philadelphia. Skinner was astonished when the merchants there gave him a higher price for the timber of his raft than for the grain and pork it carried. The rush was on. Farming became merely a sideline in the upper Delaware valley: real prosperity depended on the annual timber sale. A timberman might harvest up to a hundred acres of woodland in the fall and winter, sledding and sluicing the timber to piles near the river's edge. In early spring the raftsman bound the logs together with saplings, ropes, and iron spikes to built his raft. As soon as the ice went out, the raft, piled high with lumber, produce, or charcoal, was sent careening downriver to market.

A typical raft was 120 feet long, 25 feet wide, and drew 2 feet of water. The captain supervised four or six oarsmen—often family—on the trip. The raft was steered with huge oars balanced at its ends. As the raft approached an island, rift, or bend in the river, the captain directed the oarsmen by shouting "Pennsyvany!" or "Jersey!"

Timber rafting was the backbone of the Delaware valley economy for more than a hundred years. This raft floats downriver near Pond Eddy, New York. The raftsmen gave names to many eddies, rifts, and other places along the river. (From a postcard c. 1910, collection of the author)

A trip down the Delaware by raft was a dangerous adventure. The rafts were sent during the spring freshets, as the swift current and clearance over rocks made the trip much faster. A dam at Lackawaxen and many bridges with narrow passages between their piers provided treacherous obstacles. But Foul Rift, a rapids below Belvidere, was feared the most. Many a raft was "stove-up" as it smashed into the rocks of the mile-long rapids. The raftsmen who made it through were assured of a dowsing as their raft plunged over the final ledges.

Timber rafting was no quaint backwoods enterprise, but the backbone of the Delaware valley economy for more than a hundred years. Thousands of rafts came down every year, bringing timber for shipbuilding and construction of homes in the cities downstream. The rafts were made first of pine, then, as this resource was depleted, hemlock. There was no sense of conservation, as the timbermen cut as much as they could, as fast as they could. The good trees were gone by the 1870s, and although the industry limped along for a few years, it was essentially dead by the turn of the twentieth century. The last raft, built of inferior second-growth timber, floated alone to Easton in 1917.

The timber industry wreaked environmental havoc and literally changed the face of the Delaware. Deforestation of the hills upriver made flooding below much more frequent and severe. Lush islands were eroded down to the barren gravel bars we see today. Valuable farms on the flats became scrubby wasteland. Sediment filled the basins and clogged the channel. The devastation caused by the timber industry was lamented even in the late 1800s, yet the money the industry brought could not be forsaken. Today the forests have mostly grown back, although not with the magnificent pines and hemlocks that once stood in the upper Delaware valley.

Rafting was a tough job, and these were tough men. "Great, fierce looking fellows they were, shaggy bearded, long haired, bronzed by exposure to heat and cold and weather."[2] Some became legendary: Daniel Skinner, the first and foremost of the raftsmen, was known far and wide as "Lord High Admiral of the Delaware"; Robert "Boney" Quillen was a famed raconteur and clown prince; Deacon Mitchell raced from Hancock to Trenton in only two days.

Eddies a day's journey apart became popular stopping places, with shops, hotels, and taverns serving the hundreds of raftsmen. Hancock, at the confluence of the East and West Branches, and Tammany Flats, near Callicoon, were jammed with rafters getting underway. At Big Eddy (Narrowsburg), the rafts were so densely packed that a person could cross the river by hopping from one to the next. Dingmans Ferry was the next big way station, then Sandts Eddy just above Easton. Upper Black Eddy was most popular of all, its tavern a favorite carousing spot.

After delivering their rafts and cargo to market at Easton, Trenton, Bristol, or Philadelphia, the raftsmen had a long walk home. With their satchels full of profit, it was a walk they didn't mind.

Rifts, Eddies, and Kills—Place Names on the Delaware

The Indians called our river *Lenape-wihittuck*—the "river of the Lenape." Explorer Henry Hudson called it simply the South River (what he called the North River would later be named for him, the Hudson). Early Swedish settlers downriver knew it as "New Sweden Stream," while Dutchmen upstream called it Viskill, "the great fish river." Some English pioneers called it the Charles, after their king. But the name that stuck is derived from Thomas West, Baron de la Warr, a governor of colonial Jamestown, Virginia. Ironically, West never saw the river, bay, state, or Indian nation that were to bear his title.

There are hundreds of named places along the Delaware: cities and villages, islands, mountains, and tributary streams. Since the late 1800s, place-names have been fixed by the U.S. Geological Survey; once a name is put on a topographic map, that's pretty much it forever. Before then, however, place-names were more ephemeral. The town we know as Port Jervis was earlier called Miniskink, Mahacamac, and Deer Park. The names of geographic features, such as islands, were even more variable, often changing with sale of the property to a new owner.

Today, many "official" names in the Delaware valley are retained from the Lenape: Minisink Island, or Musconetcong River. Others have colonial Dutch origin: Weygadt, or Bush Kill (*kill* is Dutch for stream). Some are named for people who lived nearby or owned the land, such as Dingmans Ferry. In addition to "officially" named places, many locations have only traditional, local, or colloquial names. Many of these were bestowed by old-time timber raftsmen, who had a name for virtually every feature—even particular rocks—they encountered on their way down the river.

This book often refers to *rifts* and *eddies*. To old-time timber rafters, a rift was what we would today call a rapids. Bigger rapids were sometimes called *falls* (Skinners Falls, Wells Falls, and so on), especially downriver from Easton. The raftsmen paid close attention to the rifts, as failure to navigate them could lead to disaster. Some of their descriptions survive as official place names to this day (Foul Rift, Sawmill Rift), while many others can be found in historical accounts.

To modern kayakers, an eddy is the short counter-flow or dead spot downstream from a boulder or other obstruction. To the timber raftsmen, eddies were the slow stretches between rifts. The raftsmen would tie up at the eddies, where little villages grew to provide lodging and taverns. As with rifts, many of the eddies were given names, often that of the local innkeeper. Long Eddy, Pond Eddy, and Upper Black Eddy are among such communities.

The appellations used by timber raftsmen colorfully guided progress down the river. The Cellar Hole was a trap to be avoided; if water covered Calculation Rock, a raft could safely pass Jersey (to the left) of an island below. Bacon and Egg Island, Safe and Easy Eddy, Van Camps Nose, Sunfish Ripple, Loving Shore, and Woodpecker Lane, names now all but forgotten, identified places important to getting timber down to market.

More recently, anglers have been unofficially naming places along the river. Early twentieth-century author and outdoorsman Zane Grey spoke of fishing the Beer Mug, a frothy hole with lurking trout. Bard Parker Pool, Second Heaven, Cable Eddy, and House on Stilts guide the way to modern anglers.

Features along the river are as important to modern canoeists and kayakers as they were to early settlers and timber raftsmen. In addition to official names, this book uses historical and colloquial names to the extent they could be found.

Controversies, Confrontations, and Compromises

From the earliest days, people have squabbled over use and control of the Delaware River. Navigation, pollution, consumption, dams, bridges, recreation, and use of adjacent lands have vexed river users for more than 200 years.

Even before the United States came into existence, the colonies of New Jersey and Pennsylvania argued over navigation and fishing on the Delaware. "Inconveniences and mischiefs have arisen," to quote the Delaware River Compact, enacted in 1771 to solve some of the problems. The compact—which remains in effect to this day—declares that the Delaware River, from Tri-State Rock to the state of Delaware, is a "common highway," free for the use of the citizens of the bordering states. From this compact comes, for example, the rule that an angler licensed by either New Jersey or Pennsylvania may fish the Delaware anywhere between the respective riverbanks.

In the 1820s, the interests of timber rafters collided—literally—with operators of the Delaware & Hudson Canal at Lackawaxen. Heavy rafts careening downstream often struck barges at the canal crossing or hung up on the company's dam; fistfights and lawsuits ensued. Not until John Roebling constructed his famous suspension bridge to carry the canal over the river was the dispute resolved. Similar stand-offs played out wherever timber rafters met with ferries, bridges, and dams, but nowhere as dramatically as at Lackawaxen.

Controversy over use of the Delaware has raged for centuries. This 1980s placard protests diversion of river water at Point Pleasant, Pennsylvania. (Photo by the author)

Disputes over use of the Delaware have even reached the U.S. Supreme Court. In 1931, and again in 1954, the Court was called upon to apportion Delaware River water among the four states bounded by the river. In the first decision Justice Oliver Wendell Holmes famously declared, "A river is more than an amenity, it is a treasure."[3] The Delaware River Basin Commission, which supervises consumptive and other uses of the river, was born of these disputes and employs a River Master to monitor and control river flow.

There has been no controversy over use of the Delaware greater than the proposed construction of a huge dam at Tocks Island, just upstream from the Water Gap. The dam was designed to hold back floodwaters like those suffered during Hurricanes Connie and Diane in 1955. It would have created a lake 37 miles long, inundating the valley all the way to Port Jervis. Opponents formed the Save the Delaware Coalition and the Lenni Lenape League to fight the Army Corps of Engineers and construction interests, and there were more than a few ugly confrontations. Congress ultimately de-authorized the Tocks Island Dam in 1993. The lands that were to be flooded are now the Delaware Water Gap National Recreation Area, one of the most popular of our national parks.

Tempers flared again in the 1980s, when the upper Delaware was designated a National Scenic and Recreational River. Landowners feared that use of their property would be unduly restricted, while conservationists wanted to be sure the river would be protected for generations to come. A compromise was reached whereby a coalition of local governments oversees private land uses along the river and the National Park Service supervises activities on the river itself.

Controversies continue to arise among people competing for use of the Delaware, and today several citizens groups advocate its conservation. The Delaware Riverkeeper Network champions protection of the river and its tributaries along its entire length. Founded in 1988 and among the first of many riverkeepers nationwide, it grew out of Del-Aware, a citizens group opposed to diversion of river water at Point Pleasant, Pennsylvania. The Delaware Riverkeeper has recently fought for protection of horseshoe crabs in Delaware Bay, battled against dredging the Delaware Estuary, rallied citizens against irresponsible natural gas exploration in the upper basin, and advocated storm-water controls to mitigate threats of flooding.

Wild and Scenic River

Almost all of the Delaware upstream from Trenton is designated by the U.S. Congress as a Scenic and Recreational River under the national Wild and Scenic Rivers Act (1968). The upper Delaware (75 miles from Hancock to Sparrowbush) and the middle Delaware (about 40 miles within the Delaware Water Gap National Recreation Area) were so designated in 1978. The lower Delaware downstream from the Water Gap—40 intermittent miles from Martins Creek to Washington Crossing—was added in 2000. According to the act, wild and scenic rivers are those with "remarkable scenic, recreational, geologic, fish and wildlife, historic, cultural, or other similar values." Our Delaware certainly fills this bill! They are to be "preserved in free-flowing condition, and they and their immediate environments shall be protected for the benefit and enjoyment of present and future generations."

Designation of a river as "wild and scenic" is only the beginning. How to protect and preserve the river while not treading too harshly on the rights of competing interests is where things can get tricky. This has been especially true on the upper Delaware, where virtually all of the lands adjacent to the river are privately owned.

Management of the middle Delaware is less beset by controversy, as all the riverside lands are within the Delaware Water Gap National Recreation Area, a unit of the National Park Service. There are no conflicting private land uses.

As to the lower Delaware, to quote from the management plan:

The Lower Delaware River flows through the very heart of the birthplace of our nation. Every bend in the river speaks to us of history, of beauty, of opportunity. Our nation's history is revealed in the agricultural fields, forests, canals, villages, mills and inns along its path.

Guided by the Delaware River Greenway Partnership, the management plan for the lower Delaware calls for protection of water quality and of natural and historic resources, preservation of open space, and, of course, encouragement of low-impact recreation, such as canoeing and kayaking.

How Clean Is the Delaware?

Today, all of the Delaware River from Hancock to Trenton is deemed to be clean enough for fish and wildlife, and safe for recreation in and on the water. Indeed, water quality in the 120 miles from Hancock to the Water Gap is considered excellent, while from the Water Gap to Trenton the river is rated "good." The Delaware includes the longest stretch of "anti-degradation waters" in the United States. This means that the water is cleaner than regulations require and must stay that way. Canoeists and kayakers are often surprised by the crystal clarity of the upper Delaware, every rock and fish plainly visible even at six or eight feet deep.

The river was not always so clean. As long ago as 1799, a survey near Philadelphia noted that the Delaware was becoming contaminated by pollution from ships, public sewers, and wharves. Even in the upstream areas, sewage discharges and industrial wastes from Port Jervis, Stroudsburg, Easton, and Phillipsburg killed segments of the Delaware. Raw sewage dumped into the river consumed oxygen in the water, suffocating fish and other aquatic life. In the worst places, the river actually ran black and emitted the rotten-egg smell of hydrogen sulfide. River users often sued upstream communities for fouling the water that flowed down to them. The once plentiful shad and other fish were all but gone.

In 1933 a group of canoe clubs collaborated in the Great Canoe Marathon, a bid to call attention to the sorry state of Delaware River water. Ninety-four teams raced all the way from Easton to Trenton in one very long day, while thousands of spectators cheered them from the riverbanks and bridges. The cause of cleaning up the Delaware gained popular appeal, and efforts to stem the pollution were launched the length of the river. New federal laws in 1947 and 1972 established standards and required a special permit for discharge of wastes into the river, and money was granted for the construction of sewage treatment plants. By the mid-1970s, use of the river as a sewer had come to an end.

The quality of the river's water continues to improve every year. Shad and other game fish have returned in great numbers. Some local residents even complain that the river has become *too* clean, allowing for the propagation of black flies and other troublesome insects.

This is not to say that there is no pollution at all in the Delaware River. Treated effluent from village and city sewer systems is still discharged. Canoeists may notice these outfalls, usually along the length of a submerged pipe extending from the riverbank. A prominent example is the discharge at Easton, seen as a gray froth about a mile south of the city. However, this and other discharges are rapidly absorbed and cleansed. Other pollutants enter the river from non-point sources, such as fertilizer runoff from fields and suburban lawns, bacteria from livestock pens and pastures, and oily contaminants from roads and parking lots.

Invasive species have recently become a problem in the Delaware. An algae called *didymo*, or more commonly "rock snot," in some places covers the river bottom with gooey slime, inhibiting native species and disrupting the ecosystem. Canoeists and kayakers can help stop the spread of this nuisance by thoroughly cleaning the hulls of their boats.

Plain old garbage also intrudes on the river experience. Bottles and cans, plastic bags, old tires, and other detritus are sometimes left by irresponsible users or swept into the river by floodwaters. Respectful boaters never leave trash in or along the river, but always carry out more than they carried in. The National Park Service, Delaware Riverkeeper Network, and Kittatinny Canoes, among others, sponsor river cleanups during which an astonishing pile of trash is removed from the Delaware. Kittatinny Canoes reports that in 21 years of river cleanups it has retrieved more than 7,000 scrap tires, 8,000 pounds of aluminum cans, and nearly 400 tons of garbage from the river.

Although Delaware River water is clean enough for fishing and swimming, it is not fit to drink. Microorganisms in the water such as *Giardia* and *Crytosporidium* can make a person sick with "beaver fever" for weeks. River water may be drunk only if boiled for at least a minute or treated with chemical disinfectants and water filters to reduce contamination. It is safest to drink water only from a known clean source—from home or a public water supply.

Delaware River Sojourn

Reminiscent of the great canoe marathons of 1933 and 1949, hundreds of paddlers join the Delaware River Sojourn every June to foster awareness of the environmental, historical, and recreational richness of the river. Sponsored since

1995 by the Delaware River Greenway Partnership and the Delaware River Basin Commission, each year's sojourn features a particular theme—"Celebrating Native American Culture," "Bridging our Communities," and more. Canoeists and kayakers can join all or any part of a guided trip down intermittent sections of the river, including portions in the tidal Delaware estuary. Every year the sojourn names a "Lord High Admiral of the Delaware," in the tradition of timber raftsman Daniel Skinner, to honor outstanding contributions to river awareness. The sojourn has been a great success with wide participation. And what a glorious sight to see the hundreds of colorful craft easing down the river to the night's campsite!

Delaware River Water Trail

In recent years more than 150 "water trails" have been designated nationwide. There are 20 in Pennsylvania alone. The concept behind a water trail is to make a river more accessible and user-friendly, and to coordinate sometimes conflicting regulations over use of the waterway. Led by the Delaware River Greenway Partnership (DRGP), the entire Delaware River from Hancock to Trenton was designated a water trail in 2008. DRGP focuses on improved access, safety, and visitor services for the Delaware River Water Trail. In 2010 DRGP proposed a system of signage for the water trail, indicating mileage, landmarks, and access. It publishes an excellent map showing river features that could well be used as a complement to this book.

Fishing the Delaware River

No guide to the Delaware could be complete without acknowledging the thousands of fishermen and women who try their luck on the river. And more often than not, anglers are rewarded with a string of bass, a pan of trout, or a trophy muskellunge. The clean, cool water of the Delaware is a perfect home for many species of game fish.

A valid license (and special stamp if fishing for trout) is required to fish anywhere on the Delaware. When fishing from the riverbank, a license issued by the state is required; when fishing from a boat, a license issued by either adjoining state will suffice. The National Park Service and state fish and game authorities patrol the river to check for fishing licenses; a costly summons may be issued to anyone fishing without one. Licenses may be purchased at most sporting goods stores throughout the Delaware valley or through the state fish and game authorities. Fishing guide services are available along all segments of the river.

Neither anglers nor boaters have the right-of-way on the river. Sometimes, however, ugly confrontations have been known to occur. Paddlers must take care not to interfere with people fishing; common sense and courtesy will usually make for a pleasant day on the river for all. When approaching anglers, keep as much distance as possible (hopefully, the fisherman won't be standing in the only passage); if the angler is in the middle, it is usually best to pass behind her. Check to see where the angler's line is, and be sure not to cross it. When in doubt, don't hesitate to ask. Be quiet and don't scare the fish. There are certain times and places where fishing reigns, and it may be best to canoe another day. The opening of trout season on the upper Delaware or one of the local shad tournaments are probably not the best of days for a canoe trip.

The best times and places to catch the various species of game fish on the Delaware—and comprehensive lists of special regulations that may apply—can be found via state fish and game authorities or professional guides. There are several good books detailing the habits of the fish, the bait and lures to use, and the secret fishing holes for success on the Delaware. Some are listed in the bibliography of this book and may be found in Park Service and local bookstores.

The following is a summary of the major species of game fish that may be caught in the Delaware River.

Trout: The Delaware River from Hancock to Callicoon is one of the finest trout streams in the East. Both brown (to 17 inches, 1½ lb.) and rainbow (to 16 inches, 2 lb.) trout are abundant and regularly caught. The best fishing is late May and early June. First Saturday after April 11 to September 30, 14-inch minimum, limit one fish per day. Most anglers catch and release.

Shad: These robust fish (typically 15 inches, 7 lb.) migrate each spring from the sea to their spawning grounds in the Delaware. Shad can be caught in abundance as the schools move up the river; many communities have annual tournaments to catch trophy shad. All year, any size, daily limit of six.

Bass: Probably the most reliable of Delaware River game fish. Both smallmouth (most common, to 24 inches, 5 lb.) and largemouth (to 26 inches, 10 lb.) bass can be caught the entire length of the river. All year, 12-inch minimum, daily limit of five.

Striped bass: Thanks to improvement in water quality, fishing for striped bass gets better every year. Large spawning stripers (to 30 inches, 10 lb.) ascend and descend the river during June and October, and can be caught in the deeper pools; all through the summer and fall the river is a nursery for small (to 14 inches) stripers. All year, 28-inch minimum, daily limit of two.

Walleye: These bottom feeders (average 18 inches, about 4 lb.) are found in the deep holes the entire length of the river; the best fishing is on spring nights. Season begins first Saturday in May; 18-inch minimum, daily limit of three.

Pickerel: These slender fighters (20–30 inches, 5–10 lb.) are found in weedy shallows and eddies, especially in the upper reaches of the river. All year, 12-inch minimum, daily limit of five.

Muskellunge: The Pennsylvania Fish Commission stocked a few muskies near the Delaware Water Gap in the early 1970s, and a healthy population of these monsters (up to 50 inches, 40 lb.) now thrives in the river. All year, 30-inch minimum, daily limit of two.

Eel: Every summer, during dark nights, these snakelike fish (to 48 inches, 2 lb.) migrate from their home territory on the upper Delaware to the Sargasso Sea in the mid-Atlantic to spawn. This is the only species fished commercially on the Delaware; the V-shaped eel weirs are common obstacles to boaters on the upper Delaware. All year, any size, no limit.

Panfish: Sunfish, bluegills, and fallfish (to about 12 inches) are abundant throughout the Delaware. They are easily caught, even by novices. All year, any size, no limit.

Carp, catfish, suckers: These bottom feeders can be found throughout the river, especially in slow-moving and muddy water. Delaware River carp can be huge (to 48 inches), and Moby Carp is often seen. All year, any size, no limit.

The East and West Branches of the Delaware

The Lenape called the East Branch of the Delaware *Pepacton* and the West Branch *Cookquago* (later called the Mohawk's River). The streams begin at springs high in New York's Catskill Mountains, then run roughly parallel to each other until their confluence at Hancock, New York. Their flow is controlled by dams at the Pepacton and Cannonsville reservoirs, respectively, which supply water to New York City. The Delaware River Basin Commission (DRBC) manages reservoir releases for consumption by the cities and to maintain river flow and temperature for recreation and aquatic habitat.

The East and West Branches of the Delaware are renowned for trout and other fishing, and are heavily used by anglers from the riverbanks and drift boats. Several outfitters offer fishing guide services. In recent years the branches have seen more kayak, canoe, and raft traffic, and a couple of outfitters offer rental and shuttle services. Although very pretty and for the most part navigable, the branches are narrow and shallow, with a few rapids up to Class I. Sweepers and strainers (trees fallen into the water) can trap and upset a canoe and its occupants, a potentially serious hazard.

This book does not describe in detail the East and West Branches or other tributaries to the Delaware. The branches are depicted on the DRBC's latest revision of its recreation maps and in fishing guidebooks. There are four public access points on the branches, most commonly used for fishing but accessible to recreational canoeists and kayakers as well:

Mile 11.0, East Branch. Access: Fishes Eddy, New York. Maintained by the New York Department of Environmental Conservation. Limited parking, rough beach at river's edge. Access from County Road 17 at Fishes Eddy, New York.

Mile 9.5, West Branch. Access: Hale Eddy, New York. Provided by the New York Department of Environmental Conservation. Limited parking, rough access to river. Access from County Road 56 (off New York 17) at Hale Eddy, New York.

Mile 4.6, West Branch. Access: Balls Eddy, Pennsylvania. Provided by the Pennsylvania Fish and Boat Commission. Boat ramp, parking, trash disposal, privies. Access from Pennsylvania Route 191. All boats must bear a valid Pennsylvania boat registration or launch permit.

Mile 0.6, West Branch. Access: Shehawken, Pennsylvania. Provided by the Pennsylvania Fish and Boat Commission, at the mouth of Shehawken Creek and just a short distance above the confluence of the East and West Branches. Natural launch area, parking, no facilities. Access from Pennsylvania Route 191, at the junction of Pennsylvania Route 370. All boats must bear a valid Pennsylvania boat registration or launch permit. This is a good place to begin a trip on the main-stem Delaware.

Mile 330.1 to 314.9 (15.2 miles)

The Delaware River begins at the confluence of the East (Pepacton) and West (Mohawk's) Branches at Hancock, New York. This uppermost section of the Delaware River is the shallowest and most narrow. There are no major rapids and only a few riffles rated as Class I. For much of the way there are no roads along the river, and paddlers find themselves in a near wilderness. The big outfitters do not run here, and river traffic tends to be light. This section of the Delaware is popular with anglers seeking trout and other game fish.

The river flows through the Appalachian Plateau geophysical province, a broad band of shale and sandstone extending from upstate New York to northern Alabama. The foothills of New York's Catskill Mountains lie to the north of the river, and the Pocono Mountains of Pennsylvania are to the south.

In the nineteenth century, most of the timber was stripped from the surrounding hills and rafted to market in the big cities downriver. The trees have grown back, and today the banks of the Delaware are clothed in thick hardwood forest. Few people live in the valley, and the little hamlets along the river offer few services.

Many varieties of waterfowl make their home on and near the river. Mergansers—sleek ducks with tufted red heads—are often seen with their broods in the spring and early summer. Small animals, including woodchucks, muskrats, otters, and beavers, abound along the riverbanks. Deer are frequently seen near the water's edge or crossing at the shallows, and black bear are not uncommon.

There are five public access areas on the Delaware in this section,

Hancock, New York (mile 329.7)
Shingle Hollow, Pennsylvania (mile 327.5)
Buckingham, Pennsylvania (mile 325.1)
Lordville, New York (mile 321.6)
Long Eddy, New York (mile 315.5)

All of this section is within the boundaries of the Upper Delaware Scenic and Recreational River, and recreation on the river is under the jurisdiction of the National Park Service. Most lands adjacent to the river are privately owned. Park rangers and local police will ticket or arrest trespassers. Camping is allowed only at private campgrounds. Call 845-252-7100 for the Park Service report of river conditions.

River Guide

Map 1

MILE

330.1 The main stream of the Delaware River begins at the confluence of the East and West Branches. The Lenape called this place *Shehawken*, "the wedding of the waters."

The community of Hancock, New York, is one mile upstream along the East Branch. All services are available.

Point Mountain, elevation 1,380 feet, rises between the East and West Branches just above their confluence. The castle-like structure atop Point Mountain is a mausoleum built by Dr. Frank Woolsey for himself in the 1940s. However, Dr. Woolsey was not buried there, and the mausoleum is empty. There is no public access to the site.

The Upper Delaware Scenic and Recreational River begins at the confluence of the East and West Branches. From this point, recreation on the 78 miles of river down to Sparrowbush is under the jurisdiction of the National Park Service.

A spit of marshy land extends 100 yards downstream on the Pennsylvania side. There is a Class I rapids near the spit.

330.0 The slow water downstream from the confluence is known to anglers as Junction Pool, or Bard Parker Pool after a nearby medical instrument plant.

329.8 City of Hancock waste-water treatment plant, New York side. The effluent outfall—a pipe extending along the river bottom—is virtually invisible.

329.7 **Access: Hancock, New York.** Provided by the New York Department of Environmental Conservation, mainly for riverbank fishing access. There is no real boat ramp, just some short, rough trails down to the river, but adequate to launch a canoe or kayak. Ample parking, privies, and a grassy picnic area. No fee. This is the first public access below the confluence of the East and West Branches.

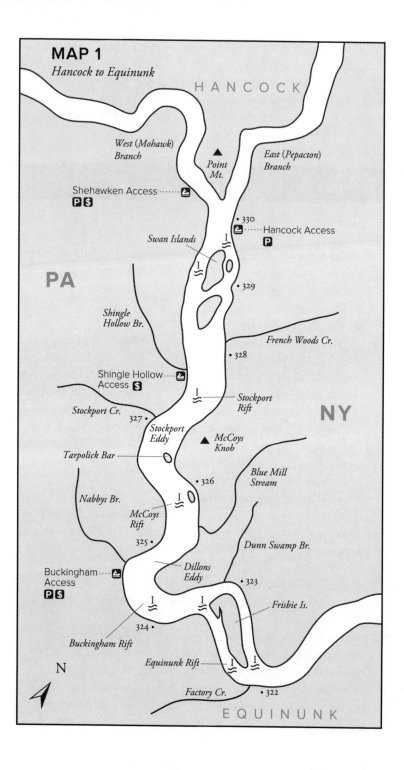

MAP 1

Hancock to Equinunk

H A N C O C K

West (Mohawk) Branch

▲ *Point Mt.*

East (Pepacton) Branch

Shehawken Access ········ 🛶
P $

• 330

🛶 ········ Hancock Access
P

Swan Islands

PA

I ≋

• 329

Shingle Hollow Br.

I ≋

French Woods Cr.

• 328

Shingle Hollow ········ 🛶
Access $

I ≋

Stockport Rift

NY

Stockport Cr.

327 •

Stockport Eddy

▲ *McCoys Knob*

Tarpolick Bar ———

Blue Mill Stream

Nabbys Br.

I ≋

• 326

McCoys Rift

Dunn Swamp Br.

325 •

Dillons Eddy

• 323

Buckingham ········ 🛶
Access
P $

I ≋

I ≋

Frisbie Is.

Buckingham Rift

324 •

N

Equinunk Rift ———

I ≋

I ≋

Factory Cr.

• 322

E Q U I N U N K

Point Mountain looms above the Hancock access area, just below the confluence of the East and West Branches of the Delaware. (Photo by the author)

Access from the end of Labaret Street (off New York 97), behind the treatment plant.

329.4 The Swan Islands begin,[1] low gravel bars extending nearly a mile. The first island is Reeds, the second Doyles. Channels to the left and right are navigable, with sinuous passages leading through the islands. A Class I rapids, known to anglers as Second Heaven, runs down the right side.

328.8 There is a grass airstrip atop the riverbank, New York side. Paddlers frequently see light planes taking off or landing.

328.5 Downstream end of the Swan Islands.

328.1 French Woods Creek enters through a marshy area, New York side.

327.7 Shingle Hollow Brook, Pennsylvania side.

Access: Shingle Hollow, Pennsylvania. Maintained by the Pennsylvania Fish and Boat Commission. Intended mainly for riverbank fishing access; rough hand-launch only. No facilities; parking is awkward along Route 191. All boats must bear a valid Pennsylvania boat registration or launch permit. Access at River Road, off Route 191. There is much better boat access, with parking, at Buckingham, three miles downriver.

327.5 River bends widely to the right.

327.3   Stockport Rift, a Class I rapids over a shallow ledge extending diagonally from the New York riverbank. The best passage is to the right.

327.1   McCoys Knob, elevation 1,800 feet, rises steeply on the New York side.

      Slow water for the next 0.5 mile is known as Stockport Eddy.

327.0   Stockport Creek enters, Pennsylvania side.

      The village of Stockport, once a thriving little community, stood at the mouth of Stockport Creek. Stockport Station, a whistle-stop on the old Erie Railroad, stood opposite on the New York side. A ferry ran between the sister villages. Both villages are no more.

326.4   Pass Tarpolick Bar, a low grassy island on the left. There are mild riffles in the channels both left and right of the island.

      The river bends sharply to the left into Tarpolick Eddy, slow water for the next 0.5 mile.

325.9   The river bends back to the right. Another little island on the left, this one called Tarpolick Jr. Stay right.

      Knights Creek meets the Delaware to the left of the island, New York side.

      McCoys Rift, Class I rapids along the island—not much to it, beware submerged rocks.

325.6   Blue Mill Stream enters under a stone-arch culvert, New York side, at a modest riffle.

325.3   The river continues its bend sharply to the right. A 500-foot-high slope rises above the river on the New York side.

      A stretch of slow water known as Dillons Eddy. A man named Dillon ran a mill at the foot of Blue Mill Stream.

324.8   Nabbys Brook enters, Pennsylvania side.

324.7   **Access: Buckingham, Pennsylvania.** Maintained by the Pennsylvania Fish and Boat Commission. Unpaved boat ramp, parking, trash disposal, privies. All boats must bear a valid Pennsylvania boat registration or launch permit. Access from Pennsylvania Route 191.

324.2   Class I rapids of Buckingham Rift; standing waves to 1½ feet. Stay to the right; the river is very shallow on the left.

324.0   The river swings to the left, with wide, barren gravel bars on both sides.

323.1   The river makes a sharp right turn at the head of Frisbie Island, a big gravel bar that extends 0.8 mile downstream. The better passage is to the right; the left is shallow and rocky. There are Class I rapids, Equinunk Rift, either way.

      Dr. Frank Frisbie was a long-time physician in Equinunk. Before Dr. Frisbie came along, this landmark was known as Equinunk Island.

Mergansers—sleek red-headed ducks—are a common sight on the upper Delaware. These ducklings are hitching a ride on mama's back. (Photo by Andy Smith)

Early settlers built their cabins on the island, thinking it a safe refuge from hostile Indians.

Steep slopes of Kilgour Mountain rise above the river, New York side.

322.3 Downstream end of Frisbie Island, with shallows and gravel bars extending a short distance further.

Easy Class I rapids along the Pennsylvania side and between the gravel bars.

322.1 Factory Creek enters, Pennsylvania side, with gravel bars extending into the river.

The creek takes its name from the old Equinunk Chemical Works, one of many "acid factories" in the area that brewed local hardwoods into high-grade charcoal, wood alcohol, and acetate of lime.

The community of Equinunk, Pennsylvania, is on the right. It offers a general store and small museum, but no easy access to or from the river. Do not trespass.

Map 2

322.0 Equinunk Creek, a good-sized stream, enters at the Pennsylvania side. *Equinunk* is the Lenape word for "trout stream."

321.9 The river makes a near-U-turn to the left into the slow water of Equinunk Eddy.

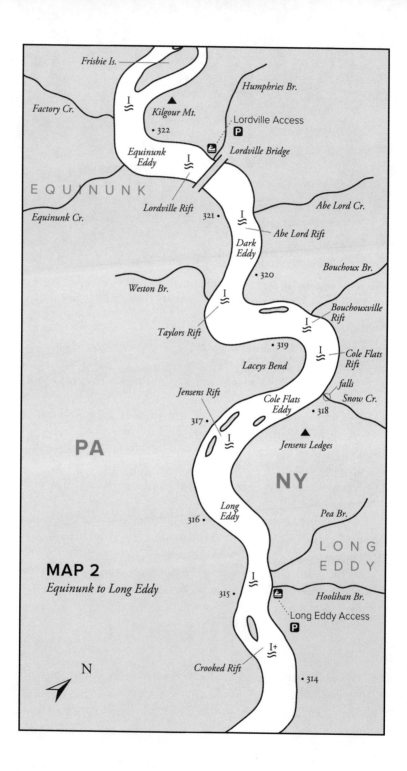

Frisbie Is.

Humphries Br.

Factory Cr.

Kilgour Mt.

Lordville Access

• 322

Equinunk Eddy

Lordville Bridge

E Q U I N U N K

Lordville Rift

321 •

Abe Lord Cr.

Abe Lord Rift

Equinunk Cr.

Dark Eddy

• 320

Bouchoux Br.

Weston Br.

Bouchouxville Rift

Taylors Rift

• 319

Cole Flats Rift

Laceys Bend

falls

Jensens Rift

Cole Flats Eddy

Snow Cr.

317 •

• 318

PA

Jensens Ledges

NY

Long Eddy

Pea Br.

316 •

L O N G

E D D Y

MAP 2

Equinunk to Long Eddy

Hoolihan Br.

315 •

Long Eddy Access

N

I+

Crooked Rift

• 314

Rocky cliffs known as Oven Rocks rise along the Pennsylvania side.

321.4 Lordville Rift, uncomplicated Class I rapids, just upstream from the bridge.

321.3 Humphries Brook enters, New York side.

Pass under the modern Lordville Bridge, constructed in 1992. A bridge built at this site in 1869 was destroyed in the Pumpkin Flood of 1903. The one-lane suspension bridge that replaced it in 1904 was demolished in 1988. A gage painted on the center pier of the current bridge measures the river level.

Access: Lordville, New York. Provided by the New York Department of Environmental Conservation. Located under the Lordville Bridge. Rough boat launch, limited parking, privies. No fee. Access off Lordville Road.

The hamlet of Lordville, New York, is on the left. No services.

320.7 Abe Lord Creek enters, New York side; the gravel bar at its mouth constricts the river to the right. Gravel and other sediment washed down the creek during floods are deposited at the mouth of the creek.

Class I rapids, Abe Lord Rift, as the current sluices along the gravel bar. Standing waves up to 2 feet. This is the biggest rapids so far.

320.5 Slow water once known as Dark Eddy.

320.0 Taylors Rift, a Class I rapids. Big rocks stick up on the left.

319.8 Weston Brook, Pennsylvania side, enters through a marshy area.

319.6 The river curves sharply left, beginning the big S of Laceys Bend. Steep wooded slopes tower 700 feet over the river on the Pennsylvania side. There are several minor (Class I) rapids through the turns.

318.8 A grassy little island nestles against the New York riverbank for about 0.1 mile. Stay right. Old-time rafters called this slip of land Pull Hair Bar—if only we knew how it got its name!

318.7 Bouchoux Brook enters, New York side, via an arched culvert under the Erie Railroad.

The gravel bar at the mouth of the creek constricts the river into the Class I rapids of Bouchouxville Rift. Stay right.

318.5 The river bends sharply right in the second turn of Laceys Bend. As is typical, the inside of the bend is shallow, here along the right (Pennsylvania) side.

Easy Class I rapids of Cole Flats Rift in the turn, continuing 0.4 mile.

318.3 Jensen Hill rises steeply on the New York side. A popular hiking trail leads to Jensens Ledges at the summit, with spectacular views of the upper Delaware valley.

Snow Creek cascades down the cliffs.

Bouchoux Trail State Forest Preserve, New York side, continuing about one mile downstream. There is no access from the river.

318.0 Cole Flats Eddy, slow water for 0.8 mile.

317.2 The river continues to be very shallow on the right; the grassy gravel islands here are submerged when the river level is above average stage.

Class I rapids known as Jensens Rift runs along the islands; stay left and be alert for submerged boulders.

317.0 Slow water of Long Eddy, continuing about 1.6 miles.

316.5 Steep evergreen slopes rise along the right.

315.2 Pea Brook enters, New York side. The river narrows to the right as gravel deposits encroach on the left.

315.0 Hoolihan Brook enters, New York side. The gravel bar at its mouth extends into the river.

314.9 **Access: Long Eddy, New York.** Maintained by the Village of Long Eddy. A paved one-lane road leads from the village to the boat launch. There is no parking at the access, but boaters may park "at your own risk" in a lot at the intersection of Route 97 and Delaware Road. No facilities, no fee.

Lunch. Long Eddy Hotel and Saloon.

Features

Scenic and Recreational River

The upper Delaware has always been scenic and recreational, but now federal law says that it must forever remain so. The U.S. Congress enacted the Wild and Scenic Rivers Act in 1968. Designated rivers "shall be preserved in free-flowing condition, and their immediate environments shall be protected for the benefit and enjoyment of present and future generations." In 1978 the Delaware from Hancock to Sparrowbush (73 miles) was named a Scenic and Recreational River under the law.

Controversy flared almost as soon as the designation was announced. Most of the lands along the river are privately held, and landowners feared that federal rules would infringe on their property rights. The Park Service's early drafts of a management plan for the upper Delaware were vehemently opposed by many residents and local governments. Some even wanted Congress to rescind the designation.

In response to these concerns, management of the river was turned over to

National Park Service rangers patrol the Upper Delaware Scenic and Recreational River, providing law enforcement, visitor information, and safety services. (Photo by the author)

the Upper Delaware Council (UDC), a panel of 20 members that includes the municipalities bordering the river, the states of Pennsylvania and New York, the Delaware River Basin Commission, and the National Park Service. The UDC's plan focuses on local control of land uses. The National Park Service owns only a few small parcels (ranger offices, and the Zane Grey Museum and Roebling Bridge at Lackawaxen) and has no authority to regulate uses of private property along the river.

On the river itself, the Park Service is boss. Park Service rangers, together with state and local police and state fish and game officers, patrol the river throughout the year. Their pale green skiffs and canoes are a familiar sight. *May I see your fishing license? Where are your PFDs? The next access is five miles ahead. Did you see the eagles?* The Park Service also sponsors activities, such as visitor services, interpretive history and nature programs, and "Volunteers in Parks," whereby citizens participate in rescue operations, boating instruction, and information services.

The management plan for the upper Delaware has not ended controversy over use of the river and adjacent lands. Some local residents feel that the Scenic and Recreational designation of the river has infringed upon their property, and visitors can still see signs shouting *Park Service Get Out!* On the other hand, many residents recognize that boating, fishing, and tourism are the economic backbone of the upper Delaware valley and welcome the opportunities brought by designation.

Fracking for Gas

"The most endangered river in America." That's what American Rivers, a national conservation group, has called the upper Delaware. The danger lies a mile below, in a rock formation known as the Marcellus shale. There is a vast amount of natural gas in the shale, and energy companies want to get it. And therein lies the problem. The Marcellus gas is tightly contained in the rock, and drillers must pressure-pump an enormous amount of water and chemicals into the formation to break the rock and free the gas. The process is called *hydraulic fracturing*, or *fracking* for short. No one knows for sure what happens to the contaminated water after it has done its job a mile down. If released at the surface, it could severely pollute the Delaware, ruining the river as a source of drinking water and wrecking the riverine habitat.

Energy companies see the Marcellus shale as one of the greatest potential sources of natural gas in the United States and have been buying up mineral rights throughout northeastern Pennsylvania and southern New York. Many landowners struggling in the current economy have been unable to resist the handsome payments offered for drilling rights. On the other hand, the value of land has gone down in some areas because of the threat of contamination at the surface. Neighbors have been pitted against neighbors.

More than a thousand exploratory wells have been drilled. Even at this preliminary stage, spills and leakages have contaminated water supplies and made people sick. A controversial film, *Gasland*, showed how in some places flames shot out of kitchen water faucets after gas wells were drilled nearby. Private water wells have exploded from gas that bubbled up from the fractured deposits below. One driller paid a stiff fine to the state of Pennsylvania for releasing toxic chemicals into the environment. Energy companies counter that fracking is safe and that the problems have been incidental to local drilling operations.

Officials of New York City, which takes almost all of its drinking water from the Delaware River watershed, say that they are in a fight for the city's life. Conservation organizations such as the Natural Resources Defense Council and Delaware Riverkeeper are fighting to protect the watershed. The state environmental agencies, the Delaware River Basin Commission, and even the U.S. Congress are casting skeptical eyes on the whole fracking business.

This drama has not yet played out. We need energy, but we need clean water more. We will welcome the day when the upper Delaware is no longer listed as the most endangered river in America.

Long Eddy to Narrowsburg

Mile 314.9 to 290.1 (24.8 miles)

Famous Skinners Falls highlights this section. A severe Class II rapids, Skinners is the starting place for many a canoe or kayak trip. There are several other rapids rated at Class I+. River outfitters launch boats as far upstream as Callicoon and offer launch/landing bases and campgrounds along the way. Canoe traffic is relatively light above Skinners Falls, but below that point the river can be very busy on summer weekends. This section is renowned for fishing, and paddlers must take care to avoid interfering with anglers. Beware the eel weirs in the river here; these are low stone walls to funnel eels into a trap. Go around the weirs if possible, and do not go through the chute at the center.

The river continues to flow through the Appalachian Plateau geophysical province. Shale bedrock is exposed in several places, most prominently at Skinners Falls. The banks of the river are almost entirely forested, although in a few areas fields have been cleared for farming. Paddlers are almost sure to see at least one bald eagle perching in the treetops or swooping to the river to catch a fish.

There are seven public access points:

Long Eddy, New York (mile 314.9)
Callicoon, New York (mile 303.1)
Callicoon, Pennsylvania (mile 302.6)
Cochecton, New York (mile 298.1)
Damascus, Pennsylvania (mile 298.0)
Skinners Falls, New York (mile 295.6)
Narrowsburg, New York (mile 290.1)

New York Route 97, the "Upper Delaware Scenic Byway," follows the river much of the way. Services can be found at the villages of Callicoon and Narrowsburg, New York. Virtually all of the land adjacent to the river is privately owned —no trespassing please! Camping is allowed only at private campgrounds.

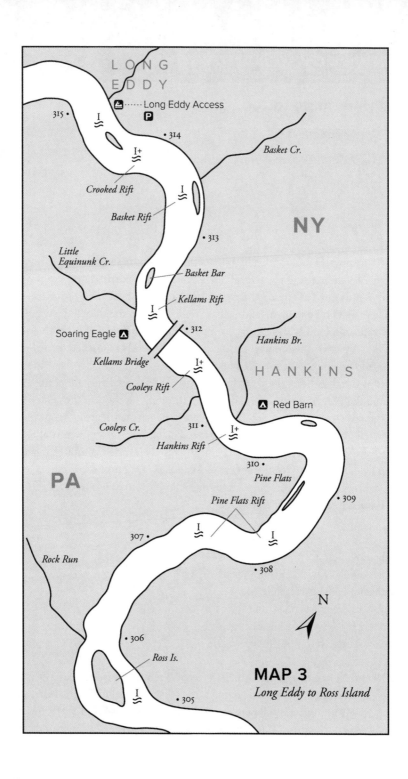

LONG
EDDY

Long Eddy Access

315

Crooked Rift

Basket Rift

Basket Cr.

NY

314

313

Little
Equinunk Cr.

Basket Bar

Kellams Rift

Soaring Eagle

312

Hankins Br.

HANKINS

Kellams Bridge

Cooleys Rift

Red Barn

Cooleys Cr.

311

Hankins Rift

310

Pine Flats

309

PA

Pine Flats Rift

307

308

Rock Run

306

Ross Is.

305

N

MAP 3
Long Eddy to Ross Island

The river here is within the Upper Delaware Scenic and Recreational River, and recreation on the river is under the jurisdiction of the National Park Service. Call 845-252-7100 for the Park Service report of river conditions.

River Guide

Map 3

314.9 **Access: Long Eddy, New York.** Maintained by the Village of Long Eddy. A paved one-lane road leads from the village to the boat launch. There is no parking at the access, but boaters may park "at your own risk" in a lot at the intersection of Route 97 and Delaware Road. No facilities and no fee.

Long Eddy was originally called Douglass City and became an important overnight stop for old-time timber rafters.

Lunch. Long Eddy Hotel and Saloon.

Enter a Class I rapids; no obstructions.

314.6 There is a small, barren gravel island in the middle of the river. Best passage is to the right (Pennsylvania side); the left channel is very shallow.

Crooked Rift, a nice Class I+ rapids, begins near the downstream end of the island—watch for submerged boulders, then standing waves to 1½ feet.

314.3 A bridge known as the Douglass High Bridge was built across the Delaware near here in 1868. It collapsed in an ice jam only 16 years later and was not rebuilt. Few traces remain.

313.5 Basket Creek enters, New York side. A gravel bar at the mouth of the creek extends to the middle of the river.

New York Route 97 crosses Basket Creek on a high concrete bridge.

Recreational maps from the Delaware River Basin Commission indicate an anglers' access at Basket Creek. Parking is awkward along Route 97, and there is no place to launch a boat.

313.4 Class I rapids of Basket Rift begin just below the mouth of the creek —very shallow.

312.5 Basket Bar, a barren gravel island extending about 0.2 mile, is tucked against the Pennsylvania side. No passage to the right, modest (Class I–) rapids on the left.

312.2 Little Equinunk Creek, a rather substantial stream, enters, Pennsylvania side.

Class I rapids called Kellams Rift, with waves up to 2 feet, along the New York side.

312.1 **Camping/outfitter.** Soaring Eagle Campground. Riverfront tent and trailer sites, showers, laundry, camp store. Soaring Eagle also rents canoes and tubes, with shuttle service.

312.0 Pass under the Kellams-Stalker, or Little Equinunk, Bridge. Constructed in 1890, this is the third-oldest extant span across the Delaware. The suspension cables hang below the road surface, an unusual configuration. The bridge deck is only one lane wide.

William Kellam ran a ferry here from 1860 until the bridge was built.

Rough trails lead up the New York riverbank to a parking area at the bridge ramp. The trails are so steep that ropes have been hung to hold onto. This is the Kellams Fishing Access, provided by the New York Department of Environmental Conservation. It is not a good place to launch or land a boat.

311.8 The bare ledges along the Pennsylvania riverbank are known as Cooleys Rocks. Cooley was a hermit, and likely refugee from the law, who lived in a cabin near here in the late 1700s.

311.4 The river narrows hard against the New York (left) side.

Enter Cooleys Rift, a Class I+ rapids—no obstructions, but big waves.

311.3 Cooleys Creek enters from a marshy area on the Pennsylvania side.

Beware the big boulders on the left.

310.8 Hankins Brook enters, New York side, at a wide gravel bar. A beautiful stone arch bridge, built in 1905 and listed on the National Register of Historic Places, crosses the creek a short distance from the river.

Begin Hankins Rift, where the gravel bar at the mouth of Hankins Brook squeezes the river hard against the Pennsylvania side. An exciting Class I+ rapids with standing waves to 2½ feet, the biggest rapids on the river so far.

310.7 Class I rapids continue over submerged boulders. Very shallow on the left.

Camping. Red Barn Campground. Riverfront tent and trailer sites, showers, laundry, camp store. Mostly seasonal campers. The campground has a rough boat ramp for canoe and kayak access.

The village of Hankins can be reached up the access road from the campground. John Hankins set up a blacksmith shop and general store

Eagles are abundant in the upper Delaware valley, and paddlers are almost sure to see at least one. This fellow is being harassed by a kingbird. (Photo by Courtenay Kling)

here in 1834. The old Erie Railroad depot still stands. Limited visitor services.

309.5   The river bends sharply to the right. Minor riffles punctuate the turn.

The broad lowlands on the Pennsylvania side are known as Pine Flats.

309.4   A small creek enters through a culvert, New York side.

308.8   A narrow gravel bar along the Pennsylvania side. Stay left.

308.0   Shallow Class I rapids of Pine Flats Rift, extending 0.5 mile; watch for boulders here and there.

307.5   Slow water for next 1.5 miles, punctuated by Class I– riffles.

305.9   Rock Run enters, Pennsylvania side, a little creek at a gravel bar.

Map 4

305.8   Ross (or Butternut) Island, a big brushy gravel bar, extends 0.6 mile. Best passage is to the left; the right channel is shallow and rocky over mild (Class I–) riffles. Joseph Ross was the first European settler at Callicoon, about 1755.

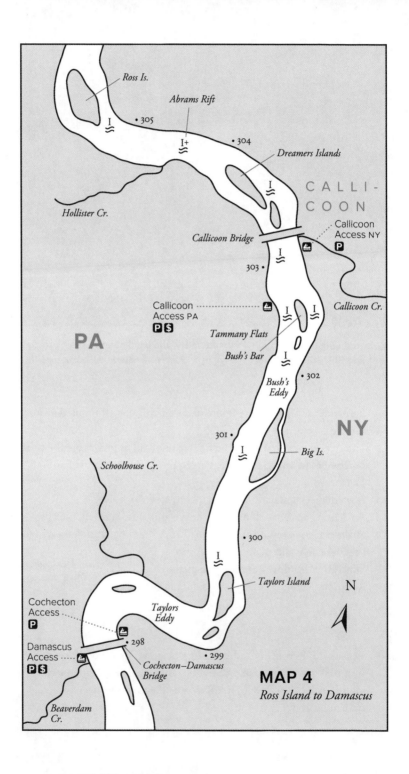

Ross Is.

Abrams Rift

• 305

• 304

Dreamers Islands

CALLI-
COON

Hollister Cr.

Callicoon Bridge

Callicoon
Access NY

P

Callicoon
Access PA

P $

303 •

Tammany Flats

Bush's Bar

Callicoon Cr.

PA

Bush's
Eddy

• 302

NY

301 •

Schoolhouse Cr.

Big Is.

• 300

Taylors Island

N

Cochecton
Access

P

Taylors
Eddy

Damascus
Access

P $

• 298

• 299

Cochecton–Damascus
Bridge

Beaverdam
Cr.

MAP 4
Ross Island to Damascus

305.5 George's Rock, big and squarish, named for timber raftsman George Abrams, sticks up from the river near the New York side.

305.2 Class I rapids in the left channel, without obstructions.

The clock tower of St. Joseph Seminary at Callicoon, built in 1904 of local bluestone, stands on the hillside ahead. The seminary closed in the 1970s, and the buildings are now occupied by a unit of the U.S. Department of Labor Job Corps.

304.6 Hollister Creek enters, Pennsylvania side. A gravel bar at the mouth of the creek extends halfway across the river.

George Abrams sluiced timber down Hollister Creek and built his rafts here.

Class I+ rapids, called Abrams Rift, at the mouth of the creek. Best right down the middle, with waves up to 2 feet.

304.0 Dreamers Islands, a series of brushy gravel bars extending 0.6 mile. Navigable either side, with Class I rapids.

303.2 Pass under the Callicoon Bridge, constructed in 1961. A steel truss bridge built in 1899 stood a short way upriver from the modern bridge.

There is a short Class I rapids under the bridge.

Callicoon Creek, a substantial stream, enters on the New York side immediately under the bridge. A wide gravel bar at the mouth of the creek extends halfway across the river.

Outfitter. Landers River Trips. The base is on the New York side, immediately downstream from the bridge and a little way up Callicoon Creek. Check in at Rivers Diner.

303.1 **Access: Callicoon, New York.** Maintained by the New York Department of Environmental Conservation. Rough boat launch, ample parking, trash disposal, and privies. No fee. From the river, look for a row of big stones just downstream from the mouth of Callicoon Creek. Access at the south end of Main Street.

The village of Callicoon, New York, population 216 (2000 census), is walking distance from the access area. Callicoon began as a center of timber rafting and grew with the arrival of the Erie Railroad in the 1840s. Many of the buildings in the downtown area were constructed in 1888, after the town was devastated by fire. *Callicoon* is old Dutch for "turkey hen."

Every July the community hosts the Callicoon Canoe Regatta, a 7.5-mile race from Callicoon to Skinners Falls, to raise money for the local youth center.

Upper Delaware Campgrounds, which once operated just below the access area, was destroyed in the 2006 flood and has not reopened.

Lunch. Callicoon advertises itself as the "dining capital of Sullivan County," and there are several restaurants along Main Street, from cafés to gourmet dining. The Rivers Diner, immediately off the Landers River Trips base, is attached to a gas station and convenience store. Pecks Grocery is a short walk from Landers and the public access area.

302.6 **Access: Callicoon, Pennsylvania.** Maintained by the Pennsylvania Fish and Boat Commission. A natural launch area, ample parking, trash disposal, and privies. All boats must bear a valid Pennsylvania registration or launch permit. Very shallow water. From the river, at the head of Bush's Bar. Vehicle access from River Road/State Route 1016.

There is a U.S. Geological Survey river gage on the Pennsylvania riverbank near the access. Base elevation is 735 feet. Best stage for boating is 3–5 feet; flood stage is 12 feet. The highest recorded flood reached 20.37 feet in 2006.

302.5 Upstream end of Bush's Bar (or Firefly Island), extending 0.3 mile, a low gravel island submerged at moderate water level. The channel to the right (Pennsylvania) side is very shallow; take the left channel. Easy Class I rapids.

302.1 Enter Bush's Eddy, slow water for the next mile.

Innkeeper George Bush ran a temperance hotel here in the mid-1800s. Raftsmen seemed to prefer the inns in Callicoon, where alcohol was served, and Bush went out of business.

Lowlands along the Pennsylvania side are known as Tammany Flats, named by pioneer Daniel Skinner, who claimed the great Lenape chief Tammany once camped nearby. It was from here in 1764 that Skinner launched his first timber raft, starting an industry that would dominate the Delaware valley economy for more than 100 years.

Look back upriver for a good view of Callicoon and St. Joseph Seminary.

301.5 A small creek enters from a marsh, New York side.

Class I rapid with no obstructions.

301.4 A dry channel (at average water level) in the marsh on the left marks the upstream end of Big Island. It is an island only at moderate or higher water. The river is very shallow along the left; stay near the Pennsylvania side of the river.

A community of Lenape lived on Big Island before colonial settlement. Many artifacts and a few graves have been found.

301.0 Class I rapids, not much to it.

300.5 Downstream end of Big Island on the left, here a more significant slough through the tall grass.

299.8 Taylors (or Plum) Island, a brushy gravel bar extending 0.4 mile. Stay right; the left channel is very shallow and may not be navigable below average water level.

A nice Class I rapids runs along the island.

299.4 Taylors Island tapers to its downstream end.

Slow water known as Taylors Eddy for the next mile. Ebenezer Taylor was an early settler, first postmaster, and tavern keeper at Cochecton.

299.2 The river bends sharply to the right. Lowlands cleared for farming on the Pennsylvania side are known as Canfield Flats.

The old Cochecton cemetery stands on the New York riverbank.

298.5 Schoolhouse Creek enters, Pennsylvania side, at gravel bars.

298.4 Easy riffles (Class I–) without obstructions.

298.3 The river bends back to the left beside a steep slope at the right.

298.1 The abutment of the old Damascus Bridge stands at the riverbank on the Pennsylvania side. A wooden bridge was built here in 1819, then rebuilt several times after succumbing to floods, decay, and ramming by timber rafts.

Access: Cochecton, New York. Provided by the New York Department of Environmental Conservation. Rough hand-launch, parking, privies. No fee. Access from Newman Road off New York Route 114 at Cochecton, just upstream from the bridge. Primarily a fishing access, it's a long carry for canoes and kayaks; there is a better boat launch at Damascus, just across the bridge.

Power lines cross the river.

298.0 Pass under the "new" steel-truss Cochecton-Damascus Bridge, built in 1952. The communities of Cochecton, New York, and Damascus, Pennsylvania, stand at opposite ends of the bridge. Although the communities once supported luxury (for the day) hotels for summer tourists, there are no services available here today.

Access: Damascus, Pennsylvania. Maintained by the Pennsylvania Fish and Boat Commission. Boat ramp, parking, trash disposal, privies. From the river, immediately downstream from the bridge. All boats must bear a valid Pennsylvania registration or launch permit. Access from Pennsylvania Route 371.

Beaverdam Creek enters, Pennsylvania side, at the access area, in a hurry to join the river.

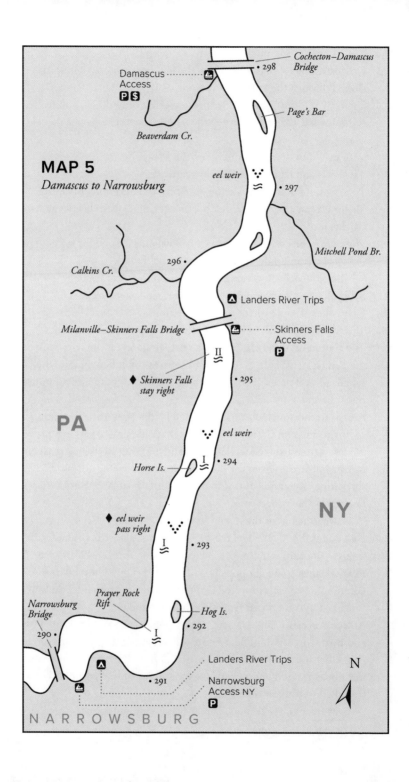

MAP 5
Damascus to Narrowsburg

Cochecton–Damascus Bridge

• 298

Damascus Access

P S

Page's Bar

Beaverdam Cr.

eel weir

• 297

Mitchell Pond Br.

• 296

Calkins Cr.

Landers River Trips

Milanville–Skinners Falls Bridge

Skinners Falls Access

P

II

◆ *Skinners Falls stay right*

• 295

eel weir

I

• 294

Horse Is.

PA

NY

◆ *eel weir pass right*

I

• 293

Prayer Rock Rift

Hog Is.

Narrowsburg Bridge

I

• 292

290 •

Landers River Trips

• 291

Narrowsburg Access NY

P

N A R R O W S B U R G

N

Map 5

297.5 Page's Bar, a brushy gravel island extending 0.2 mile, in the middle of the river. Stay right.

Fast water and riffles over shallows, next 0.4 mile.

297.2 Class I– rapids at an old eel weir.

296.9 Mitchell Pond Brook enters, New York side.

296.6 A brushy island nestles at the left side; if the water is high enough, hug the New York riverbank to explore the little channel to the left. There has been a rope swing here as long as anyone can remember—at your own risk.

River bends to the right.

295.9 Calkins Creek gurgles into the Delaware, Pennsylvania side.

295.7 **Camping/outfitter.** Landers River Trips, Skinners Falls campground and base. Riverfront tent sites and lean-tos, camp store, and restrooms with hot showers. Boat launch/landing is at a wide beach just upstream from the bridge.

Pass under the Milanville–Skinners Falls Bridge, built in 1901. This steel truss span is a throwback to horse-and-buggy days—only one lane with a wood-plank deck. Milton Skinner ran a ferry here before construction of the bridge.

A sign on the center pier of the bridge warns of the rapids ahead.

Milanville, Pennsylvania, bustled with tanneries and "acid factories" in the nineteenth century, and the little historic district boasts grand homes built by the Skinner and Calkins families. The weathered shed just off the bridge was built by Milton Skinner in 1900 and is still known simply as Skinners Barn.

National Park Service ranger offices (North District) are located at Milanville, one-quarter mile up the road from the Pennsylvania end of the bridge.

295.6 **Access: Skinners Falls, New York.** Maintained by the New York Department of Environmental Conservation. Rough hand-launch, ample parking, trash disposal, privies. A National Park Service attendant is on hand here during summer weekends. No fee. From the river, look for a wide grassy path just downstream from the bridge. Access from Milanville Road (off New York Route 97).

Outfitter. Lou's Tubes operates from the Lothian House Bed & Breakfast adjacent to the access area.

A well-worn foot trail leads from the Landers overflow parking area and Lou's tube rental shop through a field to the rocks at Skinners Falls.

Skinners Falls, a Class II rapids, is one of the most severe on the Delaware. Ledges lurk just beneath the surface, ready to grab canoes and kayaks. (Photo by the author)

295.5 Entrance Rock, a big square boulder on the left, signals the approach to Skinners Falls. Proprietors of the Lothian House call it Peace Rock. The rock is sometimes crowded with sunbathers.

295.4 **DANGER!** Skinners Falls (once known as Cochecton Falls), a Class II rapids. Although relatively short, this is one of the most severe rapids on the Delaware.

Beach your craft on the rocks at the left to scout your route. A series of flat ledges, partially submerged, guards the left side. Stay to the right, where the passage is clear with big waves. Many boats capsize or founder in this rapids. Wear your PFD!

The character of Skinners Falls changes dramatically with the water level. At its most benign, during low flows of summer, most boaters and tubers bob through without difficulty. At higher levels, Skinners becomes a raging torrent with 4-foot waves and "keeper" hydraulics, to be attempted only by fully equipped experts. If the river is higher than average, novices should consider running Skinners Falls in a raft or portaging along the ledges on the left.

Many people drowned at Skinners Falls before the National Park Service took charge of recreation on the river. Now, Park Service rangers monitor the area, and National Canoe Safety Patrol volunteers serve as lifeguards, sometimes standing by in kayaks to rescue hapless boaters.

Skinners Falls is named for the family of Daniel Skinner, "Lord High Admiral of the Delaware," who in 1764 was the first to float a timber raft to market at Philadelphia. The admiral's son Joseph Skinner ran a big sawmill here, powered by the falls.

On summer weekends the spirit of Daniel Skinner inspires an impromptu party at his namesake rapids. Up to a hundred revelers gather on the rocks to soak up the sun, wade in the shallows, fire up a barbeque, and watch people crash through the falls.

295.3 Skinners Falls ends. Ledges along the left (New York side) offer a place

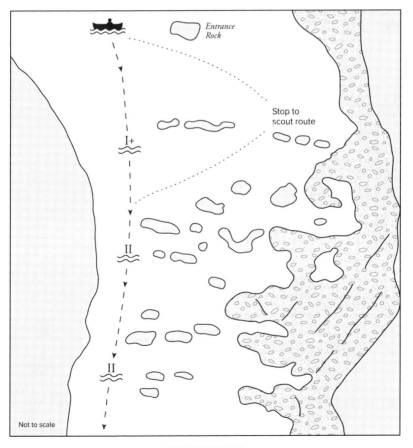

SKINNERS FALLS

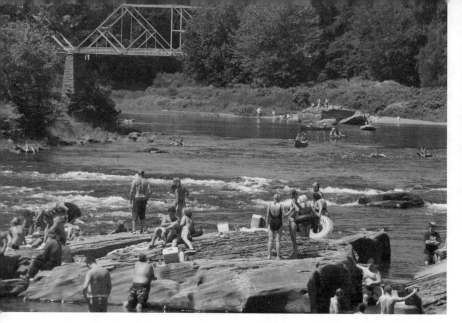

There's a party at Skinners Falls on any summer weekend. Entrance Rock and the Milanville–Skinners Falls Bridge are in the background. (Photo by the author)

to bail your canoe and gather your stuff. The right-side riverbank is steep and backs to private residences.

River is slow for the next 1.5 miles.

294.2 Beware an eel weir in the left center of the river. Passage is clear around both sides.

294.0 Horse Island, a little gravel bar in the middle as the river narrows. Class I rapids along both sides.

An old eel weir at the left side of the river can be passed over at moderate water level.

Beware rocks on the left.

293.4 Hills Brook enters, New York side.

293.3 Move to the right to skirt a big eel weir ahead.

293.2 **CAUTION!** An eel weir extends nearly across the river. Stone walls in a V configuration funnel soon-to-be-sushi into a trap at their apex. This is probably the biggest eel weir anywhere on the Delaware. Passage is best to the far right, near the Pennsylvania riverbank, over Class I rapids. Do not go through the chute; as of this writing (2010) it was blocked by an iron rail.

292.2 Hog Island, a grassy gravel bar extending 0.2 mile. Passage is clear and current swift both left and right.

291.5   The river bends sharply right.

291.3   A Class I rapids over ledges extending across the river. The main channel is in the right center, with standing waves to 1½ feet. Old-time timber rafters called this Prayer Rock Rift, the origin of the name now forgotten.

291.0   Riffles continue over ledges.

290.9   An unnamed stream enters, Pennsylvania side, at a marshy area. Gravel bars and shallows on the right.

290.5   The river bends sharply left and becomes quite narrow, with rocky cliffs along the right.

Pass under power lines marked by red balls.

290.2   **Camping/outfitter.** Landers River Trips, Narrowsburg campground and canoe base, New York side. Riverfront tent sites and lean-tos, restrooms with showers, camp store.

290.1   **Access: Narrowsburg, New York**. Maintained by the New York Department of Environmental Conservation. Paved boat ramp, ample parking, trash disposal, and privies. From the river, look for the steel bulkhead. No fee. Access from DeMauro Lane in Narrowsburg, off Sullivan County Route 24.

Walk from the access into downtown Narrowsburg, population 426 (est. 2007). The offices of the Upper Delaware Council, which manages land use in the upper Delaware River corridor, are here, and the National Park Service has an information center and bookstore on Main Street.

Lunch. There are several casual restaurants in Narrowsburg, including the Main Street Café, which features an outside deck overlooking the river.

Features

Lenni Lenape—The True People

In 1524 Native Americans in canoes paddled out to greet Italian explorer Giovanni da Verrazzano, the first white man to meet the indigenous residents of the Delaware valley. Verrazzano described them as "the most beautiful people, and having the most civil of customs." They called themselves *Lenape*, meaning "the people," or in comparison to other tribes, *Lenni-Lenape*, the "true people" or, literally, "men that are men." English settlers later called them the Delaware Indians, after naming the river in honor of Thomas West, Lord de la Warr.

The Lenape lived throughout New Jersey, eastern Pennsylvania, and southern New York State. There were three distinct tribes. Those of southern New Jersey were called *Unalachtigo*, the "people by the ocean"; inhabitants of a central area were the *Unami*, or "people down the river"; north of the Delaware Water Gap lived the *Munsee* (or *Minsi*), the "people of the stony ground." Each spoke a different dialect of the Algonquian language group and could only barely understand the others. There were perhaps about 20,000 Lenape at the time of European contact. They lived in longhouses clustered in semi-permanent villages, where they grew the "three sisters": maize, squash, and beans. In canoes dug out from poplar trees, the Lenape cruised the Delaware —known to all Indians as *Lenape-wihittuck*, the river of the Lenape—to fish and trade with their neighbors.

At first, relations between the Lenape and the new settlers were more or less cordial. The great sachem Tammany signed a treaty with William Penn at Philadelphia in 1682, guaranteeing peace between the peoples. But the pressures of encroaching settlement, most infamously in the Walking Purchase of 1737, turned the Lenape against the colonists. The Indians evacuated toward the west, but not before fighting viciously against the settlers in the French and Indian War and American Revolution.

Today, the descendants of the Unalchtigo and Unami peoples live among the Cherokees and other Indian peoples in Oklahoma, while the Munsee descendants live in Wisconsin and Ontario. Recently, people of mixed Lenape lineage who remained in Pennsylvania have formed the Lenape Nation to advocate for their culture and heritage.

The Lenape languages were very difficult for European settlers, and the newcomers are widely regarded as having butchered both pronunciation and translation. Today there are only a handful of elderly speakers of Lenape languages. Still, Lenape words survive in hundreds of place-names in the Mid-Atlantic states, including *Manhattan*, *Lehigh*, *Pocono*, and *Ramapo*.

Eels and Eel Weirs

Your favorite local sushi bar very likely offers Delaware River eel. Properly prepared—steamed, grilled, and/or smoked—eel has a delicious buttery taste. Trapping eel on the Delaware has been going on since the days of the Lenape, who perhaps enjoyed their own version of sushi. But the recent growth of Asian communities and restaurants in America has brought a renewed boom to the eel-fishing business.

Eels found in the Delaware River are "American Eels," *Anguilla rostrata*. Appearing more like snakes than the fish they are, eels are often seen swimming

As eels migrate down the Delaware in late summer, many of them are trapped in weirs like this one for delivery to market. Weirs can be hazardous to paddlers; go around the ends, not over the dams or through the chute. (Photo by Lisa Lander)

among the river-bottom rocks on the upper Delaware. They grow up to four feet long and weigh about two pounds. Delaware River eels are not "electric," so cannot give you a shock.

Eels have an unusual life cycle, one that enables fishermen to capture them by the thousands. Some fish, such as shad and salmon, live most of their lives at sea, then swim up rivers to spawn. Eels do the opposite: in the late summer, they abandon their homes in the upper Delaware and other eastern rivers and swim, at night, downstream to the ocean. Ultimately they arrive in the mid-Atlantic, where they spawn amid the floating kelp of the Sargasso Sea.

In the Delaware, eel traps, called "weirs" or "racks," are built of low stone walls in a big V pointing downstream. The migrating eels are diverted by the stone walls to a box at the point of the V, where they are captured and held until retrieved by the fishermen. Thousands of eels might be caught in a single night, bringing a nice profit to the eelers.

Canoeists and kayakers encounter many eel weirs on the Delaware upriver from Port Jervis. In the low water of early summer, eelers are often seen in the river repairing damage to the stone walls caused by the previous winter's floods and ice. The traps are usually set in August, and the largest catches come in September.

The relationship between eelers and boaters has not always been a friendly one. Eel weirs can be as much a hazard to navigation by modern canoeists as they were to old-time timber raftsmen. It is often difficult to see an eel weir when approaching from upstream, and just like the eels themselves, canoeists can be diverted by the stone walls to the point of the V. The eel trap, with its anchoring bars and rigging, can do damage to a canoe or kayak and be a danger to the boaters. On the other hand, passage of boats over the walls can dislodge the stones, undoing the eelers' hard labor. And it is not unknown for recreational boaters to open the traps and steal the catch, although severe fines and even jail time can result from such theft.

Eel weirs have always been subject to license, even in colonial times. The stone weirs were considered a hazard to navigation of timber rafts and for a time were outlawed. Today, eel traps are permitted by state fish and game authorities. Regulations limit the size of eel weirs to three-quarters of the span of the river and require that eelers place a sign upstream to direct boaters; sometimes, however, these rules are difficult to enforce, and river conditions can make compliance impractical. Boaters should try to pass around an eel weir and not go over the stone walls or through the point of the V.

Canoeists and kayakers prepare for a river trip at the New York Department of Environmental Conservation access area at Narrowsburg. Big Eddy, the deepest point on the Delaware, is just beyond the Narrowsburg Bridge. (Photo by the author)

Narrowsburg

But for the automobiles parked along busy Main Street, this little village on the Delaware seems not to have changed much in the last century. Originally known as Homan's Eddy after a pioneer settler, the community became known as Big Eddy when timber raftsmen stopped here *en masse* to patronize the hotels, restaurants, and taverns. The name Narrowsburg—for the narrowing of the river—stuck around the turn of the twentieth century. Today, it is an unincorporated hamlet within the Town of Tusten.

The Erie Railroad, built in 1847, brought permanent settlers and a business district. The centerpiece of Narrowsburg was, and still is, the Arlington Hotel, four stories high with a broad planked balcony. On his 1892 canoe adventure, J. Wallace Hoff stayed at the Arlington and remarked in his book about its hospitality and attractive waitresses.[1] Today the Arlington Hotel is listed on the National Register of Historic Places and is occupied by a National Park Service information center/bookstore and the Delaware Valley Arts Alliance. Although it has a population of less than 500, Narrowsburg boasts several shops, restaurants, motels, and other businesses. The community hosts a "country market" every summer Saturday.

Half a mile from the Delaware River bridge at Narrowsburg stands Fort Delaware, a museum of colonial history run by the Sullivan County Department of Public Works. The fort, with its log stockades and cabins, is reminiscent of the pioneer settlement at nearby Cushetunk. Costumed guides demonstrate what life on the eighteenth-century Delaware River frontier might have been like.

Mile 290.1 to 274.7 (15.4 miles)

It's an exciting ride as rapids tumble over a series of bedrock ledges. Bridge No. 9, Westcolang, Kunkelli, and Big Cedar rifts are rated as Class II, and there are 24 rapids at Class I or I+. Beginners should consider rafting this section or gaining experience in calmer water before attempting it. Many outfitters provide canoes, kayaks, and rafts for rent and shuttle, making for easy access to this exciting white water.

The river continues through the Appalachian Plateau geophysical province, with frequent outcrops of shale and sandstone bedrock. The riverbanks are clothed almost entirely in deciduous forests, with only a few areas cleared for farming or recreational use.

This section of the Delaware is the main spawning area for the American shad, an anadromous fish that lives most of its life in the ocean and then migrates into fresh water to spawn. Shad begin their annual run up the Delaware in late spring and arrive here by mid-summer. In the early decades of the twentieth century, the shad migration was almost wiped out by pollution, but in recent years the fish has made a strong comeback. Eels run in the opposite direction, downriver to spawn in the Atlantic Ocean. There are several eel weirs in this section that canoeists and kayakers must take care to avoid.

Boaters are rarely out of sight of at least one bald eagle. Once eradicated from the area, eagles have returned in great numbers and are often seen perching in treetops high over the river, looking down for their next meal of fish. The adult eagles are unmistakable, with white heads and tail feathers; juveniles are a mottled brown all over.

For the first 10 miles there are no roads and few buildings along the river, and paddling seems a wilderness experience. From just above Lackawaxen, New York Route 97 parallels the river on the left side.

The Delaware & Hudson Canal ran atop the riverbank on the New York side below Lackawaxen, where it was carried over the river on the historic Roebling

Aqueduct. Now only its traces remain. Lackawaxen was also the home of author Zane Grey, famous for his popular cowboy novels, and the site of a bloody Revolutionary War confrontation, the Battle of Minisink.

There are five public access points in this section:

Narrowsburg, New York, mile 290.1
Narrowsburg, Pennsylvania, mile 289.9
Ten Mile River (Tusten), New York, mile 283.9
Zane Grey (Lackawaxen), Pennsylvania, mile 277.6
Highland (Barryville), New York, mile 274.7

In addition, river outfitters operate from many private launch/landings along the way. This section is within the Upper Delaware Scenic and Recreational River, and boating on the river is under the jurisdiction of the National Park Service. Virtually all of the lands adjacent to the river are privately owned—no trespassing! There are several private campgrounds at the river's edge for river users.

River Guide

Map 6

290.1 **Access: Narrowsburg, New York.** Maintained by New York Department of Environmental Conservation. Paved boat ramp, ample parking, trash disposal, and privies. From the river, look for the steel bulkhead. No fee. Access from DeMauro Lane in Narrowsburg, off Sullivan County Route 24.

The river bends sharply right, constricting into a narrow passage between rocky ledges. Although tempting, it would be trespassing—not to mention dangerous—to beach here and dive off the ledges.

290.0 Pass under the arched span of the "new" Narrowsburg Bridge, constructed in 1954. A wooden covered bridge was built just upstream as early as 1811, the first bridge to span the upper Delaware. It was replaced in 1899 by a steel truss bridge and ultimately by today's green archway.

A little park with a gazebo overlooking the river atop the bluffs on the New York side commemorates Narrowsburg's war veterans.

Just downstream from the bridge the river widens into Big Eddy, the deepest water (113 feet) anywhere in the Delaware. Geologists suggest this may be the plunge pool of a glacial waterfall or perhaps a gigantic

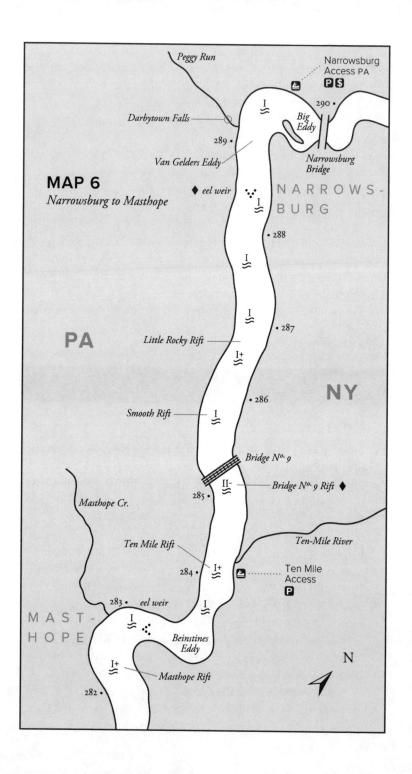

Peggy Run

Narrowsburg
Access PA
🅿 🆂

Darbytown Falls ○

I

290 •

Big
Eddy

289 •

Van Gelders Eddy

Narrowsburg
Bridge

MAP 6
Narrowsburg to Masthope

◆ *eel weir*

I

N A R R O W S -
B U R G

• 288

I

I

• 287

PA

Little Rocky Rift

I

I+

• 286

NY

Smooth Rift

I

Bridge Nᵒ· 9

II-

Bridge Nᵒ· 9 Rift ◆

285 •

Masthope Cr.

Ten-Mile River

Ten Mile Rift

I+

284 •

Ten Mile
Access
🅿

283 • *eel weir*

I

M A S T -
H O P E

I

*Beinstines
Eddy*

I+

Masthope Rift

282 •

N

scour hole. The river here moves in a slow counter-clockwise whirlpool and, along the New York riverbank, actually seems to flow upstream. Stay right to go with the flow downriver.

Several gravel islands nestle near the left side of Big Eddy. The main channel continues along the Pennsylvania side.

289.9 **Access: Narrowsburg, Pennsylvania.** Maintained by the Pennsylvania Fish and Boat Commission. Paved boat ramp, parking, privies, and trash disposal. All boats must bear a Pennsylvania boat registration or launch permit. Access from U.S. Route 652.

289.6 Class I rapids.

289.5 An unnamed stream enters, Pennsylvania side, at a wide gravel bar.

289.3 The river becomes shallow and bends sharply left into a stretch of slow water known as Van Gelders Eddy.

289.2 Darbytown Falls, on Peggy Run, plunges over the cliffs on the Pennsylvania side. It is prominent after a good rain, but just a trickle and hard to see otherwise. At 105 feet, this is one of the highest waterfalls in Pennsylvania.

In the nineteenth century timber was sluiced down the cliff via "Peggy's Runway" to build rafts in Van Gelders Eddy below.

288.7 A small stream enters, Pennsylvania side.

288.6 **CAUTION!** Beware an eel weir nearly spanning the river. Do not go through the center chute; passage is least bad along the Pennsylvania side. Class I rapids.

287.7 Class I rapids; no obstructions.

287.2 Begin Little Rocky Rift, fast water continuing about one mile. Ledges extend from the right side, gravel bars and shallows on left. Stay about left center, with standing waves to 1½ feet. Class I rapids.

286.6 Rapids increase to Class I+ at a narrows. Beware of boulders on the right; the main channel is in the left center. Diminishes to Class I after 0.2 mile.

A stretch of slow water at the end of Little Rocky Rift is called Tusten Eddy.

285.6 A short Class I rapids called Smooth Rift. It's really not so smooth— beware submerged and protruding boulders.

285.3 Watch for a "window" in the rocks on the Pennsylvania side, a mini natural bridge.

285.1 Pass under the Tusten Station Bridge (also known as Bridge No. 9), a three-truss span built to carry the Erie Railroad in 1848, now operated by the New York, Susquehanna & Western Railway. It's the ninth Erie bridge up from Port Jervis, most of them having crossed little streams.

CAUTION! Enter Bridge No. 9 Rift, a Class II− rapids, beginning under the bridge. It's pretty much a straight shot through standing waves, with a few submerged boulders. At above-average river level, the waves grow to 3 feet or more. This rapids has also been known as Tusten Rift and Little Cedar Rift.

Ten Mile River Boy Scout Camp, a 14,000-acre reservation operated by the New York City chapter, is on the New York riverbank.

284.0 The Ten Mile River enters, New York side, at a gravel bar extending into the river. Look up Ten Mile River to see a beautiful little stone arch bridge, built in 1875.

Ten Mile Rift, a Class I+ rapids—big waves. Avoid shallows on the left.

283.9 **Access: Ten Mile River (Tusten), New York.** Maintained by the National Park Service on land leased from the Boy Scout camp. A muddy launch/landing area, limited parking, picnic tables, trash disposal, and privies. A Park Service attendant is on hand during summer weekends. No fee. Access from New York Route 97 at Tusten.

Outfitter. Landers River Trips has a base adjacent to the public access area.

The Tusten Mountain Trail, a 1.8-mile loop to the summit of Tusten Mountain, begins at the river access.

The pioneer settlement of Cushetunk, near here, was wiped out by Lenape warriors in 1763 to avenge the murder of one of their chiefs. The Cushetunk settlement is re-created at Fort Delaware in Narrowsburg.

The village of Tusten, a local center of the timber and bluestone industries, once stood here. All that remains is a small church and the stone arch bridge over the Ten Mile River.

283.7 The river squeezes to a narrow channel, with a Class I rapids over a boulder ledge. There is a clear channel in left center, with standing waves to 1½ feet. Be alert for submerged rocks.

The river widens into Beinstines Eddy.

283.2 The river begins an S turn, first to the right, then to the left.

283.0 A Class I rapids at an old eel weir along the New York side. Stay right.

282.8 Masthope Creek gurgles in at the Pennsylvania side.

The river bends sharply left through another Class I rapids. Shallow and rocky on the left.

The little village of Masthope is on the Pennsylvania riverbank. According to tradition, timbermen hoped to find a tree here that would be tall enough to serve as the mast of the frigate U.S.S. *Constitution,* "Old Ironsides." Much of the timber cut here in the eighteenth and nineteenth centuries was indeed used for shipbuilding, and tall pines for masts were especially prized.

Map 7

282.2   Enter Masthope Rift, a Class I+ rapids, continuing 0.4 mile. It begins with moderate riffles over boulder ledges, then becomes more severe as the river bends to the left. Watch for boulders lurking just beneath the surface. The left side is shallow.

281.3   Grassy Swamp Brook enters, New York side.

281.2   Beware an eel weir, New York side; stay to the right.

281.1   **CAUTION!** Enter Westcolang Rift, beginning as a Class I+ rapids in a shallows peppered with submerged boulders. The rapids becomes increasingly severe, continuing 0.3 mile. Wear your PFD!

The red-roofed bungalows of Camp Colang, once a "weight-watchers" camp, can be seen on the Pennsylvania side. It remains a private camp, no trespassing.

Westcolang is derived from *Weskelang,* the Lenape name for nearby Westcolang Pond. In the nineteenth century a station stop on the Erie Railroad, called Westcolang Park, served summer tourists to the area.

280.8   After a short pause, Westcolang Rift becomes a Class II rapids in its final drop, with standing waves greater than 2 feet. Watch out for boulders on the left. Maneuvering is necessary to avoid rocks.

280.5   Westcolang Creek enters, Pennsylvania side.

The tailings of an old bluestone quarry tumble to the river's edge, New York side.

280.2   The river bends sharply left around a rocky point at Holberts Bend. William Holbert was among the first settlers of the area.

In his very first published article, Zane Grey spoke of fishing the "Beer Mug," a dark and frothy trout hole near here.[1] See if you can find it.

279.9   A rocky ledge extends from the New York (left) side; there is clear passage to the right.

279.8   A Class I rapids, continuing 0.3 mile. River is very shallow at low water level.

279.6   After a short pause, the rapids builds to Class I+. Watch for boulders lurking between the waves.

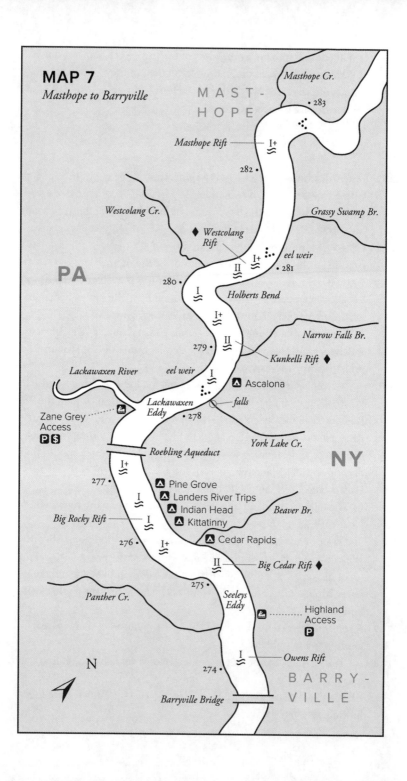

MAP 7

Masthope to Barryville

MAST-HOPE

Masthope Cr.

• 283

Masthope Rift — I+

• 282

Westcolang Cr.

Grassy Swamp Br.

◆ *Westcolang Rift*

I+ *eel weir*
II
• 281

PA

• 280

I

Holberts Bend

I+

II

Narrow Falls Br.

• 279

Kunkelli Rift ◆

Lackawaxen River

eel weir

I

△ Ascalona

Lackawaxen Eddy

falls

• 278

York Lake Cr.

NY

Zane Grey Access

P $

Roebling Aqueduct

I+

• 277

△ Pine Grove
△ Landers River Trips
△ Indian Head
△ Kittatinny

Beaver Br.

I

Big Rocky Rift — I

△ Cedar Rapids

• 276

I+

II — *Big Cedar Rift* ◆

• 275

Panther Cr.

Seeleys Eddy

Highland Access

P

N

I — *Owens Rift*

• 274

BARRY-VILLE

Barryville Bridge

279.3 There is a U.S. Geological Survey river gage in the squat little building on the New York riverbank. Base elevation is 600.22 feet. A good level ("average") for boating is 2½–4 feet. Flood stage is 17 feet, and the greatest flood was 28.97 feet in 2006. The stage of the river here is reported on the Park Service's river information line, 845-252-7100.

279.2 **CAUTION!** Kunkelli Rift (Narrow Falls), a Class II rapids. Watch out for submerged and protruding boulders. The main channel flows down the right center, with standing waves to 2 feet, but boulders often redirect the flow. The left side is too shallow for passage. Many a canoe has capsized in this rift. Hang on to your paddles and wear your PFD!

The Kunkelli family owned land along the river here. Rifts and eddies were often named by timber raftsmen in honor of hospitable local farmers.

278.9 Narrow Falls Brook enters, New York side. You won't notice it, because your attention will be focused on the big waves and boulders in the river.

278.7 The tail of Kunkelli Rapids peters out as Class I.

278.6 **Camping.** Ascalona Campgground. Riverside tent sites, privies, picnic tables. Access from the river at a wide gravel beach.

278.4 There is a smallish eel weir at the left side. Stay to the right, in Class I rapids.

278.3 Slow water of Lackawaxen Eddy, for the next 0.6 mile.

New York Route 97 approaches closely on the left, the first major road to do so since Narrowsburg.

278.2 York Lake Creek tumbles down the cliffs on the New York side over a very pretty waterfall.

277.7 The Lackawaxen River enters, Pennsylvania side, a major tributary to the Delaware. *Lackawaxen* is the Lenape word for "swift water," and the river indeed presents Class II–III rapids to skilled kayakers.

The Erie Railroad tracks cross the Lackawaxen over a high steel trestle a short way upstream from the Delaware.

277.6 **Access: Zane Grey (Lackawaxen), Pennsylvania.** Maintained by the Pennsylvania Fish and Boat Commission. Paved boat ramp, ample parking, picnic tables, telephone. A National Park Service attendant is on hand during summer weekends. All boats must show a valid Pennsylvania registration or launch permit. Access at Lackawaxen Scenic Drive, off Pennsylvania Route 590.

The Zane Grey Museum, home of author Zane Grey, stands just above the access area. Grey penned many tales of the Old West in his study above the river here.

The 2010 Delaware River Sojourn approaches the amazing Roebling Aqueduct at Lackawaxen, Pennsylvania, the oldest suspension bridge extant in America. The bridge was built in 1849 to carry the Delaware & Hudson Canal over the river. (Photo by Laurie Ramie)

A short walk along the road (heading downstream) passes historic Union Cemetery and the grave of a soldier killed during the Revolutionary War at the Battle of Minisink, fought here July 22, 1779. American militia were routed by Loyalist and Iroquois forces.

The road continues one-quarter mile to the amazing Roebling Aqueduct. It is well worth a stop here to view this extraordinary landmark.

The village of Lackawaxen, Pennsylvania, within walking distance, has a general store but no other services.

277.3 Pass under the Roebling Aqueduct, built in 1849 to carry the Delaware & Hudson Canal over the Delaware. This bridge is a National Historic Landmark, the oldest wire-cable suspension bridge in North America, and the oldest bridge of any kind across the Delaware.

A riffle near the Pennsylvania side of the river just upstream from the bridge is caused by the remnants of a dam built to impound water for the canal. The old dam was a major obstacle to timber raftsmen and early canoeists. Wooden cribs for the old dam can be seen on the river bottom. Passage may be barred by a string of buoys.

There is a wide gravel bar on the left just downstream from the bridge.

A Class I+ rapids, with tortuous channels and standing waves, begins under the Roebling Bridge.

Stone walls of the Delaware & Hudson Canal rise from the New York riverbank. Remnants of the canal can be seen occasionally from this point all the way to Port Jervis.

277.1   The little village of Minisink Ford stands on the New York riverbank. The river is shallow enough here for crossing by horses and light wagons, and was used as such until construction of the bridges.

This place was also known as Brant's Crossing. It was here that American militia tried to ambush Joseph Brant's raiders as they forded the Delaware, igniting the Battle of Minisink in 1779.

276.9   A Class I rapids, continuing 0.3 mile. Very shallow on the right— beware submerged rocks.

276.5   Bald Eagle Observation Site, New York riverbank, a little wooden shed at a turnout from New York Route 97 (no access from the river). Once virtually extinct in the upper Delaware valley, bald eagles have made a dramatic comeback in recent years. Thanks to wildlife protection laws, habitat management, and transplantation from Alaska and Canada, more than 100 eagles now winter in the upper Delaware, and several are known to have established nests. Boaters are likely to see many eagles on a voyage down the river in this section.

276.2   Enter aptly named Big Rocky Rift, a Class I rapids, continuing 0.7 mile. Boulders protrude on the right.

275.8   **Camping.** Kittatinny Canoes, Pine Grove Campground, left side. Tent sites, privies, picnic tables (an annex to Kittatinny Campground 0.5 mile downriver).

275.7   **Camping/outfitter.** Landers River Trips, Minisink Ford base and campground. Riverside tent sites, lean-tos, camp store, showers, restrooms.

275.6   After a brief respite, Big Rocky Rift ends as Class I+ rapids. A stony ledge extends diagonally upstream from the New York side. The main channel is in the right center, with standing waves to 1½ feet.
Camping/outfitter. Indian Head Canoes has a campground at its base on the river. Tent sites, lean-tos, cabins, camp store.

275.5   Cook's Eddy, slow water for 0.3 mile. Don your PFD and secure your gear for the rapids ahead.

275.4   **Camping/outfitter.** Kittatinny Canoes, Kittatinny Campground and river base ("Luke's Landing"). River- and stream-front campsites, game areas, laundry, camp store.

Rafters and kayakers make their way through Big Cedar Rift, a Class II rapids near Barryville. Rafts are a good choice for novices or when the river is running high. (Photo by the author)

275.2   Beaver Brook enters, New York side, at the head of Big Cedar Rift.
Camping/outfitter. Cedar Rapids Kayak and Canoe campground and river base. Riverfront tent sites, restrooms, showers, all facilities. Beach your boat on the rocks at the mouth of Beaver Brook.
Lunch. Cedar Rapids Inn, New York side. Famous for breakfast/brunch on summer weekends.
CAUTION! Enter Big Cedar Rift (Cedar Rapids), an exciting Class II rapids continuing 0.2 mile. The river tumbles over two ledges, then opens into scattered boulders. Quick maneuvering is required to avoid upset against the rocks; there is no obvious course through. Many boats get hung up on the rocks or capsize in the big waves. Wear your PFD!

275.0   The final ledge of Big Cedar Rift, with a clear channel at the left middle. At low water the ledges block passage on the right. Haystack waves to 2 feet.

Slow water of Seeleys Eddy, extending one mile, begins at the tail of Big Cedar Rift.

274.7 **Access: Highland (Barryville), New York.** Maintained by the New York Department of Environmental Conservation. Rough hand-launch canoe/kayak access, parking, privies. No fee. From the river, look for a dirt road leading down from Route 97. Access at a big turnout on Route 97.

Roebling's Amazing Bridge

Most of the great bridges—the Brooklyn, George Washington, Verrazano Narrows, and Golden Gate—are suspension bridges, with the roadway hung from cables spanning the river. And so is the little bridge at Lackawaxen. Completed in 1849, it is the oldest suspension bridge in America.

The great stone piers and heavy steel cables of the Lackawaxen bridge seem unnecessarily massive for the one-lane roadway. But the little bridge had to be strong, for it was made to carry a canal. The Delaware & Hudson Canal was built in 1829 to ship coal from Pennsylvania to tidewater on the Hudson River. At Lackawaxen the proprietors built a dam to impound the Delaware so barges could be towed across. But this crossing caused a bottleneck on both the river and the canal and was impassable when the river ran high or was icy. Worse, huge timber rafts careening downriver often crashed into the barges as they crossed, sparking fistfights and lawsuits.

The canal company consulted John Augustus Roebling, a German-born engineer. His idea at Lackawaxen was to build the canal over the water. Steel suspension cables, eight inches in diameter, were spun at the site and strung across

Roebling's aqueduct at Lackawaxen before reconstruction in 1995, revealing the massive cables that held the weight of the Delaware & Hudson Canal. (Photo by the author)

the Delaware. The canal itself—6 feet deep and 20 feet across—was suspended from the cables. Conventional construction would have required five stone piers, but Roebling's suspension design needed only three. There was plenty of room for timber rafts and ice flows to pass beneath. Roebling's experience at the Lackawaxen crossing laid the foundation for his design of the Brooklyn Bridge in 1883.

Competition from railroads eventually pushed the canal out of business. In 1898 the water was drained from the crossing and a plank road installed. A succession of private owners collected tolls for horses and buggies, then automobiles. The National Park Service acquired the old bridge in 1979 as part of the Upper Delaware National Scenic and Recreational River project and restored it in 1995 to look as it did in the heyday of the canal.

When modern visitors drive their "land barges" over the bridge, or even when walking, they might feel the deck swaying and bouncing beneath them. Yet the strength of the bridge is undiminished; pedestrians and automobiles have hardly begun to tax the piers, cables, and fittings installed by John Roebling 160 years ago. Engineering students are frequently seen inspecting the bridge, as if on a pilgrimage to this milestone of their trade. There are parking areas at both ends of the bridge, pedestrian walkways across, and a small museum and information center at the New York end.

Zane Grey and the Wild West

The banks of the Delaware do not seem a likely place to inspire legends of the Old West. But it was here at Lackawaxen that Zane Grey wrote more than 60 books about cowboys and Indians, cavalry and bandits.

Grey was born in Zanesville, Ohio, in 1872. He grew up to love sports and even played minor league baseball. Although educated as a dentist, Grey longed for the great outdoors, especially fishing and canoeing on the upper Delaware River. His first published article, in *Recreation* magazine in 1902, was titled "A Day on the Delaware." By 1905 Dr. Grey had saved enough to build a big house on the banks of the river at Lackawaxen.

Grey was inspired to write popular fiction about the Old West after spending time in 1907 at the Arizona ranch of C. J. "Buffalo" Jones, a noted Western storyteller of the time. Over the next 14 years, at his home in Lackawaxen, Grey turned out dozens of novels, including *Riders of the Purple Sage* and *Desert Gold*. In many ways, Zane Grey invented what we think of as the romantic Old West. His book *The Lone Star Ranger* inspired the *Lone Ranger* radio and television series, while *King of the Royal Mounted* became the *Sergeant Preston* series. More than 100 million copies of his books were sold, and Zane Gray was

Zane Grey wrote popular stories of the Old West at his home near the river at Lacka-waxen. Grey's very first published article was about fishing on the Delaware. (Photo by the author)

among the most popular authors in the world. In 1918 he moved to Hollywood, where he was involved in the production of movies based on his books. He died in 1939.

Zane Grey's home at Lackawaxen is maintained by the National Park Service as a museum. Photos and paintings of Western scenery and people, Indian clothing and artifacts, Grey's manuscripts, letters, and articles, and other treasures and memorabilia are on display.

The Battle of Minisink

Forty-seven Revolutionary War militiamen were killed in a pitched battle near Lackawaxen on July 22, 1779. For 43 years their bones laid about the forests and fields near the banks of the Delaware.

The upper Delaware valley was a wilderness at the time of the American Revolution. British forces and their Indian allies waged a campaign of terror on this frontier, attacking the sparse settlements and leaving bloody carnage behind.

Many of these raids were led by Joseph Brant, a Mohawk war chieftain and colonel in the British Army. On July 20, 1779, Brant's raiders attacked the little settlement at Minisink (now Port Jervis). Four settlers were killed, and houses and barns were burned. Lieutenant Colonel Benjamin Tusten of the New York

The Battle of Minisink raged in the forest around Lackawaxen in 1779. American militiamen were routed by British and allied Indian soldiers. This monument stands a short walk from the Zane Grey access area. (Photo by the author)

militia at Goshen quickly mustered 120 volunteers to chase Brant's raiders as they retreated up the valley.

On the morning of July 22, Tusten's militia waited in ambush at Minisink Ford. But as Brant's raiders began to cross the Delaware a nervous militiaman fired too soon, spoiling the surprise. The battle was on. Fighting was fierce and lasted throughout the day, but the New York volunteers were no match for Brant's experienced soldiers. Forty-seven Americans, including Colonel Tusten, were killed, while only eight of Brant's raiders were lost.

Not until 1822 were the bones of the dead collected and buried. The skeleton of a last soldier was found in 1847 near the Lackawaxen River and interred in an "unknown soldier's" grave at St. Mark's Lutheran Church, a short walk down the road from the Zane Grey river access.

Minisink Battleground County Park is located on County Road 168, about one mile up the hill from Route 97 and the old Lackawaxen bridge. This park, site of most of the fighting, tells the story of the Battle of Minisink by interpretive displays, self-guided trails, and monuments marking the locations of important events. It offers picnic sites with barbeque grills, restrooms, and an interpretive center. There is no camping in the park.

Mile 274.7 to 255.6 (19.1 miles)

White water starts off with a bang at the Class II Shohola Rift, then continues through eight more Class I+ or II rapids. Beginners should consider rafting this section. Many outfitters run here, and on summer weekends plenty of people are out enjoying the river via canoes, kayaks, rafts, and tubes.

New York Route 97, the "Upper Delaware Scenic Byway," follows the river between Barryville and Port Jervis. The Erie Railroad tracks run atop the Pennsylvania riverbank, and the Delaware & Hudson Canal once paralleled the river on the New York side. The villages of Barryville and Pond Eddy, New York, offer limited services; Port Jervis, New York, and Matamoras, Pennsylvania, at the end of this section, are fair-sized communities with all services available.

The river continues through the Appalachian Plateau geophysical province. Shale and sandstone bedrock is prominently exposed in several places, most notably at Hawks Nest, where cliffs tower several hundred feet above the river's edge. The riverbanks are heavily forested until approaching the urbanized areas of Port Jervis and Matamoras.

There are five public access areas in this section:

Highland, New York, mile 274.7
Mongaup, New York, mile 261.2
Sparrowbush, New York, mile 258.2
Matamoras, Pennsylvania, mile 256.0
West End Beach, Port Jervis, New York, mile 255.6

Virtually all of the lands adjacent to the river are privately owned; please do not trespass. Camping is allowed at many private campgrounds and at one primitive camping area on Pennsylvania state forest lands.

The river in this section (to Sparrowbush) is part of the Upper Delaware Scenic and Recreational River, under the jurisdiction of the National Park Service. Call 845-252-7100 for the Park Service report of river conditions.

Map 8

274.7 Access: Highland (Barryville), New York. Maintained by the New York Department of Environmental Conservation. Hand-launch boat access, parking, privies. No fee. Access at a wide turnout off New York Route 97.

Continue in Seeleys Eddy, slow water for the next 0.6 mile. William Seeley was among the first settlers in the area.

274.5 Camping/outfitter. Wild and Scenic River Tours has riverfront tent sites at its Barryville canoe base.

274.3 Little Halfway Brook enters, New York side.

274.2 Panther Creek enters, Pennsylvania side.

274.1 Enter Owens Rift, a Class I rapids continuing 0.4 mile. The final drop is Class I+, with big waves on the left side of the river.

273.7 A short Class I rapids, shallow with lots of rocks.

Stone abutments of the old Shohola Bridge, built in 1855 and closed in 1941, stand at both riverbanks.

273.5 Pass under the new Barryville-Shohola Bridge, opened to traffic in 2007. This is the fifth bridge to span the river here. The first, a single-lane wooden suspension bridge, was built in 1855 but lasted only three years before falling in a windstorm. A steel truss bridge stood here from 1941 until it was dismantled in 2007, making way for the modern steel-and-concrete structure.

Canoeists can beach their craft on the rocks under the New York end of the bridge and walk a grassy trail to a parking area and services in Barryville. This is not a public boat launch.

The villages of Barryville, New York, and Shohola, Pennsylvania, stand at opposite ends of the bridge.

On July 15, 1864, a train carrying Confederate prisoners on their way to internment at Elmira, New York, smashed head-on into a south-bound coal train on the Pennsylvania riverbank near here. Fifty-one prisoners, 17 guards, and several train crew were killed.

The Shohola Caboose Museum, run by the Shohola Railroad and Historical Society, is located one-quarter mile up Pennsylvania Route 434 from the Pennsylvania end of the bridge. The Civil War train wreck is commemorated, among other exhibits.

Lunch. Barryville, New York: Clancy's Diner and ice cream; Carriage House Restaurant and Motel (formerly Reber's).

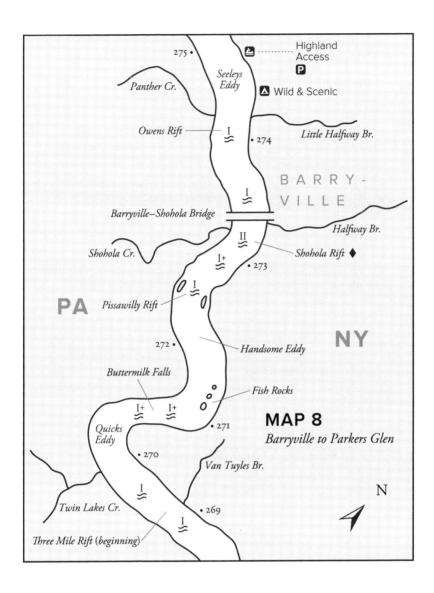

MAP 8
Barryville to Parkers Glen

N

Halfway Brook enters, New York side, just downstream from the
bridge. Gravel bars and shallows on the left.

273.4 **CAUTION!** Begin Shohola Rift, a challenging Class II rapids extending
0.4 mile. The clearest channel begins on the left.

273.3 Shohola Creek enters, Pennsylvania side, from a steep ravine. Shohola
Falls, a wide cascade dropping 40 feet over several ledges, is located on
Shohola Creek about 1.5 miles from the river (just off U.S. Route 6).

Rapids become more severe, with boulders obstructing the channel. The river is deepest in the center, but even there paddlers must navigate among boulders.

273.1 Note the fine stone walls along the New York riverbank, remnants of the Delaware & Hudson Canal.

272.9 There is a wide ledge along the left bank just at the end of Shohola Rift, a good place to pull over and bail canoes of the water taken on while passing through the rapids.

272.5 A Class I rapids over boulders and ledges at a squeeze in the river; best passage is down the middle. This rocky little rapids is known as Pissawilly Rift.

272.4 The river makes a sweeping turn to the left into Handsome Eddy, slow water for one mile.

The tracks of the Erie Railroad (today operated by the New York, Susquehanna & Western Railway) run high on the bluffs to the right.

271.5 Camp Tel-Yehudah, a private camp, on the New York riverbank.

271.6 The river swings back to the right.

271.5 Stay to the right; the center and left are very shallow.

Boulders called the Fish Rocks protrude in a line down the middle. The largest of them, near the New York riverbank, is known as Canope's Rock. Canope was a Lenape man ambushed and murdered by infamous "Indian slayer" Tom Quick while fishing here.

271.3 Begin Buttermilk Falls, a Class I+ rapids over a series of ledges, continuing 0.7 mile. Watch for protruding and submerged boulders.

270.7 The last and most severe drop of Buttermilk Falls. The main current runs from left to center, but leads directly toward a big submerged boulder in the very middle of the river. Big waves!

270.3 The river makes a right-angle turn to the left. Steep bluffs on the right and broad ledges along the left.

This short stretch of slow water is called Quicks (Eckharts) Eddy. The National Park Service once maintained a river rest stop on the New York riverbank here, but the land has been sold. No trespassing.

The Park Service's Barryville office, locally known as the "Coop," is along New York Route 97 here, but a couple hundred yards from the river.

270.0 Twin Lakes Creek (once known as Carrs Rock Brook) enters, Pennsylvania side.

In April 1868 the rail bridge over Twin Lakes Creek gave way, pitching an Erie passenger train from the cliffs into the river. Forty passengers were killed and another 75 injured.

The community of Parkers Glen, in the 1800s a center of the local bluestone industry, once stood above the railroad on the Pennsylvania riverbank. Today only a cemetery and a few foundations remain (no access from the river).

Map 9

269.9　Three-mile Rift begins, intermittent rapids continuing almost to Pond Eddy. This first section was dubbed Lost Channel Rift by J. Wallace Hoff on his 1892 trip down the Delaware.[1] Pick your way over shallows and among boulders.

Note the massive stone walls supporting the slope below the Erie Railroad tracks, New York side, laid by hand in 1848.

269.5　A Class I rapids, no obstructions.

269.3　There is a small parking area along New York Route 97 atop the bluffs, with picnic tables and trash barrels. Not a boat launch, and there is no access to or from the river.

269.1　Van Tuyles Brook enters, New York side.

268.8　Beware an eel weir in the center of the river; do not go through the center chute. Gravel bars and shallows on the left; passage to the right is best.

268.7　**Outfitters.** Landers River Trips, Pond Eddy base, New York side.

Kittatinny Canoes, Pond Eddy base, New York side.

268.6　A Class I rapids without obstructions. Be on the lookout for boulders. The river is very shallow.

268.4　**Camping/outfitter.** Jerry's Three River Canoes has campsites at its base on New York Route 97.

267.7　The final stretch of Three-mile Rift, here a Class I+ rapids. Paddlers will surely bump and grind on submerged rocks in the shallow water. The rapids go on for 0.5 mile, one of the longest on the river.

Bluffs of Little Hawks Nest rise above the river on the left.

266.7　Wide ledges extend into the river from the Pennsylvania side, with cliffs rising about 20 feet above the ledges. The river bends to the left. **Camping/outfitter.** Indian Head Canoes operates a campground (tent sites and lean-tos) at its Pond Eddy base.

266.4　Pond Eddy Brook enters, Pennsylvania side, via a picturesque stone tunnel beneath the Erie tracks. The river bends sharply to the left.

A small brushy island near the left (New York) side.

265.8　Mill Brook enters, New York side.

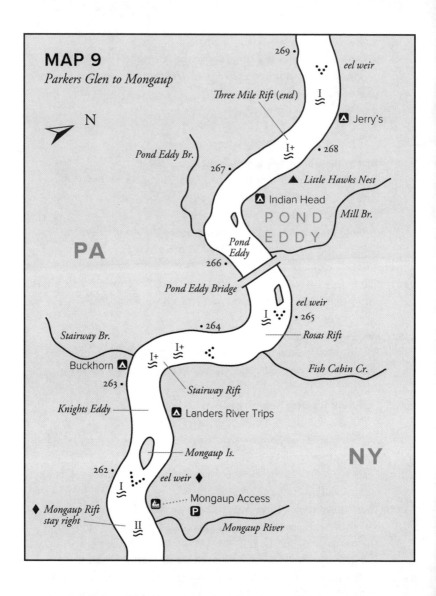

MAP 9
Parkers Glen to Mongaup

N

eel weir

269 •

Three Mile Rift (end)

I

🔺 Jerry's

• 268

Pond Eddy Br.

I+

267 •

🔺 *Little Hawks Nest*

🔺 Indian Head

P O N D

Mill Br.

E D D Y

Pond Eddy

PA

266 •

Pond Eddy Bridge

eel weir

I

• 265

• 264

Rosas Rift

Stairway Br.

Fish Cabin Cr.

Buckhorn 🔺

I+

I+

263 •

Stairway Rift

Knights Eddy

🔺 Landers River Trips

Mongaup Is.

262 •

NY

eel weir ♦

I

🛶 ...... Mongaup Access

♦ *Mongaup Rift*

🅿

stay right

II

Mongaup River

Although there is no "official" access, services in Pond Eddy, New York, can be reached via a *steep* trail to New York Route 97 at the mouth of Mill Brook. Beach your canoe on the rocks.

265.6 Pass under the Pond Eddy Bridge, built in 1903, a double-truss steel span with a one-lane wooden roadway. A wire-rope suspension bridge built here in 1870 was destroyed in the Pumpkin Flood of 1903. This old bridge carries fewer cars than any other on the Delaware;

there is only a small community on the Pennsylvania side and no through traffic.

The village of Pond Eddy, once called Flagstone, was a center of the local bluestone slate industry. A huge slab quarried here was placed in front of City Hall in New York City.

Lunch. Pond Eddy, New York: Nolan's River Inn and the Mill Brook Inn. The Mill Brook Inn has been here for more than 150 years and was once popular with timber raftsmen and canal crews.

265.1   Broad ledges are exposed at low water near the New York (left) side, as the river bends sharply to the right.

265.0   River bends to the right into the Class I rapids of Rosas Rift, with protruding and submerged boulders across the river, continuing 0.4 mile.

Stay right to avoid an eel weir on the left.

264.1   **Outfitter.** Kittatinny Canoes landing (Knights Eddy), New York side.

264.0   Fish Cabin Creek enters, New York side.

263.9   There's an old eel weir on the New York (left) side; stay to the right. As of this writing (2010), it was not in use.

263.6   Enter Stairway Rift, a succession of three ledges with increasingly severe Class I+ rapids. Rocky bluffs along the Pennsylvania side can be imagined as a giant staircase. Best passage is to the left. Standing waves to 1½ feet foreshadow what's to come around the next few bends.

Stairway Rift begins the most exciting string of rapids on the Delaware. The next five miles will give canoeists, kayakers, and rafters a wild ride though five Class I+ and II rapids, with only brief respites in the eddies between. Wear your PFD and do not take it off until the ride is over.

Route 97 runs very close at the New York riverbank, supported here and there by remnant walls of the old Delaware & Hudson Canal.

263.3   Stairway Brook enters, Pennsylvania side, at the final ledge of the rapids.

263.2   **Camping.** Buckhorn Natural Area (Delaware State Forest, Pennsylvania). Primitive camping by permit from the National Park Service.

The camping area is not marked and is hard to find from the river. Beach your boat on the riverbank just below Stairway Rift.

263.1   Enter Knights Eddy; slow-moving water continues 0.8 mile. "Captain" John Knight was a well-known timber raftsman.

262.5   **Camping/outfitter.** Landers River Trips, Knights Eddy campground and river base. Primitive tent sites and lean-tos for canoeists and kayakers, New York side. Water and privies only.

262.4   The river is bounded on both sides by slabs of shale bedrock.

262.3 Upstream end of Mongaup Island, a brushy gravel bar extending 0.2 mile. Stay right; the left channel seems clear but will put you into the maw of an eel weir.

262.1 There are Class I rapids in the channel to the right of Mongaup Island. **CAUTION!** An eel weir nearly spans the river just below Mongaup Island. Stay as far right as possible, although shallow.

Slow water for the next 0.7 mile.

Map 10

261.2 **Access: Mongaup, New York.** Maintained by the New York Department of Environmental Conservation. Hand-launch boat landing, ample parking, privies. Boats must be carried about 100 yards along a dirt trail from the parking area to the river. A National Park Service attendant is on hand during summer weekends. No fee. Access from New York Route 97.

Mongaup was a way station on the old Delaware & Hudson Canal. A stone lift lock can be seen in the woods across Route 97.

261.1 The Mongaup River enters, New York side, in a torrent of white water.

Canoeists and kayakers play in the big waves at Mongaup Rift, a Class II rapids. It's not uncommon to capsize here; wear your PFD! (Photo by Courtenay Kling)

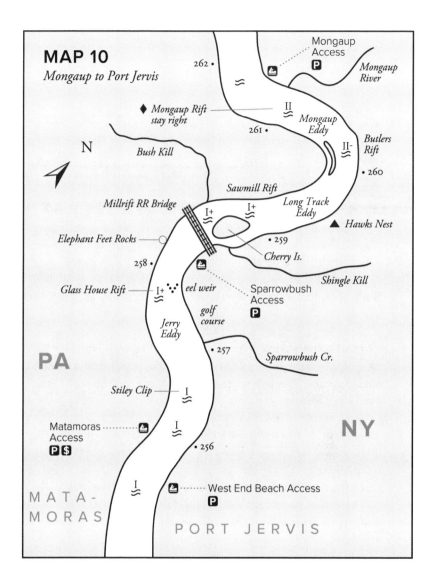

MAP 10
Mongaup to Port Jervis

Mongaup
Access

262 •

Mongaup
River

II
Mongaup
Eddy

♦ Mongaup Rift
stay right

261 •

Butlers
Rift

II-

N

Bush Kill

• 260

Sawmill Rift

Long Track
Eddy

Millrift RR Bridge

I+   I+

▲ Hawks Nest

Elephant Feet Rocks —○

• 259

258 •

Cherry Is.

Shingle Kill

Glass House Rift —   I+   eel weir

Sparrowbush
Access

Jerry
Eddy

golf
course

PA

• 257

Sparrowbush Cr.

Stiley Clip —   I

Matamoras
Access

I

NY

• 256

I

MATA-
MORAS

West End Beach Access

PORT JERVIS

CAUTION! Enter Mongaup Rift, a Class II rapids. Scout the rapids
from either riverbank to plan your route through. This one is a thriller!
Wear your PFD; many paddlers founder or capsize in the big waves.

    Ledges and shallows extend from the New York (left) side, with
the main flow of the river squeezed to the Pennsylvania (right) side.
The rapids begin over a boulder ledge, then funnel into a chute where
the biggest standing waves (3+ feet) on the Delaware are formed. The

channel through the chute is clear, but open canoes will almost surely take on water in the 3-foot haystacks.

A huge stone-and-concrete abutment supports the Erie Railroad tracks on the Pennsylvania side. It is possible to scramble up to a wide ledge to watch boaters pass through the rapids.

260.9 Whew, you've made it through the Mongaup! Pull over to shallows at either side to bail your canoe. Slow water of Mongaup Eddy for the next 0.8 mile.

260.1 The river bends sharply to the right. A large gravel bar known as Butlers Island is on the right side.

Enter Butlers Rift, Class II– rapids extending about one-quarter mile. The main current flows near the New York (left) side with occasional hidden boulders; standing waves 2½ feet high make for a wild ride. Stay right to avoid the heaviest of the rapids.

General Butler was a Loyalist associate of Chief Joseph Brant, leader of the British and Iroquois raiding party at the Battle of Minisink in 1779.

Rock ledges extend from the left.

Hawks Nest Mountain rises steeply from the river on the New York side. New York Route 97 snakes along the cliffs with a view down to the river, one of the most spectacular sections of roadway in the eastern United States.

The base of the cliffs was known as the Cellar Hole to timber raftsmen, a trap for rafts in high water. Raftsmen struggled to stay near the Pennsylvania side to avoid being dashed against the wall of the Delaware & Hudson Canal. The canal ran against the cliffs 40 feet above the river, an astonishing feat of engineering. Remnants of the canal walls can be seen along the river's edge, New York side.

259.9 Enter Long Track Eddy. The Erie tracks run atop the Pennsylvania riverbank.

259.7 Hay Rock, so-called because a ferry hauled hay here for a nearby farm, juts prominently from the cliffs on the New York side.

258.9 Upstream end of Cherry Island. Stay to the right for the best ride through Sawmill Rift; the left channel is very shallow.

Enter Sawmill Rift, a strong Class I+ rapids, with the best passage down the right center. Big waves and lots of rocks!

258.6 Downstream end of Cherry Island.

Shingle Kill enters, New York side.

Sawmill Rift continues after a brief pause, still a strong Class I+ rapids. Boulders lurk below the water line, and shallows extend from

New York Route 97 winds along the cliffs of Hawks Nest Mountain, one of the most spectacular drives in the eastern United States. The rapids of Butlers Rift and Sawmill Rift run through the river far below. (Photo by Andy Smith)

the downstream tip of Cherry Island. The best passage, with standing waves to 2 feet, is down the middle.

The little community of Millrift, Pennsylvania, is very close to the water on the right. A ferry operated here in the nineteenth century.

Bush Kill enters, Pennsylvania side. There are two more tributaries named Bush Kill farther downriver. *Kill* is old Dutch for "stream."

The perils of Sawmill Rift were remembered in a little ditty by raftsman raconteur Boney Quillen:

We swung around Old Butler's,
No danger did we fear;

Until we come to Sawmill Rift—
And went plumb against the pier.[2]

258.3 Unless you are careful, you too will go plumb against the pier
of the Millrift Railroad Bridge (Bridge No. 2). A wooden trestle
for the Erie Railroad was built here in 1850, replaced later by the
present steel span. Today the old Erie line is operated by the
New York, Susquehanna & Western Railway.

The railroad bridge marks the downstream boundary of the
Upper Delaware Scenic and Recreational River.

258.2 **Access: Sparrowbush, New York.** Maintained by the New York
Department of Environmental Conservation. A natural beach for
boat launch, limited parking, no facilities. No fee. Access from
Hook Road off New York Route 97. Locally known as Fireman's
Beach, the site is often used by swimmers.

Remnants of the Delaware & Hudson Canal are found beside
the dirt road that leads to the access area.

Cliffs aptly known as Elephant Feet Rocks rise from the water
on the Pennsylvania side.

258.0 A sign painted on the rocks, right side, warns boaters to "Stay
Right." Do so.

257.9 An eel weir extends nearly across the river. Do not go through the
center chute or over the stone wings of the weir; stay as close to
the cliffs at the Pennsylvania (right) side as possible.

Enter Glass House Rift, a Class I+ rapids. Stay on the right;
there are shallows, gravel bars, and the eel weir on the left.
The rapids ends with big standing waves beneath towering
Glass House Cliffs.

In the early 1800s a glass factory operated atop the cliffs. Using
river sand as its raw material, the factory produced window panes
for use in Philadelphia and New York City.

A broad gravel bar extends from the New York side.

257.7 Enter Jerry Eddy, slow water for the next mile.

Eddy Farm Resort and golf course, left (New York) side.

257.1 Sparrowbush Creek enters, New York side.

256.5 **Outfitters.** Several river outfitters end their trips here, with landings on both sides:

Silver Canoes, Sparrowbush, New York.
Whitewater Willies, Sparrowbush, New York.
Indian Head Canoes, Matamoras, Pennsylvania.

Kittatinny Canoes, Matamoras, Pennsylvania.
Landers River Trips, Matamoras, Pennsylvania.
Jerry's Three River Canoes, Matamoras, Pennsylvania.

256.4 Class I rapids with choppy waves, continuing intermittently for nearly a mile. Old-time raftsmen called this Stiley Clip. Not difficult; beware of boulders on the right.

256.0 **Access: Matamoras, Pennsylvania.** Maintained by the Pennsylvania Fish and Boat Commission. A wide paved ramp, ample parking, privies, trash disposal, water. All boats must bear a valid Pennsylvania registration or launch permit.

Modest Class I rapids.

255.8 Look ahead to the High Point monument atop the Kittatinny Ridge. At 1,803 feet, High Point is the highest peak in the state of New Jersey.

255.6 **Access: West End Beach, Port Jervis, New York.** Maintained by the City of Port Jervis. A sandy boat ramp, ample parking, roped and guarded swimming area, restrooms. Access from Ferry Street, Port Jervis. No fee. Private boat launch is permitted, but commercial access is not.

This is the site of the old Mapes Ferry, one of several nineteenth-century crossings at Port Jervis.

Features

Delaware & Hudson Canal

Fine stone walls rise above the New York riverbank from Lackawaxen to Sparrowbush, the remnants of a canal built to carry coal from Pennsylvania to the Hudson River.

Anthracite coal found in the Pocono Mountains was black gold to entrepreneurs of the early 1800s. But it was a long, hard way from the Poconos to market in New York City. In 1823 William Wurtz chartered the Delaware & Hudson Company to build a canal from Honesdale, Pennsylvania, to Rondout, New York, a total of 108 miles. Twenty-five hundred men labored under the direction of engineer John Jervis to dig the trench, lay stone walls, and build the locks and aqueducts. The first barges passed through the canal in 1828.

Profits soared as tens of thousands of tons of coal, timber, grain, and cement were barged to the Hudson River and New York City. The upper Delaware valley was alive with the raucous shouts of bargemen and the braying of mules. Yet it wasn't long before new-fangled railroads took business from the canal.

A mule-drawn barge awaits passage through a lock on the Delaware & Hudson Canal in this view c. 1890. The canal ran 40 feet above the river against the cliffs of Hawks Nest. Only remnants of the walls remain. (Photo courtesy of the Delaware & Hudson Canal Historical Society)

And as it aged, the canal became harder to keep up. Floods, cave-ins, and other disasters slowed traffic and cost too much to repair. Tourist excursions on the canal were popular near the end of its life, but these only postponed the inevitable. The canal was drained in 1898.

Early canoeists on the upper Delaware paddled alongside "the ever-attendant noise of horns and shoutings, together with the choice vocabulary of captains and mule drivers," as J. Wallace Hoff described the scene in 1892.[3] Today, few traces of the canal remain: abandoned locks along the road, foundations of a lock tender's home, a shallow trench in the forest. In a few places, retaining walls hand-laid for the canal now support New York Route 97. And John Roebling's aqueduct at Lackawaxen, built to carry the canal across the Delaware, stands as a National Historic Landmark. The Delaware & Hudson Canal Historical Society runs a museum at High Falls, New York, where visitors can get a taste of life on the old canal.

The Erie Railroad

New York & Erie Railroad president Benjamin Loder promised that trains would run to Port Jervis before 1848. On New Years Eve the locomotive *Eleazar Lord* moved into position east of the Neversink River. But the tracks over the trestle were not yet complete. Well after dark the crew, with local citizens pitching in, worked to lay the rails. At 17 minutes before midnight the line to Port Jervis was finished, and the little train chugged into town to begin a grand party. Loder had kept his word.

North of Port Jervis the Erie was to wind along the Delaware River. The rails had to be laid on the rocky Pennsylvania side because the Delaware & Hudson Canal already occupied the relatively gentle New York side. Workmen hung in baskets over the river to blast the rock away, hauled up to safety only when the fuse was ignited. Massive stone walls were built to buttress the rail grade, in places 50 feet above the river.

There was no love lost between the rail crews and the canal bargemen across the river. The men knew that their employers would be competing and that their livelihoods were at stake. Rail crews learned to time their blasts to shower bargemen with dust and debris. Canalers stole equipment and sabotaged construction of the tracks. Local taverns saw many a brawl between the sides, and sometimes shots were fired over the river. Yet railroad construction progressed rapidly. The line was completed to Lake Erie in 1851, linking the cities of the East with the Midwest.

Early days on the railroad were hazardous. The worst crash occurred during the Civil War, when a train carrying Confederate prisoners slammed into a locomotive hauling 50 cars of coal. Seventy-five souls perished in the wreck, their remains buried in a common grave along the tracks near Shohola. Terrible wrecks also occurred at Parkers Glen, Millrift, and Port Jervis.

Many of the villages in the upper Delaware valley grew around the Erie line. Hancock, Callicoon, Narrowsburg, Shohola, Millrift, and Port Jervis thrived because of their locations by the tracks. Each of these towns and hamlets boasted a depot, many of which remain standing.

The Erie line has changed hands, and names, many times over the years. The tracks are now operated by the New York, Susquehanna & Western Railway, with local freight run by the Central New York Railroad. There is less traffic than there once was, and no regular passenger service. Still, campers are often awakened by the squeal of a late-night freight train rumbling along the Delaware on the old Erie line.

Port Jervis

How can a city so far from the sea be called a "port"? The answer lies in its history: the community was an important layover for barges on the old Delaware & Hudson Canal, engineered in the 1820s by John B. Jervis.

The Lenape called the confluence of the Neversink and Delaware Rivers

Mahacamac. They grew corn and squash, hunted game, fished for eel and shad, and canoed the Delaware. In about 1690 a Dutch blacksmith named Abrahamse Tietsoort arrived, and before long little settlements had sprouted at Deer Park and Mahacamack. The village was sacked by Joseph Brant's raiders during the American Revolution, then remained a wilderness outpost until Jervis routed the canal through the area in 1828. Port Jervis became a railroad town when the Erie arrived in 1848, home to freight yards, machine shops, warehouses, and employees. Although the city has declined since the heyday of the canal and the Erie, it remains the commercial center of the tri-state region.

The link across the river between Port Jervis and Pike County, Pennsylvania, has always been a vital one. Ferries began to run soon after the first settlers arrived, and a bridge was built in 1852. Yet no crossing was as strange as the one that occurred in 1868, when the circus came to town. Tippoo the elephant was too heavy for the bridge, so his handler prodded him to ford the Delaware. Just then, a 140-foot timber raft careened around the bend, aimed straight toward the pachyderm. The panicked raftsmen dove off to swim ashore. Tippoo and the raft were left to fight it out alone. When the raft collided with the elephant, it pivoted and, with a shove from Tippoo, was dashed apart on the rocks. Tippoo himself was none the worse for wear, and the circus went on the next day.[4]

Today, Port Jervis and its sister city, Matamoras, Pennsylvania, offer all services to visitors and tourists. There are good hotels, restaurants, grocery stores, and a hospital. Artifacts of colonial history are displayed at Fort Decker, maintained by the Minisink Valley Historical Society and open to the public on an irregular basis. The majestic old Erie depot, abandoned for many years, has been renovated and stands a few blocks from the Mid-Delaware Bridge. Port Jervis is today the terminus of the Metro North Railroad, a commuter line that runs to Suffern, New York, with connections to New York City.

Mile 255.6 to 238.6 (17.0 miles)

The river changes dramatically as it bends sharply south at Port Jervis. The white water of the previous 40 miles is left behind, and the river becomes wider and deeper. Only one rapids, found in the tortuous channels around Quicks Island, presents any real difficulty. This section is excellent for beginners. Several outfitters offer canoes, kayaks, rafts, and tubes for rent and shuttle, although traffic is lighter than above Port Jervis.

The river is deflected south at Port Jervis by the hard rock of the Ridge and Valley geophysical province, a band of wrinkled mountains that extends from Vermont to Alabama. As you face downstream, the Kittatinny Ridge is on your left, and the Pocono Mountain portion of the Appalachian Plateau is on your right.

The islands in this section are quite different from the low gravel bars farther upriver. Here many of the islands rise 15 or 20 feet on high silty banks and are inundated only during the highest floods. The islands are cloaked with lush forests of poplar trees and an undergrowth of ferns. These river islands were deposited when the great continental glacier melted about 15,000 years ago, swelling the flow of the river with gravel and silt. The river basin itself is filled with the stony debris left by the melting glacier, and bedrock is exposed in few places.

The river valley here was once inhabited by the Lenape, or Delaware Indians. They called the area *Minisink*, aptly meaning "stony ground." The Lenape were here when European settlers first arrived in the valley, and archaeological exploration has revealed much earlier habitation.

With the exception of the first few miles, the river and adjacent lands in this section are within the Delaware Water Gap National Recreation Area (DWGNRA), and the National Park Service supervises recreation on the river. The river here has been designated by the U.S. Congress as the Middle Delaware National Scenic River and is subject to special protections.

Port Jervis, New York, and Matamoras and Milford, Pennsylvania, are the

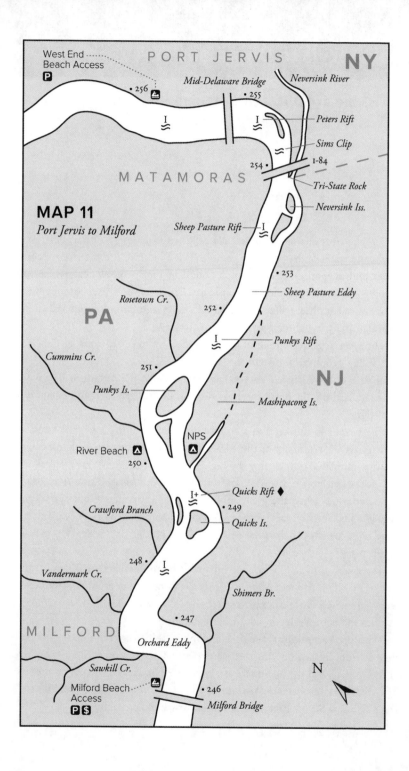

West End
Beach Access
🅿

• 256

PORT JERVIS

Mid-Delaware Bridge

NY

Neversink River

• 255

Peters Rift

Sims Clip

MATAMORAS

254 •

I-84

Tri-State Rock

Neversink Iss.

MAP 11
Port Jervis to Milford

Sheep Pasture Rift

• 253

Sheep Pasture Eddy

Rosetown Cr.

252 •

PA

Punkys Rift

Cummins Cr.

251 •

NJ

Punkys Is.

Mashipacong Is.

NPS

River Beach 🏕

250 •

Quicks Rift ◆

Crawford Branch

I+

• 249

Quicks Is.

248 •

I

Vandermark Cr.

Shimers Br.

• 247

MILFORD

Orchard Eddy

Sawkill Cr.

Milford Beach
Access
🅿 💲

• 246

Milford Bridge

N

main towns in this area. U.S. Route 209 roughly parallels the river on the Pennsylvania side. The New Jersey side is sparsely populated, and virtually no services are available.

Camping for one night only via canoe/kayak is permitted at designated sites on the riverbanks within the DWGNRA. Be prepared to rough it: each site has a metal fire grate, and some have a privy, but that's all. Rangers will issue tickets to persons camping at unauthorized locations or not on a river trip. Because there is no road access, your fellow campers will also be paddlers. Note: most campsites on the river islands were obliterated in the 2004–2006 floods, and the Park Service has not reopened them. Private, full-service campgrounds may be found at Matamoras and near Milford.

There are four public access sites in this section:

West End Beach, Port Jervis, New York, mile 255.6
Milford Beach, Pennsylvania, mile 246.2
Namonock, New Jersey, mile 241.9
Dingmans Ferry, Pennsylvania, mile 238.6

River Guide

Map 11

255.6 **Access: West End Beach, New York.** Maintained by the City of Port Jervis. Unpaved boat ramp, ample parking, guarded swimming area, restrooms. No fee. Private boat launching is permitted, but commercial access is not. Access from Ferry Street, Port Jervis.

This is the site of the old Westfall (Mapes) Ferry, which crossed here until construction of a bridge in 1852.

255.5 Bridge abutments on both riverbanks and the remnant of a pier in the center of the river mark the temporary location of the Mid-Delaware Bridge during construction of the present bridge in 1939. The old bridge was floated upriver and anchored here while the new bridge was built.

Power lines buzz overhead.

255.4 The river widens and becomes quite shallow, with a moderate riffle over the gravel bottom. There is an old eel weir near the New York riverbank; as of this writing (2010), it is not in use.

255.1 Pass under the Mid-Delaware Bridge, built in 1939, the fourth bridge to span the river here. The first bridge was constructed in 1852 to carry both horse-drawn wagons and the Erie Railroad.

The twin cities of Matamoras, Pennsylvania (est. pop. 2,624, 2009), and Port Jervis, New York (est. pop. 9,136, 2009), stand at opposite ends of the bridge. There is no access from the river at the bridge crossing. **Lunch.** Flo-Jean's restaurant, a local landmark since 1929, incorporates the old toll house on the Port Jervis end of the bridge.

Shallows or gravel bars on the left.

There is a U.S. Geological Survey river gage on the Pennsylvania riverbank just downstream from the bridge. River stage measured here is used by the Geological Survey, National Weather Service, and Delaware River Basin Commission to monitor the flow of the river. Base elevation is 415.35 feet. Good stage for boating is 3–6 feet. Flood stage is 18 feet, and the greatest flood measured here was 25.5 feet, in 1904.

254.9 Numbers painted on a concrete bulkhead, New York side, indicate elevation above sea level.

254.6 Class I rapids of Peters Rift, at a submerged ledge extending halfway across the river. Clearest passage is right down the middle.

254.4 The river makes a sharp turn to the right. Shallows or gravel bars hug the outside of the turn; stay right.

Bare shale ledges plate the bluff at the New York riverbank. During high water the river boils up against these ledges as it bends hard to the right. This was a trouble spot for old-time timber rafters, who called it Sims Clip. A "clip" was a stroke of the steering oar, and rafters had to clip hard to avoid being jammed onto the ledges. The place is named for Simeon Westfall, a prominent pioneer and raftsman. Old Sim, along with many other Westfalls, is buried in the cemetery above the rocks.

253.9 Pass under a high concrete-and-steel bridge carrying Interstate 84, completed in 1973.

253.8 The Neversink River enters on the left. A principal tributary of the Delaware, the Neversink is renowned for Class III and IV white water that rages through a gorge upstream. *Neversink* is derived from the Lenape *Navasink*, meaning "at the point." The Lenape called the river itself *Mahacamac*, also an early name for the community of Port Jervis.

The peninsula at the confluence of the Neversink and the Delaware is called Carpenters Point. Benjamin Carpenter ran a ferry between the point and Matamoras, Pennsylvania, in the 1700s and early 1800s.

Beautiful Laurel Grove cemetery occupies most of the peninsula. The founding families of the area, including Deckers, Quicks, and Westfalls, are buried here. The grave of ferryman Benjamin Carpenter, dated 1826, can be found at the very end of the cemetery, under the I-84 bridge.

The boundaries of New Jersey, New York, and Pennsylvania meet at Tri-States Rock, on Carpenters Point near Port Jervis. (Photo by the author)

Tri-States Rock, a small granite monument with a bronze benchmark embedded on top, stands near the water's edge at the very tip of Carpenters Point. Tri-States Rock marks the intersection of the boundaries of New York, New Jersey, and Pennsylvania. The little monument, placed here in 1882, is actually located in three states. A larger monument higher on the rocks (under the I-84 bridge) commemorates the engineers who surveyed the boundary.

253.7 Neversink (or Sims) Islands, left side, extending 0.6 mile. The main flow of the river is to the right, but the little channel to the left of the islands is navigable, with Class I rapids.

253.5 A Class I rapids known as Sheep Pasture Rift, continuing 0.3 mile. Standing waves to 1½ feet and a few submerged boulders. The remnant of an eel weir can be seen at the end of the rapids; as of this writing (2010), it was not in use.

253.2 The river slows into Sheep Pasture Eddy.

253.0 Cleared land along the New Jersey (left) riverbank was once a golf course, now abandoned.

252.4 A gravel clearing on the left marks the upstream end of Mashipacong Island, extending 2.5 miles downstream. The channel between the island and the New Jersey riverbank is just a swampy pass through the forest known as *Benakill*, old Dutch for "minnow stream."

252.2 Punkys Rift, a Class I rapids with moderate standing waves, flows right to left, then left to right. Very shallow; beware submerged boulders peppered throughout.

251.6 Delaware Valley High School and athletic fields, Pennsylvania side.

251.1 Upstream end of Punkys Island, extending 1.2 miles. Passage is good either side, with mild riffles.

Punkys Island and Rift got their name when ripened pumpkins, snatched from their vines by an October flood, snagged here to form a bouncing orange dam across the channel.

Rosetown Creek enters, Pennsylvania side.

250.4 Cummins Creek, long ago known as Quicks Mill Creek, joins the Delaware on the Pennsylvania side.

In 1756 Tom Quick Sr. was ambushed and killed near here by Lenape warriors, an event that fueled a life-long campaign of cruel vengeance by his son Tom Quick Jr., the "Avenger of the Delaware."

250.3 **Camping/outfitter.** Kittatinny Canoes, River Beach campground and river base, Pennsylvania side, at a broad sandy beach. Full facilities. Road access from U.S. Route 209.

249.9 Punkys Island tapers to its downstream end; fast water with no obstructions.

The Delaware Water Gap National Recreation Area and Middle Delaware National Scenic River begin here. From this point to just south of the Delaware Water Gap use of the river and adjacent lands is under the jurisdiction of the National Park Service.

249.8 A power line marked by red balls crosses the river.

249.5 **Camping.** Mashipacong Island campsite. An NPS primitive campsite near the end of the island. No facilities.

249.3 Downstream end of Mashipacong Island, usually just a dry, gravelly channel on the left.

249.0 Mays Bar extends about 0.2 mile along the Pennsylvania side.

248.9 Quicks Island, a brushy gravel bar extending 0.3 mile, to the left of Mays Bar.

CAUTION! Enter Quicks Rift, a Class I+ rapids, the trickiest to be found in this section. The main current zigzags left, then right, through a narrow channel along the New Jersey riverbank. Standing waves to 2 feet. Stay close to the island to avoid being pushed against the riverbank.

The sudden change of direction generates wicked cross-currents, boils, and whirlpools capable of upsetting a canoe or pushing it into the riverbank. Sweepers (logs or trees fallen from the shoreline) may be a hazard. Wear your PFD.

The passage along the Pennsylvania (right) side of Quicks Island is easier, a straight shot along the tail of Mays Bar over a cobbled bottom with nice standing waves; at low water, however, it may be too shallow.

Quicks Island and Rift are named for Tom Quick, infamous "Avenger of the Delaware."

248.3 Crawford Branch enters, Pennsylvania side.

248.0 A Class I rapids over shallows. Watch for scattered submerged boulders.

247.9 Enter Orchard Eddy, slow water continuing well past Milford.

247.3 Vandermark Creek enters at a constriction of the river, Pennsylvania side.

247.0 Sawkill Creek enters, Pennsylvania side. Sawkill Falls, also known as Pinchot Falls, one of the most spectacular cascades in the region, is found on this creek about one mile from the Delaware near Grey Towers, the estate of "father of conservation" Gifford Pinchot.

246.5 Shimers Brook enters, New Jersey side.

246.2 **Access: Milford Beach, Pennsylvania.** A major day-use area maintained by the National Park Service. Paved boat ramp, ample parking, restrooms, drinking water, telephone, picnic tables, and swimming beach. Fee: $7 per vehicle weekdays / $10 weekends (2010). Access from U.S. Route 209 at Milford, Pennsylvania.

Milford Beach is the northern terminus of the McDade Recreation Trail, a hiker/bicycle path extending 37 miles down to the Hialeah Picnic Area.

The community of Milford, Pennsylvania (est. pop. 1,210, 2009), is about one mile up the beach access road. All services are available, including restaurants and groceries.

A concrete bridge abutment on the Pennsylvania side and its rock counterpart across the river mark the location of the old Milford-Montague Bridge. A wooden covered bridge was built here in 1826, a suspension bridge in 1869, and a steel truss span in 1889, ultimately replaced in 1953 by the modern concrete bridge slightly downstream.

This is the site of Wells Ferry, which crossed the Delaware in the late eighteenth and early nineteenth centuries, before construction of the first bridge. The village of Milford was initially known as Wells Ferry (not to be confused with Wells Ferry downriver at New Hope).

The 20-foot-tall concrete tower standing atop the Pennsylvania bridge abutment houses a gage to measure the flow of the river. Base elevation is 369.33 feet. Good boating stage is 5–8 feet; flood stage is 25 feet. The greatest flood at this point on the river was 35.5 feet, in 1903.

According to 1931 and 1954 rulings of the U.S. Supreme Court, New York may draw water from the Delaware watershed for consumption in New York City so long as flow to downstream cities in New Jersey and Pennsylvania is not impaired. A River Master employed by the Delaware River Basin Commission constantly monitors the flow of the river here, allocating consumption among the states.

Map 12

245.9   Pass under the "new" Milford-Montague Toll Bridge, opened to traffic in 1953. When it was first constructed, this bridge was recognized as one of the most beautiful steel bridges in the country.

245.7   White Brook enters, New Jersey side.

245.0   Upstream end of Minisink Island, continuing 1.8 miles. *Minisink*, roughly meaning "stony ground," is the Lenape name for the tri-state area. There was a big Lenape village on Minisink Island when European settlers arrived in the late seventeenth century.

Brinks Rift, a Class I rapids, runs down the main channel to the right of the island. There are standing waves to 1½ feet, no obstructions.

The left channel is navigable at average water levels and offers a spell of "little river" paddling down the sloughs.

244.8   A rocky escarpment known simply as The Cliff towers 500 feet above the river along the Pennsylvania side.

244.6   Everetts Island, in the channel to the left (New Jersey side) of Minisink Island.

243.9   Raymondskill Creek enters, Pennsylvania side.

Famous Raymondskill Falls—one of the highest and most spectacular in Pennsylvania—is found on this creek about a mile from the river. It's well worth a stop on your way to or from a river trip.

The Battle of Conashaugh, a skirmish during the American Revolution, occurred near here in 1780. Thirteen American militia and several civilians were killed in a raid led by Joseph Brant, a Mohawk Indian and colonel in the British Army.

243.3   Downstream end of Minisink Island. There is an exposed gravel bar where the channels rejoin.

This slow stretch of river was once known as Death Eddy. Seven

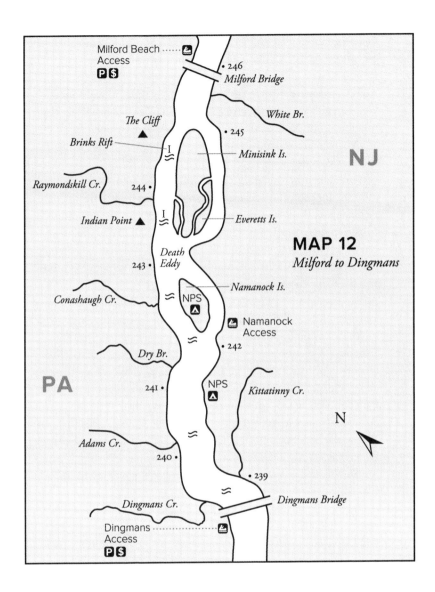

Milford Beach ......
Access
🅿️ 🆘

• 246
Milford Bridge

White Br.

The Cliff
▲

Brinks Rift

• 245

Minisink Is.

NJ

I

Raymondskill Cr.

244 •

Indian Point ▲

I

Everetts Is.

MAP 12
Milford to Dingmans

*Death
Eddy*

243 •

Namanock Is.

Conashaugh Cr.

NPS
⛺

🏖️ Namanock
Access

Dry Br.

• 242

PA

241 •

NPS
⛺

Kittatinny Cr.

N

Adams Cr.

240 •

• 239

Dingmans Bridge

Dingmans Cr.

Dingmans ....
Access
🅿️ 🆘

🏖️

pioneers in pursuit of a Lenape raiding party were themselves
ambushed and killed at the river's edge here in 1778.

The cliffs along the Pennsylvania side are called Indian Point and
Pow Wow Hill.

242.7 Upstream end of Namanock Island, extending one mile. Channels to
the left and right are passable without obstructions; minor riffles.

242.5 Conashaugh Creek enters, Pennsylvania side.

242.1 **Camping.** Namanock canoe campsites. Four primitive Park Service sites on Namanock Island, about 0.1 mile apart. Fire pits, privies, no other facilities.

241.9 **Access: Namanock, New Jersey.** Maintained by the National Park Service. Rough hand-launch area, small parking area, picnic tables; no other facilities. No fee. Access from Sussex County Route 521.

Downstream end of Namanock Island. The river moves slowly for the next 1.6 miles.

Fort Namanock, one of six forts built by eighteenth-century pioneers for protection against Indian raids, was located near here. Remnants of the fort were obliterated when the land was acquired for construction of the Tocks Island Dam.

241.3 Dry Brook enters, Pennsylvania side.

240.8 **Camping.** Sandyston canoe camping area, New Jersey side. Six primitive sites, spaced about 0.1 mile apart; privies.

240.3 Adams Creek enters, Pennsylvania side. A trail leads from U.S. Route 209 along Adams Creek to spectacular "secret" waterfalls.

Moderate riffle with no obstructions.

239.2 Dingmans Creek enters, Pennsylvania side. Famous Dingmans Falls and Silver Thread Falls are on this creek about 1.5 miles from the river, accessible via Dingmans Creek Road in Dingmans Ferry. The National Park Service has a visitor center at Dingmans Falls.

239.1 Kittatinny Creek joins the Delaware at the New Jersey side.

238.7 Pass under Dingmans Bridge. This picturesque span, owned by the Dingmans Choice and Delaware Bridge Company, is the only extant private toll bridge across the Delaware and one of only a handful in the United States.

Andrew Dingman ran a ferry here as early as 1738. The wooden covered bridges built here, the first in 1836, repeatedly collapsed in flood, wind, or fire. The present steel span dates to 1900. Tolls on the "new" bridge were assessed as follows:

2 horse wagon	25 cents
1 horse wagon	18 cents
horseless carriage	40 cents
horse and rider	10 cents
horse sled	6 cents
footman	2 cents
bicycle	5 cents
tandem	6 cents
cattle	3 cents

Most bridges across the Delaware were once privately owned. The one at Dingmans Ferry, built in 1900, is the only private toll bridge remaining and one of only a handful in America. (Photo by the author)

There was, and still is, no charge for children going to school or people going to church on Sundays. The toll for a horseless carriage today is one dollar.

The ancient stone home of Judge Andrew Dingman III, built in 1803, stands sentinel at the Pennsylvania end of the bridge. The village of Dingmans Ferry, once a raftsmen's hangout and a vacation haven, is all but gone.

238.6 **Access: Dingmans Ferry, Pennsylvania.** Operated by the National Park Service. A wide, paved boat ramp, plenty of parking, restrooms, telephones, and trash disposal. Fee: $7 per vehicle weekdays / $10 weekends (2010). Access from Dingmans Ferry Road, one mile from U.S. 209. **Outfitter.** Kittatinny Canoes landing, adjacent to the public access.

Features

Tom Quick, the Avenger of the Delaware

According to *Ripley's Believe It Or Not,* Tom Quick killed more Indians after he died than he did during his lifetime. Known in legend as the "Avenger of the Delaware," he was in real life a psychotic killer who wrecked havoc on the Minisink frontier.

When Europeans settlers arrived in the Delaware Valley, they were greeted in the Lenape tradition of hospitality. But good relations did not last long. Tensions arose over land-grabs and incursions on hunting grounds. By the time of the French and Indian War (1754–1763), many Lenape sided against the English and Dutch settlers, hoping to drive them from the Minisink. Although the settlers built stone forts along the Delaware for protection, no one was safe.

Dutchman Tom Quick Sr. came to the Minisink in 1733 and lived peaceably with his aboriginal neighbors until the war. Then, on a cold winter day in 1756, Quick and his two sons, John and Tom Jr., were ambushed by Lenape warriors near their mill at Cummins Creek. The Quicks tried to run across the Delaware for safety, but Tom Sr., old and gouty, could not keep up. As the boys escaped, the Indians fell upon the elder Quick, brutally killing and scalping him. Traumatized, Tom Quick Jr. vowed never to let an Indian escape from him alive.

Tom Quick was cunning and merciless in his mission of vengeance, often befriending Indians before killing them when he had the chance. In the most infamous tale, Tom was splitting logs for a fence as seven Indians came upon him, intent on taking him away. Tom asked the Indians to help him split the last log. As Quick drove a wedge into the log, he instructed the Indians to pull it apart with their hands. When the Indians complied, Quick knocked the wedge from the log to snap it tight on his victims' fingers. Tom then dispatched the seven at his leisure. Quick's own mother said that Tom had not been "right in the head" since witnessing his father's cruel death.

Tom Quick died of smallpox in 1796, his only regret that he had not killed more Lenape. Gleeful Indians took his clothing and bits of flesh to show their brethren that Quick at last was surely gone—but many of them became infected and succumbed to the disease that had killed their tormentor.

The legend of Tom Quick still sparks controversy in the Delaware valley. In 1904 a granite monument was erected at Quick's burial site in Milford, portraying him as the heroic "Avenger of the Delaware." But in 1997, amid protests by the Lenape Nation and other citizens, the monument was vandalized and now languishes in storage. The site, on Sarah Street, is marked by ornamental plants and a plaque. Quick's remains are still buried there.

Gifford Pinchot, the "Father of Conservation"

High above Milford, by the tumbling waters of Sawkill Creek, stands Grey Towers. This castle-like home was the residence of Gifford Pinchot (1865–1946), the first Chief of the U.S. Forest Service.

Until the end of the nineteenth century, forestry in America amounted to "cut as much as possible, as fast as possible"—leaving barren wastelands across much of the continent. Nowhere was such devastation more complete than in the upper Delaware valley, where by the 1880s virtually all useable timber had been slashed down and rafted to market.

Enter Gifford Pinchot, a wealthy scion of his father's lumber business. Growing up to love the woods and encouraged by his father, Pinchot studied "scientific forestry" in France after college. Back in America, he was hired to manage the lands at the Vanderbilt estate, Biltmore, in North Carolina, where he was among the first in America to use professional forest management techniques. President Theodore Roosevelt took note, creating the U.S. Forest Service and making Pinchot its chief. Under Roosevelt and Pinchot, vast areas of the American West were designated as National Forests.

Pinchot was guided by the philosophy that natural resources should be managed for the greatest use in the long run. But there were rivals within the growing conservation movement. Foremost among them was John Muir, founder of the Sierra Club, who advocated preservation of dwindling resources. Muir opposed plans to build a dam at Hetch Hetchy, a Yosemite-like valley in California. But Pinchot, who did not support preservation of lands for wilderness or scenery, argued that the reservoir would provide the best use in the long run. Pinchot prevailed, and the Hetch Hetchy valley was lost. Ironically, the same philosophical battle was later fought in Pinchot's own front yard. Advocates of the Tocks Island Dam championed Pinchot's managed use concept, while preservationists claimed that the magnificent Delaware valley would be forever lost if the dam were to be built. Today, John Muir's philosophy of preservation is seen in many programs of the National Park Service, while Gifford Pinchot's legacy of managed use guides the U.S. Forest Service. After his 10 years as chief of the Forest Service, Pinchot served two terms as governor of Pennsylvania between 1923 and 1935, and is recalled by many as one of the great governors of that state.

Pinchot lived at Grey Towers in Milford until his death in 1946. Now owned by the U.S. Forest Service, the mansion is a National Historic Landmark, and parts of it are open to the public. The site is often used for Forest Service conferences and seminars. Go through a gate across the lane on a shaded trail to Sawkill Falls, one of the most magnificent of waterfalls along the Pocono front. The falls is located on private property of the Pinchot family; visitors are permitted with the understanding that private property must be respected.

Milford, Pennsylvania

Milford was once named the "prettiest county seat in America."[1] Grassy alleyways bisect wide boulevards lined with tall shade trees and quaint

Victorian homes. The public buildings are constructed of local bluestone, many with tall steeples or bell towers. Climb "The Knob" at the south end of town for a spectacular view of the Delaware valley and the village below.

According to tradition, Milford was founded in 1733 when Dutch immigrant Tom Quick Sr. settled at the mouth of Sawkill Creek. The community became known as Wells Ferry, then later earned its present name because of sawmills in the glen to the south of town. Milford has been a haven for vacationers and tourists since the mid-nineteenth century. Some prominent people have called it home, including conservationist Gifford Pinchot and philosopher Charles Saunders Peirce.

The Pike County Historical Society has a museum in The Columns mansion on U.S. Route 209. The most unusual item on display is the blood-stained flag upon which Abraham Lincoln's head rested after he was shot at Ford's Theatre in Washington, D.C. There are dozens of artifacts of the Lenape and their forebears, old farm tools, photo albums, and volumes of genealogy. The little museum is reminiscent of your grandparents' attic, where collections are so crammed together it's difficult to tell where the arrowheads end and the farm tools begin.

Milford may be reached from the Delaware at the Milford Beach access. All services are available, including fine restaurants at the Hotel Fauchere, Dimmicks Inn, Tom Quick Inn, and the more casual Milford Diner.

Mile 238.6 to 218.0 (20.6 miles)

There is a wilderness aspect to the river here, which is entirely within the Delaware Water Gap National Recreation Area. Virtually all private and commercial structures were removed in the 1960s and 1970s to prepare for the Tocks Island Dam and reservoir. The controversial project was eventually abandoned, and the U.S. government turned over nearly 70,000 acres to the National Park Service. The scenery is magnificent, and access is easy. The few rapids—Fiddlers Elbow, Mary and Sambo, and Depew Island—are not severe. This is an excellent section for novices. Several outfitters offer canoes, kayaks, rafts, and tubes for hire, with shuttle service.

This river section is long, and slow eddies are the rule. When the wind blows from the southwest, as it often does, vigorous paddling is required to make any headway at all. To attempt the whole reach in a single day requires stamina of muscle and mind. Fortunately, there are enough access points and camping areas to break up the trip or to paddle only selected portions.

The Kittatinny Ridge rises sharply on the New Jersey side, while the rolling Pocono Mountains loom above the river on the Pennsylvania side. The large, heavily forested river islands are favored nesting places for waterfowl and other birds. Many species of hawks ride the updrafts along the Kittatinny during their autumn migration, and birdwatchers flock to the area to witness this spectacle.

U.S. Route 209 roughly parallels the river in Pennsylvania, and the historic Old Mine Road, said to be one of the oldest continuously used highways in America, approaches the river on the New Jersey riverbank. There are no substantial communities on either side and no commercial services.

The National Park Service maintains five access areas:

Dingmans Ferry, Pennsylvania, mile 238.6
Eshback, Pennsylvania, mile 231.3
Bushkill, Pennsylvania, mile 227.9

Poxono (Pahaquarry), New Jersey, mile 219.7
Smithfield Beach, Pennsylvania, mile 218.0

Camping for one night via canoe/kayak is permitted at designated primitive sites on the riverbanks within the National Recreation Area. Rangers will issue tickets to campers at unauthorized locations or not on a river trip. Sites are marked by a Park Service camp sign. There are two group campsites, available by prior reservation, along the riverbanks at Walpack Bend, and a private, full-service campground at Dingmans Ferry. *Note:* some of the campsites on the river islands were obliterated in the 2004–2006 floods, and the Park Service has not reopened them.

River Guide

Map 13

238.6 **Access: Dingmans Ferry, Pennsylvania.** Operated by the National Park Service. A wide, paved boat ramp, plenty of parking, restrooms, telephones, and trash disposal. Fee: $7 per vehicle weekdays / $10 weekends (2010). Access at Dingmans Bridge, one mile from U.S. Route 209.
   Outfitter. Kittatinny Canoes landing, adjacent to the public access area.
   The Dingman family ran ferries and bridges here for more than 150 years.
   Dingmans Eddy, wide and slow, continues 1.6 miles. Dingmans Eddy was a favored stopping place for timber raftsmen, many of whom enjoyed the lodging and taverns at the village of Dingmans Ferry.
   The McDade River Trail, for hikers and bicyclists, continues along the Pennsylvania riverbank.

238.3 **Camping/outfitter.** Dingmans Campground, operated under a permit from the National Park Service. Access from the river (very shallow) and U.S. Route 209. Full facilities, including riverfront tent sites. Dingmans Campground also offers canoes and kayaks for rent, with shuttle service beginning or ending at the campground.

237.3 A series of shallow riffles (Class I–) across the width of the river; watch for submerged rocks.

236.8 **Camping.** Dingmans Shallows campsite, Pennsylvania side. One site, no facilities or road access.

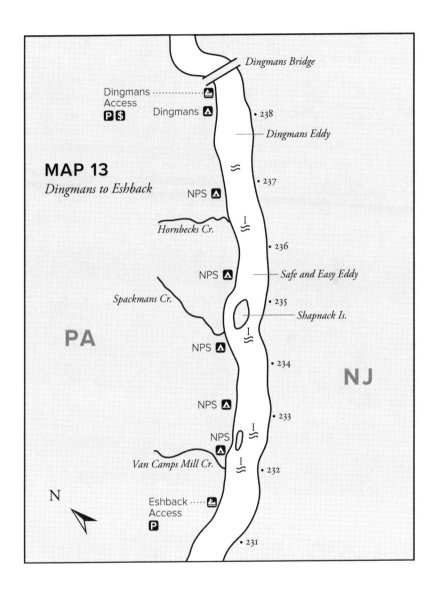

MAP 13
Dingmans to Eshback

Dingmans Bridge

Dingmans Access

Dingmans

Dingmans Eddy

• 238

• 237

NPS

Hornbecks Cr.

• 236

NPS

Safe and Easy Eddy

Spackmans Cr.

• 235

Shapnack Is.

PA

NPS

• 234

NJ

NPS

NPS

• 233

Van Camps Mill Cr.

• 232

N

Eshback Access

• 231

236.5   Another easy riffle.

236.3   Class I rapids on the left. The middle right of the river is shallow and crowded with submerged rocks streaked with paint from passing boats.

   The deepest channel from here to Walpack Bend tends to be nearer the New Jersey (left) riverbank.

236.2   Hornbecks Creek enters through a marsh, Pennsylvania side.

A two-mile trail along Hornbecks Creek from U.S. Route 209 offers one of the most spectacular waterfall hikes in the Mid-Atlantic region. A series of falls, long known as Indian Ladders, includes three over 25 feet high, plus a dozen more over 10 feet high.

235.4 Easy riffle; best passage is on the left side.

235.2 **Camping.** Hornbecks river campsite, Pennsylvania side. Three primitive sites, about 0.1 mile apart; no facilities or road access.

A slow stretch of water known as Safe and Easy Eddy.

234.9 Shapnack Island, a brushy gravel bar continuing 0.5 mile. We don't know why old-time timber rafters called it Bacon and Egg Island. The main channel is on the left; the slough to the right is too shallow for passage.

There are Class I rapids along the island; shallow, watch for submerged rocks.

233.9 Easy riffle (Class I−) over shallows.

233.3 Spackmans Creek enters, Pennsylvania side, just downstream from Shapnack Island.

There is a short Class I rapids with a clear channel near the New Jersey side.

233.2 **Camping.** Jerry Lees river campsite, Pennsylvania side. Two primitive sites about 0.1 mile apart.

232.9 Easy Class I rapids, continuing 0.5 mile. Continue to stay left.

232.5 The river is narrow and straight for the next mile.

The Old Mine Road closely parallels the river on the New Jersey side.

The rapids pick up speed along Shapanack Bar, a little gravel island near the Pennsylvania side; standing waves to 1½ feet.

232.1 **Camping.** Mill Creek river campsite, Pennsylvania side. One primitive site; no facilities or road access.

232.0 Van Camps Mill Creek enters, Pennsylvania side. A waterfall known as Tumbling Waters is about a mile upstream, reached via a trail at the Pocono Environmental Education Center.

Map 14

231.3 **Access: Eshback, Pennsylvania.** Maintained by the National Park Service. Rough boat ramp, limited parking, privies, and trash disposal. No fee. Access via a long gravel road from U.S. Route 209.

230.5 Buck Bar, in the center of the river. The right channel is barely passable; left channel is narrower but deep enough.

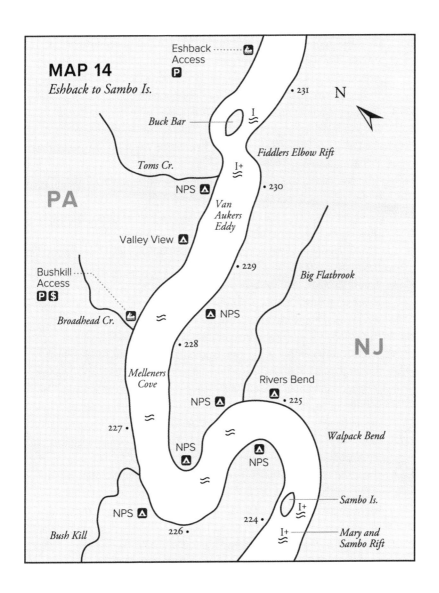

MAP 14

Eshback to Sambo Is.

Eshback Access

PA

N

• 231

Buck Bar

Fiddlers Elbow Rift

Toms Cr.

NPS

• 230

Van Aukers Eddy

Valley View

Bushkill Access

• 229

Big Flatbrook

Broadhead Cr.

NPS

• 228

NJ

Melleners Cove

Rivers Bend

• 225

NPS

227 •

NPS

Walpack Bend

NPS

Sambo Is.

NPS

224 •

I+

Bush Kill

226 •

I+

Mary and Sambo Rift

Class I rapids flow to the left of the island, with moderate waves.

230.0 Enter Fiddlers Elbow Rift as the river bends sharply to the left, then back to the right. Class I+ rapids with no obstructions and standing waves to 2 feet, continuing 0.4 mile. This one is fun!

229.8 Toms Creek enters, Pennsylvania side.

Camping. Toms Creek river campsites, Pennsylvania side. Four primitive sites about 0.1 mile apart; no facilities or road access.

229.7 Beware whirlpools, boils, and shifting currents at the end of Fiddlers Elbow. Try not to crash into the shale ledges on the left (New Jersey) side.

Begin Van Aukers Eddy, slow water for a mile or so.

229.4 **Camping.** Valley View Group Campsites, Pennsylvania riverbank. Restrooms, firepits, picnic tables. By advance reservation only from the Delaware Water Gap National Recreation Area. Road access from U.S. Route 209.

228.6 The river bends slightly right in a long, easy riffle; watch for submerged rocks.

228.4 **Camping.** Ratcliffs river campsites, New Jersey side. Three primitive sites; no facilities or road access.

U.S. Route 209 is very close to the river for the next 0.4 mile, Pennsylvania side.

227.9 **Access: Bushkill, Pennsylvania.** Maintained by the National Park Service. Paved boat ramp, ample parking, water, restrooms. Fee: $7 per vehicle weekdays / $10 weekends (2010). Access from U.S. Route 209.

227.8 Broadhead Creek (not to be confused with Brodhead Creek, at Stroudsburg) enters at a gravel bar, Pennsylvania side. Mild riffles.

227.6 Site of Rosenkranz Ferry, one of the last to ply the Delaware. The ferry remained in operation until 1945, when its overhead cable was cut by a low-flying airplane. A trace of the road to the ferry, Rosenkranz Lane, can be seen in the forest on the New Jersey side.

227.5 Slow water of Melleners Cove. In the nineteenth-century Mellener ran a hotel for raftsmen on the New Jersey riverbank.

226.8 Bush Kill enters, Pennsylvania side, with broad gravel shallows extending halfway across the river. Bush Kill, a substantial tributary to the Delaware, is famed for trout fishing. *Kill* is the old Dutch word for "stream."

226.6 The river swings left into Walpack Bend, a great S turn where the river cuts through the hard rock of Walpack Ridge. The bend is really a small water gap, geologically similar to the Delaware Water Gap 16 miles downriver. The rocks nearby yield many fossils.

226.5 **Camping.** Peters river campsites, New Jersey side. Ten sites with privies; no other facilities. A lovely site tucked in the curve of Walpack Bend.

226.4 **Camping.** Bushkill Creek river campsites, Pennsylvania side. One primitive site; no facilities or road access.

226.2 Shale ledges along the New Jersey riverbank are stacked like piles of books; the most prominent is known as Bible Rock.

226.0 Fast water—beware of boulders lurking just below the surface.

Timber raftsmen called the steep, shady slopes on the Pennsylvania (right) side Greenland. The evergreen rhododendron and mountain laurel bushes that blanket the riverbank were a welcome respite from the grays of late winter, when the rafts came down. The still-verdant slopes are in glorious blossom every spring.

225.5 **Camping.** Quinns river campsite, New Jersey side. Seven primitive campsites; no facilities or road access.

225.2 Big Flatbrook, a "trout stream of no mean reputation,"[1] enters at the New Jersey side. The New Jersey Division of Fish and Wildlife reports that three species of native trout (brook, brown, and rainbow) run wild in Big Flatbrook. The stream is lined with anglers every April.

The whirlpool-like eddy where Big Flatbrook joins the Delaware was known to the Lenape as *Wahlpeck*, hence the name of the township. Alternatively, *Walpeek* means "deep water." Take your pick.

The village of Flatbrookville once stood nearby. It was razed in preparation for the Tocks Island Dam.

Walpack Ferry operated here in the 1800s.

225.1 Begin the right turn out of Walpack Bend as the current increases.

225.0 **Camping.** Rivers Bend Group Campsites, New Jersey riverbank. By advance reservation only through the Delaware Water Gap National Recreation Area.

224.8 **Camping.** Freeman Point river campsites, Pennsylvania side. Three primitive sites about 0.1 mile apart; no facilities or road access.

Map 15

224.5 Sambo Island, a small gravel bar, on the right. Clear passage to the left of the island.

A rock slide on the New Jersey side exposes the red shale of the Bloomsburg Formation, one of several layers of rock that form the Kittatinny Ridge.

224.4 Begin Mary and Sambo Rift, a Class I+ rapids continuing 0.6 mile; three sets of increasingly severe rapids separated by swift pools. There is no clear channel, and paddlers must navigate around many barely submerged boulders.

According to legend, the name of this rift commemorates the "drowning of two lovers who once upon a time went a-wooing on a raft."[2] The placed seems cursed, as a fisherman also drowned near here in 2008.

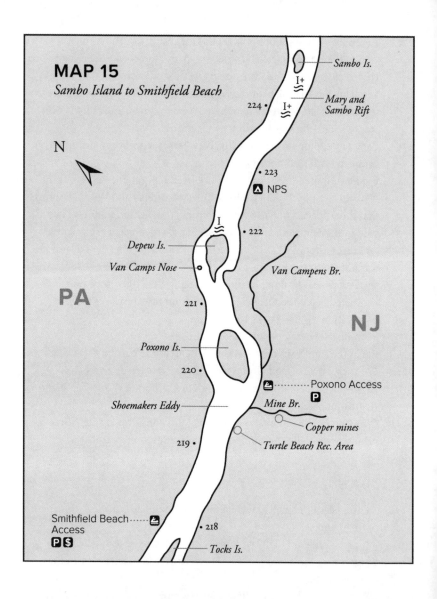

MAP 15
Sambo Island to Smithfield Beach

N

Sambo Is.

I+

Mary and
Sambo Rift

224 •

I+

• 223

▲ NPS

I

• 222

Depew Is.

Van Camps Nose ○

Van Campens Br.

PA

221 •

NJ

Poxono Is.

220 •

▲ ········· Poxono Access

Shoemakers Eddy

P

Mine Br.

○ — Copper mines

219 •

Turtle Beach Rec. Area

Smithfield Beach ······· ▲
Access

• 218

P $

Tocks Is.

223.8 Mary and Sambo Rift ends with 2-foot standing waves and big rocks.

222.7 **Camping.** Hamilton river campsite, New Jersey side. Several primitive campsites with privies; no road access.

222.6 Pass under high-tension power lines, with a right-of-way up Kittatinny Ridge to the east.

222.0 Upstream end of Depew Island. Stay right; the left channel is dry at low water levels.

There is a Class I rapids in the right passage, making an S turn around the point of the island; there are no obstructions but standing waves to 2 feet. Beware of being pushed against the Pennsylvania riverbank.

Depew Island is named for Nicolas DePew, who settled in this area in 1727.

221.6 A great boulder known as Van Camps Nose sticks up from the river, Pennsylvania side. Old-time timber rafters pulled hard left to avoid it.

221.4 A mild riffle (Class I–) at the end of Depew Island.

Until 2004 there was an access/recreation area at the New Jersey riverbank here (Depew Recreation Site). However, it was washed away in the 2004, 2005, and 2006 floods, and has been replaced by Turtle Beach a little way downriver.

220.5 Begin Poxono Island (formerly Opohanough or Mine House Island). At moderate water level the left channel is dry and impassable, just a brushy path through the forest. The current is swift in the main channel.

219.9 The river widens into Shoemakers Eddy immediately downstream of Poxono Island.

219.8 A small gravel bar, right side of the river.

219.7 **Access: Poxono (Pahaquarry), New Jersey.** Maintained by the National Park Service. A steep, paved ramp, limited parking, trash disposal. No fee. From the river, just at the foot of Poxono Island. Access from the Old Mine Road. This site once served as the waterfront of old Boy Scouts Camp Cowaw.

Van Campens Brook enters from behind Poxono Island, New Jersey side. A short distance up the brook is Van Campens Glen, a protected natural area where the stream cascades through a beautiful hemlock ravine. There are picnic facilities and hiking trails in the glen.

The Old Mine Road runs atop the New Jersey bluff.

A ferry owned by the Shoemaker, Fisher, and Dimmick families ran here in the 1800s.

219.5 Shoemakers Eddy continues, slow water for the next mile. The New Jersey side of the river, marked by buoys, is reserved for unpowered craft; motorboats and Jet Skis use the Pennsylvania side. Canoes and kayaks stay left!

Mine Brook enters, New Jersey side.

Adits and shafts of nineteenth-century copper mines are found on a short trail leading up along the stream from a parking area atop the New Jersey riverbank. Entrance to the mines is barred, but the mine holes are amazing to see. Dutch settlers began mining for copper here in the 1600s. Never profitable, the mines were ultimately abandoned forever by 1917.

This was also the site of Camp Pahaquarra. Boy Scouts summered here from 1925 until 1971, when the land was acquired by the National Park Service. Remnants of camp buildings can be found in the forest. Today's small parking area was the camp parade ground.

The riverbank along the Pennsylvania side was once called Loving Shore, apparently because the current tended to push timber rafts to that side. The soft soils collapse easily into the river during floods.

219.3 Turtle Beach recreation area, New Jersey side. This swimming and picnic area was opened in 2010, replacing the Depew Recreation Site upstream. Features include a beach with seasonal lifeguards, a bathhouse with restrooms, and a picnic area. There is no developed boat access. Fee: $7 per vehicle weekdays / $10 weekends (2010).

A nearby site initially proposed for the new beach was found to be inhabited by endangered bog turtles, resulting in a new location and a new name.

219.4 Traces of a road can be seen at the river's edge, once leading to Shoemakers Ferry, crossing here until 1927.

The abandoned Coppermine Inn / Union Hotel, a popular hostelry for more than 100 years, still stands not far from the river. The old inn closed when the government acquired the land for the Tocks Island Dam.

218.0 **Access: Smithfield Beach, Pennsylvania.** Maintained by the National Park Service. Paved boat ramp, separate canoe launch area, parking, water, restrooms, picnicking, telephones, trash disposal, swimming beach. This is a very popular day-use area. Fee: $7 per vehicle weekdays / $10 weekends (2010). Access from River Road, Smithfield Township.

Features

The Old Mine Road

Is the Old Mine Road really the oldest highway in America? In many places unpaved and only one lane wide, this little road runs about 100 miles from the Delaware Water Gap northward to Kingston, on the Hudson River. Legend has it that Dutch settlers made the road to haul copper from mines at Pahaquarry, and there are records of Dutch explorers hunting for minerals in the Minisink as early as 1626. English pioneers, chasing rumors about mines far upriver, in 1730 found a thriving and long-established community at Pahaquarry.

Little villages grew as settlers named DePew, Van Campen, Rosenkrantz, and Decker came to the area, and the road became a thoroughfare of commerce and communication. Generations lived and died near the road. Battles between settlers and Indians, then between Revolutionaries and the British, were fought around it. Merchants, artists, soldiers, statesmen, and adventurers passed along the road and contributed to its colorful history.

The Old Mine Road runs close to the Delaware from the Water Gap north to Dingmans Ferry. A drive along it is like a trip back through time. Abandoned mine holes can be seen near the Poxono access; people dug for a long time, but not much copper was actually found. Foundations of buildings hulk in the forest, razed when the land was acquired to build Tocks Island Dam. Ironically, the land is in a more primitive state today than it has been for 200 years.

A few landmarks still remain. Isaac Van Campen's magnificent stone house, built about 1746, has been restored by the National Park Service. A path up the hill leads to the Old Shapanack burying ground, where the 1776 gravestone of Anna Symmes, mother-in-law of U.S. President William Henry Harrison, stands among others in the forest. Generations of children learned their ABCs in the single room of the old Calno School. And at Millbrook Village, life in the old Minisink region has been captured for modern-day visitors via re-enactments and demonstrations. The Delaware Water Gap National Recreation Area offers extensive information and detailed guides about the Old Mine Road.

The Grandfathers

Early European settlers in the Delaware Valley were met by the Lenape, whose very name means "the people." The people understood that their ancestors had lived in the valley for many centuries. To neighboring tribes, the Lenape were the "grandfathers," revered as the original people from whom all others had descended.

Serious archaeology of the ancient peoples of the Delaware Valley began in the 1960s and 1970s, when the land was acquired by the federal government to build the Tocks Island Dam. Dr. Herbert Kraft of Seton Hall University led excavations at Harry's Farm (near Tocks Island) and Minisink Island. These locales were attractive to the ancients for the same reasons they are today—springs of clean water, safety from all but the greatest floods, abundant fish and game, and easy canoe access to the Delaware.

The first people in the Delaware Valley, Paleo-Indians, came soon after the glacier retreated 12,000 years ago; their fluted spear points have been found at Pahaquarry. The ancient ones might have included even the great wooly mammoth on their menu. Later cultures called Archaic, Kittatinny, and Lackawaxen spanned thousands of years, each distinguished by the form of its projectiles and pottery.

A revolutionary new culture known as Woodland blossomed at about A.D. 200. These were the Lenape and their direct ancestors. At Harry's Farm many refuse pits containing pottery, food remains, tools, ornaments, and other clues to early Lenape culture have been discovered. Archaeologists have also found several Indian graves near Minisink Island, the bodies "facing the setting sun, knowing that the land of the spirits lies in the southwest, in the country of good hunting."[3]

It is not unusual even today to find an arrowhead or some other stone artifact along the banks of the Delaware. Federal law prohibits removal of Indian artifacts from public land, and any find should be reported to the National Park Service. Modern visitors can see collections of Indian artifacts at High Point State Park in New Jersey, the Pike County Historical Society in Milford, Pennsylvania, and the New Jersey State Museum at Trenton.

Delaware Water Gap National Recreation Area

A huge lake, with big marinas for powerboats and beaches crowded with swimmers—such was the vision for the reservoir behind Tocks Island Dam, to be built for control of floodwaters on the Delaware River. To prepare the area, the government razed more than 3,000 homes and other buildings and forced more than 12,000 residents to leave. When environmental opposition and mounting costs finally put a stop to the project, the Park Service unexpectedly found itself with 70,000 acres of nearly uninhabited land, abundant with wildlife, historic sites, trails, and a gorgeous free-flowing river. Today, the Delaware Water Gap National Recreation Area is one of the most popular of all units of the National Park Service, with more than 5 million visitors each year.

Families flock to the picnic grounds at Smithfield, Milford, and the new Turtle Beach. Each has a seasonally guarded swimming area in the river, barbeque grills, restrooms, and wide expanses of grass. There are more secluded picnic areas at Hialeah and Toms Creek in Pennsylvania and at Van Campens Glen and Watergate in New Jersey.

More adventurous visitors hike some of the trails, including the Appalachian Trail in New Jersey and the new McDade River Trail for hikers and bicyclists in Pennsylvania. The waterfalls at Dingmans, Childs Park, and Raymondskill are tourist magnets, and there are "secret" falls along trails up Hornbecks, Adams, and other creeks.

Interested in history and the arts? Trace the Old Mine Road (described above), or visit Millbrook Village, with its authentic blacksmith, gristmill, schoolhouse, and general store; Millbrook Days are celebrated the first weekend of October. At the Peters Valley Crafts Center artists create inspired works in pottery, metals, wood, and glass. The Peters Valley crafts fair is held every autumn.

But the centerpiece of the Delaware Water Gap National Recreation Area, its very essence, is the river. The Park Service provides seven access points for canoes and kayaks, licenses river outfitters, patrols river safety, and maintains dozens of campsites for river users.

It's hard to imagine that all this would have been under water if the dam had been built. Yet, ironically, preparation for the dam saved the river and the valley. While commercial and residential development has intensified just outside the park's boundaries, the land and river it protects remains today as accessible, pristine, and inviting as ever.

Mile 218.0 to 194.1 (23.9 miles)

The famous Delaware Water Gap and the severe rapids at Foul Rift dominate this section. At the Water Gap the river has gouged a 1,300-foot-deep cleft in the Kittatinny Ridge. At Foul Rift, the river drops 23 feet in two miles over sharp limestone ledges, one of the most hazardous rapids on the Delaware. Commercial outfitters do not run below the Water Gap, and river traffic is usually light.

After breaking through the Kittatinny Ridge, the Delaware is a mountain river no longer. Forests give way to cleared farmland, and here and there industrial centers rise from the riverbanks. There are giant power stations and cement plants at Martins Creek and Portland, and chemical factories at Belvidere. Above the Water Gap, the rustic Old Mine Road parallels the river; below the Gap, Interstate 80, U.S. Route 46, and Pennsylvania Route 611 run alongside. Recreation on the river below the Water Gap becomes more motor-oriented; powerboats, Jet Skis, and pontoon boats are popular, canoes and kayaks less so. Homes and vacation cottages line the riverbanks in many areas.

The first 10 miles of this section are within the Delaware Water Gap National Recreation Area and the Middle Delaware National Scenic River, part of the National Park system. The Appalachian Trial, a continuous footpath from Georgia to Maine, crosses the Delaware River on the Interstate 80 bridge.

There are seven public access areas in this section:

Smithfield Beach, Pennsylvania, mile 218.0
Worthington State Forest, New Jersey, mile 214.9
Kittatinny Point, New Jersey, mile 211.6
Portland, Pennsylvania, mile 207.6
Doe Hollow, Pennsylvania, mile 198.9
Belvidere, New Jersey, mile 197.8
Martins Creek, Pennsylvania, mile 194.1

Camping for one night only via canoe or kayak is permitted at designated primitive campsites on the riverbanks within the National Recreation Area. Sites are marked by a Park Service camp sign. Camping is also permitted at Worthington State Forest and at several private campgrounds. There are commercial services at Delaware Water Gap and Portland, Pennsylvania, and at Belvidere, New Jersey.

River Guide

Map 16

218.0 **Access: Smithfield Beach, Pennsylvania** Maintained by the National Park Service. A paved boat ramp, a hand-launch area for canoes and kayaks, parking, water, restrooms, picnicking, telephones, trash disposal, and a swimming beach. Fee: $7 per vehicle weekdays / $10 weekends (2010). Access from River Road, Smithfield Township. This is a very popular day-use area.

217.6 Upstream end of Tocks Island. Channels on either side are navigable, with swift current and short riffles, though the left channel is narrower.
The Old Mine Road runs very close atop the New Jersey riverbank.

217.3 Big Tocks and Little Tocks Creeks enter, New Jersey side.

217.0 Downstream end of Tocks Island.
This is the site of the proposed Tocks Island Dam. In the 1960s, the Army Corps of Engineers began preparations for construction of a dam here to hold back floodwaters like those suffered during Hurricanes Connie and Diane in 1955. The dam would have impounded the Delaware all the way up to Port Jervis. Public opposition eventually prevailed, and the dam project was scrapped. The lands that were acquired for the reservoir now make up the Delaware Water Gap National Recreation Area.

216.9 A high-tension power line crackles overhead.

216.7 **Camping.** Walters river campsite, Pennsylvania side. One primitive site; no facilities or road access.

216.6 A small island nestles against the Pennsylvania riverbank; a stream enters behind the island.

216.5 Labar Island, continuing 0.5 mile. Channels to the left and right are passable without obstructions.
Camping. Hialeah Island river campsite, Pennsylvania side. Two primitive sites to the right of Labar Island; no facilities or road access.

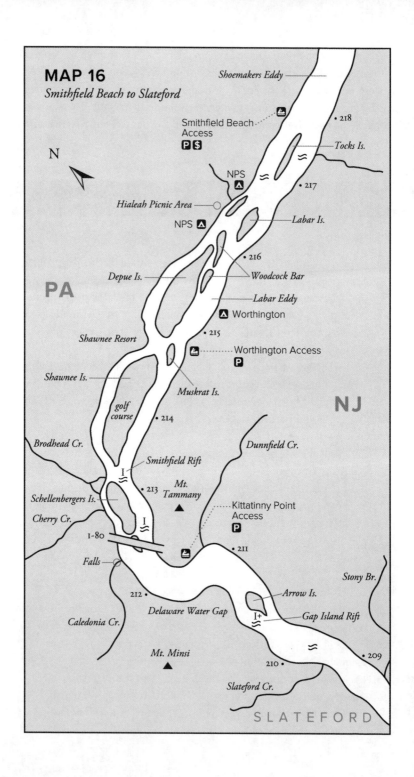

MAP 16
Smithfield Beach to Slateford

N

Shoemakers Eddy

• 218

Smithfield Beach
Access

Tocks Is.

NPS

• 217

Hialeah Picnic Area

Labar Is.

NPS

• 216

Depue Is.

Woodcock Bar

Labar Eddy

Worthington

PA

• 215

Shawnee Resort

Worthington Access

Shawnee Is.

Muskrat Is.

NJ

golf
course

• 214

Brodhead Cr.

Dunnfield Cr.

Smithfield Rift

Schellenbergers Is.

• 213

Mt.
Tammany

Kittatinny Point
Access

Cherry Cr.

I-80

• 211

Falls

Stony Br.

212 •

Arrow Is.

Delaware Water Gap

I+

Gap Island Rift

Caledonia Cr.

• 209

Mt. Minsi

210 •

Slateford Cr.

S L A T E F O R D

The Hialeah Picnic Area, maintained by the National Park Service, is atop the Pennsylvania riverbank. Watch for the red brick foundations of razed cottages. There are picnic tables and privies. The riverbank is very steep and not suitable for launching boats, but paddlers can scramble up to the picnic area. Access from River Road, Smithfield Township.

Hialeah Picnic Area marks the southern end of the McDade River Trail for hikers and bicyclists.

216.1　Upstream end of Woodcock Bar, a slender island extending diagonally downstream. The main channel is on the left, over shallows. The channel to the right is navigable, though at low water its entrance is blocked by gravel bars.

215.9　Upstream end of Depue Island (not to be confused with Depew Island upriver), in the right channel behind Woodcock Bar. Depue Island extends one mile downstream against the Pennsylvania side. The main channel is to the left, but the narrow right channel is passable. Depue Island is privately owned—no trespassing.

In 2008 a developer proposed to build a hotel and recreation complex on Depue Island. As of 2010, no action had been taken. The island was inundated in the 2004, 2005, and 2006 floods.

215.8　A slow stretch of water called Labar Eddy, continuing about two miles along Depue and Shawnee Islands.

Camping. Worthington State Forest campground, atop the bluffs on the New Jersey riverbank. Camper registration is at the office at the Worthington access area, one mile downstream.

There is a U.S. Geological Survey river gage here, a green metal box on stilts at the riverside edge of the campground. Base elevation is 293 feet above sea level. Good boating stage is 5–8 feet; flood stage is 21 feet. The maximum flood here was 37.4 feet, in 1955.

214.9　Downstream end of Depue Island, along the Pennsylvania riverbank.

Access: Worthington State Forest, New Jersey. Maintained by the New Jersey State Park Service. A paved boat ramp, restrooms, trash disposal, telephones, and fresh water. The state forest office is a few feet from the boat ramp. No fee. Access from Old Mine Road.

This is the site of Walkers Ferry, a nineteenth-century crossing.

Camping. Worthington State Forest (New Jersey) has about 70 campsites on the river's edge between mile 215.5 and mile 214.5. A cluster of wooded sites just downstream from the boat launch is designated for tent camping only, the sites of choice for canoe/kayak camping from the river. Restrooms, showers, and potable water. Group campsites are also available. Worthington State Forest is very popular with car campers, and it is often difficult to find an available site on weekends; reserve ahead of time.

The Douglas Trail leads up from the campground along a waterfalling stream to beautiful Sunfish Pond atop Kittatinny Ridge. In the 1960s Supreme Court Justice and ardent conservationist William O. Douglas led a hike here to promote protection of Sunfish Pond, at that time slated to become a pumped storage reservoir for the Tocks Island Dam project.

214.8 Shawnee Point, between Depue Island upstream and Shawnee Island downstream, is on the Pennsylvania side opposite the Worthington access.

The Shawnee Inn, white with a red roof, stands near the point. It is the last of the great resort hotels on the Delaware River. Vacation havens at the Delaware Water Gap and Shohola disappeared decades ago, but the Shawnee Inn has kept up with the times. Developed by C. C. Worthington in 1910 as the Buckwood Inn, the Shawnee became known as one of the finest golf resorts in the country, hosting the PGA championship tournament in 1938. In the 1940s the property was taken over by big-band leader Fred Waring. The Shawnee Inn today is a complete resort community, with the 100-room inn, private cottages, timeshare condominiums, golf, swimming, nightclub entertainment, and the Delaware River. The famous Shawnee Playhouse is nearby in the community of Shawnee-on-Delaware.

Outfitter. Shawnee River Trips landing and river base, at a steep gravel boat ramp. Not a public access.

Muskrat Island, a skinny sand bar with big trees, on the left (New Jersey) side. The channel to the left is clear. There is a moderate current in the main channel on the right.

214.7 Upstream end of Shawnee Island, extending 1.2 miles along the Pennsylvania side. The main flow of the river runs to the left of the island, but the narrow channel to the right is navigable. The second and seventeenth holes of the famous Shawnee golf course cross the channel shortly after its entrance, and the river bottom is often littered with errant golf balls. Shawnee Island is privately owned—no trespassing.

213.6 Downstream end of Shawnee Island.

Pass under a power line marked by red balls.

213.4 Brodhead Creek enters, Pennsylvania side. The creek has built up gravel bars that extend two-thirds of the way across the river. Thirty-seven campers at Camp Davis, on Brodhead Creek in Stroudsburg, were drowned during the 1955 flood spawned by Hurricanes Connie and Diane.

213.3   Two stone piers are all that remain of a New York, Susquehanna & Western Railroad trestle, destroyed in the 1955 flood.

Ledges on the New Jersey side are covered with graffiti.

Upstream end of Schellenbergers Island, extending 0.5 mile. Stay left; the channel on the Pennsylvania side is dry at average water level. Long ago there was a little amusement park on the island, with swimming and waterslides.

213.2   Smithfield Rift, a Class I rapids with standing waves to 1½ feet, runs along the New Jersey side for 0.3 mile.

Cherry Creek enters, Pennsylvania side, into the channel to the right of Schellenbergers Island.

212.7   A couple of small gravel bars along the right extend under the Interstate 80 bridge. Continue to stay left.

212.6   There is a Class I rapids in the main channel near the New Jersey side, with standing waves to 1½ feet and no obstructions.

212.4   Pass under the Delaware Water Gap Toll Bridge carrying Interstate 80, constructed in 1953.

The river has gouged a 1,300-foot cleft in the Kittatinny Ridge at the famous Delaware Water Gap. It's Mount Minsi to the right and Mount Tammany to the left. (Photo by the author)

The Appalachian Trail, extending from Georgia to Maine, crosses the Delaware on this bridge.

212.3 Caledonia Creek tumbles down the rocks on the Pennsylvania side, a nice waterfall after a rain.

212.1 The river bends sharply left, entering the famous Delaware Water Gap. Hemlock woods cover the steep slopes of Mount Minsi on the Pennsylvania side, named for the northern clan of the Lenape. After a rain, runoff tumbles down Minsi via several waterfalls.

Resort Point overlook, a roadside (Route 611) scenic viewing area high atop the Pennsylvania riverbank, is maintained by the National Park Service. This was the site of the Kittatinny House, a lavish resort hotel built in 1836. Until it closed in 1932, vacationers came via rail from New York and Philadelphia to enjoy the scenery of the Delaware Water Gap. The hotel operated a little steamboat, also named *Kittatinny*, for excursions on the river.

The village of Delaware Water Gap, Pennsylvania, stands on the bluffs to the right.

211.6 **Access: Kittatinny Point, New Jersey.** Maintained by the National Park Service. A sandy beach with a corduroy boat ramp (hand-launch only), ample parking, restrooms, picnic tables. No fee. At this writing (2010) the Park Service had plans to expand and improve this access.

The Park Service's Kittatinny Point Visitor Center offers information services and a bookstore atop the bluff above the beach. The visitor center was rebuilt in 2007 after near-destruction in the 2006 floods.

This was the site of Karamac, a resort camp that operated until the 1950s. Today's boat launch was the camp's swimming beach.
Lunch. It's a 1.5-mile walk across the I-80 bridge—along the Appalachian Trail—into the village of Delaware Water Gap, Pennsylvania, home to the Water Gap Diner and the Village Farmer & Bakery.

211.5 Dunnfield Creek enters, New Jersey side. The Appalachian Trail leads up the creek to beautiful Sunfish Pond and, eventually, to Maine.

If you have a good imagination, the stone visage of Chief Tammany, with forest headdress, can be seen in Indian Profile Rock, where the cliffs meet the sky on the New Jersey side.

211.0 Steep cliffs and talus slopes rise high over the river, both sides. It's Mount Minsi (elev. 1,461 feet) on the Pennsylvania side, and Mount Tammany (elev. 1,527 feet), named for the great Lenape chief, on the New Jersey side. There are rugged hikes to the tops of both mountains, with spectacular views from the summits.

210.9 Point of Gap overlook, a roadside (Pennsylvania Route 611) scenic viewing area atop the Pennsylvania riverbank. Hiking trails lead up Mount Minsi. There is no river access.

210.8 Arrow Island, roughly shaped like an arrowhead, extending 0.3 mile.

Class I+ rapids with big standing waves run along both sides of the island, known to timber rafters as Gap Island Rift.

210.5 The rapids abate to Class I. Rocky ledges extend from the Pennsylvania side. Beware of barely submerged boulders on the right for the next 0.2 mile.

Arrow Island overlook, a roadside (Pennsylvania Route 611) scenic viewing area, atop the Pennsylvania riverbank. Maintained by the National Park Service. There is no access from the river.

209.5 Slateford Creek enters, Pennsylvania side, constricting the river at a wide gravel bar river.

The confluence of Slateford Creek marks the southern boundary of the Delaware Water Gap National Recreation Area. National Park Service jurisdiction ends here. Downstream from this point most of the lands along the river, including islands, are privately owned.

The boundary of the Middle Delaware Scenic River also ends here.

209.4 Site of Deckers Ferry, another nineteenth-century crossing.

The community of Slateford, Pennsylvania, runs along the bluffs on the Pennsylvania side for 0.7 mile. No access from the river. The village was home to workers at the nearby slate quarries.

Map 17

208.9 Stony Brook enters, New Jersey side, nearly under the railroad bridge. Its wide gravel bar extends 0.1 mile downstream.

The river is squeezed to the right. Dills Rift begins as Class I rapids.

At one time there were slate quarries on both sides of the river. The excellent slate mined here was used for roofing and schoolroom blackboards.

208.8 Pass under the compound arches of the Delaware River Viaduct (also known as the Lackawanna Cutoff), a rail bridge built between 1908 and 1911 by the Delaware, Lackawanna & Western Railroad. The bridge is no longer in use. Reminiscent of a Roman aqueduct, it is one of the most unusual and beautiful bridges to span the Delaware.

Dills Rift increases to a Class I+ rapids under the bridge, flowing from left to right with a few boulders. Standing waves to 2 feet continue 0.1 mile.

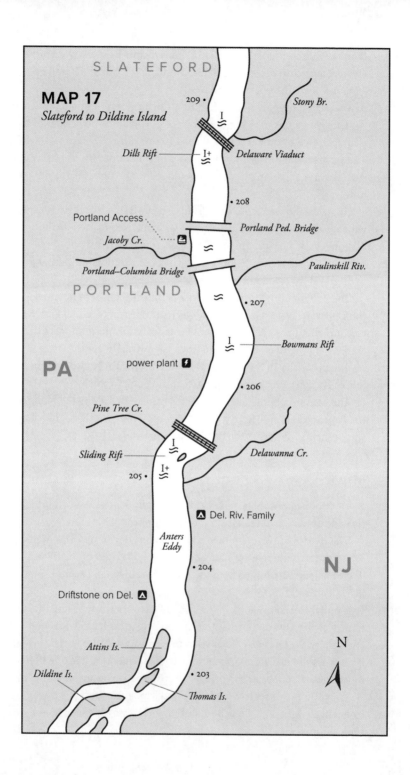

MAP 17
Slateford to Dildine Island

S L A T E F O R D

209 •

Stony Br.

I

Dills Rift ——— I+

Delaware Viaduct

• 208

Portland Access

Portland Ped. Bridge

Jacoby Cr.

Portland–Columbia Bridge

P O R T L A N D

Paulinskill Riv.

• 207

PA

I

Bowmans Rift

power plant ⚡

• 206

Pine Tree Cr.

I

Sliding Rift ———

Delawanna Cr.

205 • I+

▲ Del. Riv. Family

Anters Eddy

NJ

• 204

Driftstone on Del. ▲

Attins Is.

N

Dildine Is.

• 203

Thomas Is.

The spectacular Delaware Viaduct, carrying a now-abandoned spur of the Lackawanna Railroad, crosses the river just below the Delaware Water Gap. (Photo by the author)

207.7 Pass under the Portland-Columbia Pedestrian Bridge. A covered wooden bridge was built here in 1869. It survived the great Pumpkin Flood of 1903 and a tornado in 1929, but could not withstand Hurricanes Connie and Diane in 1955. At the time of its demise it was the last remaining covered bridge to span the Delaware. People say that the ghost of bridgemaster Charlie Newbaker, who stood by in uniform as he watched his bridge wash away, continues on guard whenever the river rises.

The present four-span steel bridge was completed in 1958 on the piers and abutments that supported the old covered bridge and is open only to pedestrians. The original toll house, and Newbaker home, stands at the Pennsylvania end of the bridge.

Dills Ferry crossed here before the bridge was built.

207.6 **Access: Portland, Pennsylvania,** on land of the Delaware River Joint Bridge Commission, right under the pedestrian bridge. A steep gravel ramp but no other facilities. Parking is awkward on Route 611 in downtown Portland. No fee.

The communities of Columbia, New Jersey, and Portland, Pennsylvania, stand at opposite ends of the bridge. Limestone quarried in the vicinity is used in the manufacture of Portland cement.

Lunch. Portland Family Restaurant, Portland, Pennsylvania, 100 yards south of the pedestrian bridge.

207.5 Jacoby Creek enters, Pennsylvania side, at a wide gravel bar.

A modest riffle (Class I–) begins, extending about a mile.

207.4 Pass under the Portland-Columbia Toll Bridge, opened to traffic in 1953. This bridge was constructed to replace the aging covered bridge upstream.

207.2 The Paulinskill River enters, New Jersey side, a significant tributary to the Delaware. It's a nice little canoe/kayak river in its own right and is popular for fly-fishing.

Bowman's Rift begins, here just mild riffles (Class I–).

206.8 The boat ramp and picnic area on land owned by GenOn Energy are closed to public use. No access.

In recent years at least one pair of bald eagles has nested near here, and eagles are occasionally seen from the river

206.6 Bowman's Rift builds to Class I rapids, a diagonal ledge as the river bends to the right, continuing 0.4 mile. Watch for rocks. Best passage is on the Pennsylvania (right) side.

206.4 High-tension power lines overhead.

206.2 A gigantic coal-fueled power plant, with two high smokestacks, stands on the Pennsylvania riverbank. Operated by GenOn Energy as of 2010.

206.1 A concrete cooling-water outfall extends from the power plant into the middle of the river—stay way clear to the left.

205.6 Pass under the five-span steel truss bridge of the old Delaware, Lackawanna & Western Railroad, constructed in 1914. The bridge is no longer in use.

An earlier bridge stood just downstream, built in 1855 for the railroad. When the "new" rail bridge opened in 1914, the Reverend Darlington acquired the old span and ran it as a toll bridge for cars. Darlington's Bridge was ultimately closed and dismantled in 1954. Few traces remain.

Pine Tree Creek enters, Pennsylvania side.

205.5 There is a small gravel island on the left side of the river just below the bridge.

Little Delawanna Creek joins the river, New Jersey side.

205.3 Sliding Rift, beginning as a Class I rapids with standing waves to 1½ feet, runs along the Pennsylvania side. The left three-quarters of the river is very shallow.

Abandoned buildings of Eagles Nest, a private camp, stand on the New Jersey riverbank. The camp closed in the 1990s.

205.1 Delawanna Creek enters, New Jersey side.

205.0 Rapids increase to Class I+ along the Pennsylvania side. Be wary of a few just-submerged boulders.

204.9 Enter Anters Eddy, slow water continuing 2.5 miles downstream.

204.7 Site of Meyers (Hartzells) Ferry. In the early twentieth century a timber raft careening downstream crashed into and upset the ferry, causing the deaths of four ferry passengers. The trace of Ferry Lane can be seen at the river's edge, New Jersey side.

204.6 **Camping/outfitter.** Delaware River Family Campgrounds, Ramseyburg, New Jersey. A private campground with tent sites accessible from the river; all facilities. Access from New Jersey Route 46. Canoes, kayaks, rafts, and tubes are available for rent and shuttle.

203.6 **Camping/outfitter.** Driftstone on the Delaware, Mt. Bethel, Pennsylvania. Riverfront tent and trailer sites. A wooden dock marked *No Trespassing* serves as boat access for campers. Canoes and kayaks, with river shuttle, are available to campground customers. Access from River Road, Mt. Bethel, Pennsylvania.

203.5 Upstream end of Attins Island, extending 0.4 mile. The main channel is to the left, with mild riffles. Here begins a maze of islands extending two miles downstream

203.1 Thomas Island begins as Attins Island comes to its end. The main channel continues on the left, but the slough between the islands is navigable. A handful of summer cottages dot Thomas Island.

202.7 The site of Manunka Chunk, once an important rail junction, New Jersey side.

Meyers Ferry at Ramseyburg, New Jersey, one of dozens that crossed the Delaware from the 1700s to the early 1900s. Meyers Ferry ceased to run after it was rammed by a timber raft, killing four passengers. (From a postcard c. 1915, collection of the author)

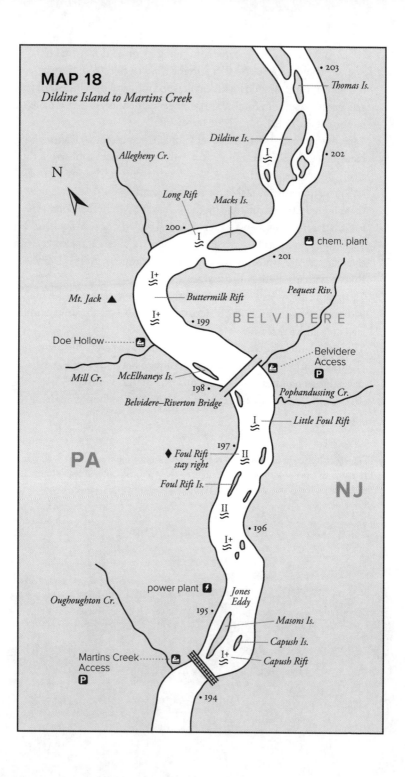

MAP 18

Dildine Island to Martins Creek

N

• 203
Thomas Is.

Dildine Is.

I

• 202

Allegheny Cr.

Long Rift   *Macks Is.*

chem. plant

200 •
I

• 201

I+

Mt. Jack ▲   *Buttermilk Rift*

Pequest Riv.

BELVIDERE

I+

• 199

Doe Hollow

Belvidere
Access

P

Mill Cr.   *McElhaneys Is.*

198 •

Pophandussing Cr.

Belvidere–Riverton Bridge

I   *Little Foul Rift*

PA

197 •
II

♦ *Foul Rift*
stay right

Foul Rift Is.

NJ

II

• 196

I+

power plant

Jones
Eddy

Oughoughton Cr.

195 •

Masons Is.

Capush Is.

Martins Creek
Access

P

I+   *Capush Rift*

• 194

Map 18

202.6 Upstream end of Dildine Island, extending about one mile. Paddlers can go to either side. The deeper channel is to the right, with a nice Class I rapids around gravel bars near the end of the island. The New Jersey side leads into the maze of Macks Bars, little islets with winding passages between. It can be fun to explore the little channels.

The Manunka Chunk House, a luxury hotel, occupied the island in the nineteenth and early twentieth centuries. The hotel burned to the ground in 1938. Today private cottages and boat landings dot Dildine Island.

201.9 There is a small island in the right (Pennsylvania) channel; go to either side for a nice Class I rapids.

Rapids also begin in the left-hand channels.

201.7 King Cole Grove, a long-time riverside ice cream stop and snack bar on U.S. Route 46 (New Jersey side), once a favorite of river users, alas has closed.

201.6 Downstream end of Dildine Island.

201.3 The river bends sharply right.

The great continental glacier came as far as this point, pushing loose rocks ahead of it and leaving them here as its *terminal moraine.* Fifteen thousand years ago the lands north of this point were under a mile of ice. The moraine extends from Staten Island, across New Jersey, through Pennsylvania, and into Ohio and the Midwest.

The huge complexes on the New Jersey side are chemical works operated by Roche and BASF. A water intake is marked by a buoy advising *Stay Away!* The BASF plant was slated to close in late 2010.

201.1 Pass under high-tension power lines.

200.9 Upstream end of half-mile-long Macks Island.

Long Rift, a Class I rapids, flows between the island and the Pennsylvania riverbank. The rift begins with a series of waves, then tumbles over a little ledge 100 yards downstream. There is a second ledge near the end of the island. The left (New Jersey) channel is navigable but shallow and rocky.

Mount Jack County Park (Northhampton County, Pennsylvania) runs along the riverbank, Pennsylvania side. No access from the river.

200.6 Mount Jack river rest, Pennsylvania side. Not an access or boat launch, just a little clearing along the riverbank. No facilities, but it is public land, and paddlers can take a break.

200.3 A huge gravel bar sticks out into the river from the New Jersey side.

A small, unnamed creek enters at the Pennsylvania side.

199.7 Allegheny Creek enters, Pennsylvania side, with a gravel bar constricting the river by nearly one-half.

The steep slopes of Mount Jack rise on the Pennsylvania side.

The current is funneled into a big V at the New Jersey side, with standing waves to 2 feet. So begins Buttermilk Rift, a tricky Class I+ rapids. The main channel flows from the New Jersey (left) side to the center of the river. Near the Pennsylvania side the channel is peppered with boulders, requiring skillful maneuvering.

199.5 The second ledge of Buttermilk Rift. Watch for ragged ledges along the right.

Little Mill Creek enters, Pennsylvania side.

199.3 The third and final ledge of Buttermilk Rift. The main channel is in the middle, with standing waves to 2 feet. Submerged ledges extend from both banks.

198.9 **Access: Doe Hollow, Pennsylvania.** Maintained by Northhampton County Parks. A steep trail from Riverton Road leads down to the river. This is mainly intended for walk-in anglers. Limited and awkward parking. No fee. Better to use the Belvidere access just downstream for boat launch/landing.

Mill Creek enters, Pennsylvania side.

198.3 McElhaneys Island nestles near the Pennsylvania side. The narrow slough to the right (Pennsylvania side) of the island is not passable when the river level is low.

197.9 Pass under the Belvidere-Riverton Bridge. The abutments and piers were constructed in 1836 to support a wooden bridge. The present four-span steel structure was built in 1904 after the old bridge was destroyed in the Pumpkin Flood of 1903. It was in this vicinity that the raging river tore pumpkins from their vines, littering the riverbanks downstream and giving the flood its name.

The communities of Riverton, Pennsylvania, and Belvidere, New Jersey (seat of Warren County), stand at opposite ends of the bridge.

The Pequest River, a significant tributary, enters at the New Jersey side immediately downstream from the bridge.

The Martins Creek Land Management Area and Tekening Hiking Trails, owned and maintained by PPL Corporation, begin here along the Pennsylvania side. There is a parking area 0.3 mile up the Belvidere Highway (Pennsylvania 1004) from the Belvidere-Riverton Bridge. A blue-blazed trail leads along the river for a birds-eye view of Foul Rift, one mile downstream. There is no easy access from the river.

Approaching Foul Rift, a long and choppy Class II rapids below Belvidere, New Jersey. Stay right and wear your PFD! The stacks and cooling towers of PPL Corporation's power plant at Martins Creek loom in the distance. (Photo by the author)

197.8 **Access: Belvidere, New Jersey.** Maintained by the New Jersey Division of Fish, Game and Shellfisheries. A gravel boat ramp, parking, and privies. No fee. Access from Front Street in Belvidere. From the river, look for a gravel ramp just below the bridge and the Pequest River. *Note*: Recreational maps from the Delaware River Basin Commission omit this access, but it is open and in use as of 2010.

This is a good place to launch for a short run through the Foul Rift rapids, with a landing at Martins Creek access below.

Lunch. Riverton, Pennsylvania: Riverton Hotel and Restaurant, at the Pennsylvania end of the bridge. Belvidere, New Jersey: Belvidere Coffee Shop and Skoogy's Deli (one block from the river).

197.7 There is a U.S. Geological Survey river gage at a tiny brown shed just above the New Jersey riverbank. Base elevation is 225.75 feet above sea level. Good boating stage is 4–6 feet; flood stage is 22 feet. The greatest flood on record was 30.2 feet, in 1955.

197.5 Pophandussing Creek enters, New Jersey side.

The gigantic cooling towers of PPL Corporation's Martins Creek power plant loom ahead.

197.3 A rocky ledge at the left marks the beginning of Little Foul Rift, a Class I rapids continuing 0.4 mile. Passage is best right down the middle. This little rapids is just a tease of what's to come.

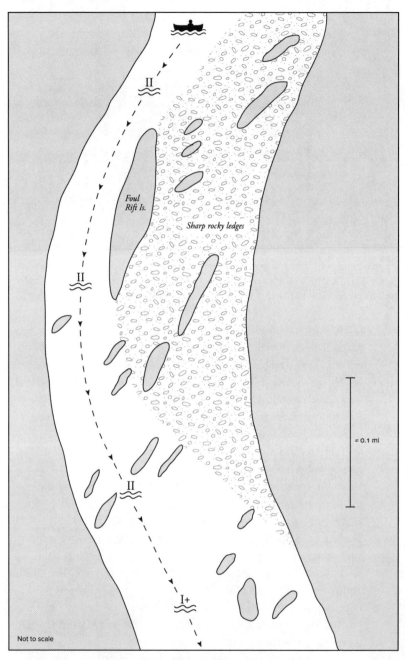

Foul Rift Is.

Sharp rocky ledges

II

II

II

I+

= 0.1 mi

Not to scale

FOUL RIFT

196.9 **CAUTION!** Enter Foul Rift, beginning as Class I but building quickly to a Class II rapids. Stay to the right (Pennsylvania side).

The fall of Little Foul and Big Foul Rift together measures 23 feet over 1.75 miles, making these the longest and steepest rapids on the Delaware.[1] There is no good place to pull up if you swamp or overturn, and no easy way to portage. Secure your gear and wear your PFD! Commercial outfitters do not run Foul Rift.

Foul Rift—or, simply, The Big Foul—was especially feared by old-time timber raftsmen, and many a raft was "stove up" on the rocks. It is not the pitch of the rapids or the big waves that made Foul Rift so infamous, but the sharp limestone ledges. An apt description was given by an early adventurer:

> But more threatening than the tall rocks, that looked like a disorganized Stonehenge, was the terrible nature of the bedrock. We could steer between the teeth we saw, but suddenly became aware of unseen teeth that lay in wait to lacerate the boats beneath the water line.[2]

As early as 1791 there were efforts to clear Foul Rift for better passage by timber rafts and Durham boats. Today's paddlers might notice drill holes where rocks and ledges have been blasted away. These projects defanged Foul Rift to some extent, and at average water level the rapids is just a long set of choppy waves. Still, canoeists and kayakers must take care—the rocks remain sharp, and there is little refuge if you swamp or overturn.

Stay to the right; the left is guarded by nasty ledges.

196.4 Foul Rift Island, a long, jagged ledge, extends 0.1 mile. *Stay right!* The narrow channel to the right of the island has few obstructions and is the safest route, but with big waves. There is nothing but trouble to the left, where sharp ledges lurk. Serious Class II rapids.

196.2 More ledges extend from the New Jersey riverbank. The current flows from left to right. Rapids become more severe, with many submerged and protruding rocks. Continue to stay right.

195.6 The final ledge of Foul Rift, reaching all the way across the river with a sudden drop of about 2 feet into big waves. At low water, parts of the ledge are exposed, revealing a gap into big standing waves in the center. Aim for the gap. This ledge was a boat-buster for timber rafts.

195.4 Ledges and islets extend from the New Jersey riverbank for the next 0.2 mile at the end of Foul Rift. Clearest channel remains along the Pennsylvania side.

195.3 Enter Jones Eddy. Timber raftsmen pulled up here to collect their equipment and composure. Modern paddlers can do likewise. There is a sandy beach on the right (Pennsylvania) side that seems custom-made for the purpose (just beyond a few private homes above the riverbank). In the old days, a man would sell whisky from his rowboat to calm the nerves of shaken raftsmen; alas, the whiskey man has gone.

195.2 Pass under power lines marked by red balls.

Foul Rift Ferry ran here in the nineteenth century.

195.0 PPL Corporation's Martins Creek power plant is on the Pennsylvania riverbank. The twin giant cooling towers are landmarks for miles around. Despite the appearance of the cooling towers, the plant is not nuclear-powered but is fired by oil or natural gas.

There are two water intakes for the power plant at the Pennsylvania riverbank, marked by signs: *DANGER—do not approach within 200 feet.* Stay away if you don't want to be sucked into the power plant.

194.6 Upstream end of Masons Island on the right, extending 0.3 mile. Go to the left of the island; the slough to the right is impassable at low water.

A little gravel bar in the middle of the river is called Capush Island. At above-average river levels it is under water.

Capush Rift starts as Class I but builds quickly to a Class I+ rapids. Go between Masons and Capush Islands, then look for a way down the middle. The river tumbles over a couple of ledges where paddlers will have to avoid protruding and submerged rocks. Standing waves to 2 feet. A challenging little rapids!

194.2 Pass under a bridge carrying the Roxburg branch of the old Belvidere-Delaware Railroad, constructed in 1952 for rail access to the power plant.

Capush Rift ends under the bridge, with standing waves to 2 feet in the middle and left of the river.

194.1 **Access: Martins Creek, Pennsylvania.** Open to public access courtesy of PPL Corporation. A sandy boat ramp, day parking, trash disposal, picnic tables, and privies. The gate to the area is locked from 9:00 p.m. to 7:00 a.m. Camping and overnight parking are not permitted. No fee. Access from Martins Creek–Belvidere Highway (Pennsylvania 1004) to DePues Ferry Road near Martins Creek, Pennsylvania.

The Tocks Island Dam

Tocks Island is just a little sliver of land. Canoeists and kayakers pass by it with hardly a notice. Yet here raged the greatest battle ever over the use and future of the Delaware River.

The twin hurricanes of 1955 brought horrendous floods to the Delaware valley, causing the deaths of more than 100 people. Residents demanded that something be done. So the Delaware River Basin Commission and the U.S. Army Corps of Engineers proposed that a great dam be built at Tocks Island. In addition to holding back the next great flood, the dam would make electric power and provide drinking water for the cities downriver. The 37-mile reservoir behind it—all the way up to Port Jervis—was seen by some as a new paradise for motorboating.

The government began buying (and condemning) land that would be inundated by the reservoir. People were forced to leave their homes, in some cases driven from property that had been in their families for generations. Signs went up: *The Lord Giveth, and the Government Taketh Away.* Hippies (so some said) moved into the abandoned homes. There were ugly confrontations among the locals, the squatters, and the Corps. Bulldozers were called in to raze homes as residents ran into the forest.

Meanwhile, the opposition organized. The Save the Delaware Coalition and Lenni-Lenape League gathered signatures and filed lawsuits. Environmental studies proved the reservoir would quickly fill with silt, choke with algae, leave ugly mud flats at its edges, and drown historic and natural resources. It would not have saved the lives lost in the big floods. And the dam would wipe out 37 miles of spectacular river travel.

In the summer of 1974 New Jersey Governor Brendan Byrne canoed the river leading to the site of the proposed dam. The Youth Conservation Corps (YCC) cleaned up Tocks Island itself, ferrying off five truckloads of trash. Kittatinny Canoes graciously loaned 40 canoes for Byrne's expedition. The athletic governor took the bow in one, a state trooper in the stern. Then the rest of the party—dignitaries, reporters, the YCC—paddled out. At least 100 craft joined the flotilla as demonstrators and onlookers came along. Byrne completed his voyage with a short speech at Tocks Island amid a throng of demonstrators carrying signs that spoke their minds: *Doom the Dam.*

A decision had to be made, and Byrne charged his commissioner of Environmental Protection, David Bardin, with making the call. Bardin, an avid outdoorsman, had read the studies and been to the hearings. But he also wanted a private visit to get a better feel of the place. Guided by teenagers from the YCC, Bardin hiked the Appalachian Trail from the Delaware Water Gap to Millbrook. He saw scores of canoes making their way through the rapids in the river far below. Every hiker he talked to knew about the dam, and all were opposed to it. Then, as Bardin logged his name in the trail register near Rattle-snake Spring, he told his young guides that he would use the same pen to sign his report to the governor—in opposition to the dam.

The next week the governors of the Delaware River Basin Commission voted to discontinue the Tocks Island Dam project, and in 1992 authorization for the dam was forever rescinded by Congress. The Delaware will remain a free-flowing river.

Delaware Water Gap

The Delaware Water Gap is the most famous and spectacular natural feature along the river. Here the river has cut through the hard rock of the Kit-tatinny Ridge to form a cleft 1,300 feet deep, 1,500 yards across at the top, and 300 yards across at the bottom.

Geologists tell us how the water gap was formed. Hundreds of millions of years ago, during the Silurian period, the continents of Europe and North America were jammed together. Great rivers flowed down from mountains in Europe, depositing layers of pebbles, sand, silt, and limestone over what is now eastern North America. The layers of rock heaved and folded as the continents separated, building high mountains. A great river flowed through these ancient mountains; over the eons it eroded down through a weak spot in the rock to form the Delaware Water Gap. Glaciers in more recent geologic history shaped the gap into its present form.

In 1833 a roadside inn called Kittatinny House opened at the foot of Mount Minsi on the Pennsylvania side. Before long, fast trains were depositing tour-ists from New York and Philadelphia for weekend getaways on the river. By 1877 Kittatinny House and the competing Water Gap House had grown to ornate Victorian resorts with hundreds of rooms. On the New Jersey side, Camp Karamac hosted tourists at the site of today's Kittatinny Point visitor center. All of the resorts offered canoes for use by their patrons, and there was even a little steamboat for excursions up to Bushkill. But by the turn of the twentieth century the tourists began to move on. The grand hotels disap-peared one by one, and the Kittatinny House itself burned to the ground in 1931. Today only its foundation remains, near Resort Point overlook on Penn-sylvania Route 611.

There are trails to the summits of Mount Minsi on the Pennsylvania side

PUB. BY I. H. BLANCHARD CO. N.Y.

THE KITTATINNY HOUSE

The Kittatinny House, a bygone luxury resort at the Delaware Water Gap. The excursion steamer *Kittatinny* churns in the foreground. (From a postcard c. 1915, collection of the author)

and Mount Tammany on the New Jersey side. It's a tough hike to the top—but what a view of the river and valley far below!

The Appalachian Trail

White rectangles 2½ inches wide by 6 inches tall are painted along the walkway on the Interstate 80 bridge at the Delaware Water Gap. From the Pennsylvania end of the bridge, the blazes lead up Mount Minsi and all the way to Springer Mountain, Georgia. From the New Jersey end, they follow Dunnfield Creek, ramble past Sunfish Pond atop Kittatinny Ridge, and eventually lead to Mount Katahdin in Maine. The blazes mark the Appalachian Trail (AT), a footpath that extends 2,161 miles along the ridge tops from Georgia to Maine.

The AT is not, as some think, an old Indian trail. The first section of the AT was cleared at Bear Mountain, New York, in 1923, and the last in 1937, when the Civilian Conservation Corps axed through the swamps of Maine. The corridor of the trail is protected by federal law, and in New Jersey it is all on public land.

Until the 1970s only a handful of people had hiked the entire length of the AT. But now, every year, hundreds of "thru-hikers" can proudly claim the coveted *Georgia to Maine* patch for their backpacks. Most thru-hikers start in Georgia in early spring, then work their way north with the season, to arrive in Maine just as snow begins to fall. To keep this timetable, the thru-hikers must cross the Delaware in June or July.

Thru-hikers are easy to spot. Unlike many day hikers, they don't seem to be in a hurry, yet cover the ground fast. They long ago shed excess weight from their backpacks. Some joke that they look like Tyrannosaurus Rex, with hugely muscled legs and limp, under-used arms. Thru-hikers take a "trail name," used in the shelter logbooks and among their brothers and sisters on the trail. Each has his or her own reason for hiking the AT, and many have become the stuff of legend. The "Barefoot Sisters" hiked the entire trail *sans* shoes, then turned around and hiked back; Jim "the Geek" carried his cat Ziggy, who became famous for cleaning up the mice at shelters all along the way; and in 1990 Bill Irwin inspired international awe when he hiked the trail end-to-end and mostly alone—even though he was completely blind.

The Appalachian Trail is like a village 2,100 miles long by six feet wide. In a way, our Delaware River is a similar village, 200 miles long. The villages meet here at the Water Gap; as you pass beneath, be sure to give a wave!

Mile 194.1 to 168.3 (25.8 miles)

Highlights of this section include Weygadt Gap—also known as the Little Water Gap—and the Forks of the Delaware, where the Lehigh River joins the Delaware. There are Class I+ rapids at Weygadt Rift, Durham Falls, and Lynns Falls. It's a long slog to paddle the entire length of this section in one day, so it might be better to break it up into shorter trips. This section is relatively little used by canoeists and kaykers, although some areas are very popular with powerboaters. Outfitters do not regularly operate in this section. Still, the adventurous will find excellent paddling, dramatic scenery, and fascinating historic features.

The river continues to flow through the Ridge and Valley geophysical province, cutting through a couple of small water gaps. Just below Riegelsville the river leaves the Ridge and Valley and enters the Piedmont, a broad band of rolling hills extending from New Jersey to northern Georgia. The red sandstone Palisades of the Delaware rise 500 feet above the river between Riegelsville and Upper Black Eddy.

Farmlands and forest continue to dominate the countryside along the river, with the exception of the twin cities of Phillipsburg, New Jersey, and Easton, Pennsylvania. In some areas, the river seems far from civilization; in others, cottages and private boat docks dot the riverbanks. Pennsylvania Routes 611 and 32 parallel the river on the Pennsylvania side most of the way. The old Delaware Canal, now a state park, runs atop the riverbank on the Pennsylvania side below Easton.

There are eight public access points in this section:

Martins Creek, Pennsylvania, mile 194.1
Sandts Eddy, Pennsylvania., mile 189.3
Frost Hollow, Pennsylvania, mile 186.4
Phillipsburg, New Jersey, mile 183.9

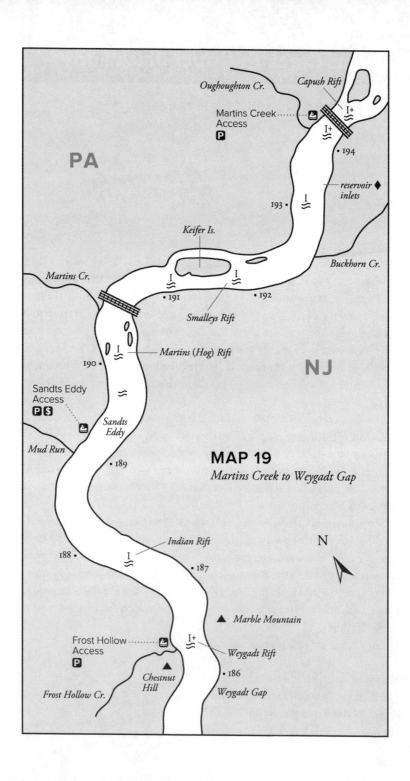

Oughoughton Cr.

Capush Rift

Martins Creek
Access

🅿

I+

I+

PA

• 194

reservoir
inlets ◆

193 •

I

Buckhorn Cr.

Keifer Is.

Martins Cr.

I

I

• 191

• 192

Smalleys Rift

NJ

I

Martins (Hog) Rift

190 •

Sandts Eddy
Access

🅿 💲

Sandts
Eddy

Mud Run

• 189

MAP 19
Martins Creek to Weygadt Gap

Indian Rift

188 •

I

• 187

N

▲ Marble Mountain

Frost Hollow
Access

🅿

I+

Weygadt Rift

• 186

▲
Chestnut
Hill

Weygadt Gap

Frost Hollow Cr.

Scott Park (Easton), Pennsylvania, mile 183.7
Riegelsville, New Jersey, mile 175.0
Riegelsville, Pennsylvania, mile 174.0
Upper Black Eddy, Pennsylvania, mile 168.3

Portions of the river are within the Lower Delaware Wild and Scenic River. However, most lands adjacent to the river are privately owned—no trespassing. There are no campgrounds immediately along the river.

River Guide

Map 19

194.1 **Access: Martins Creek, Pennsylvania.** Provided courtesy of the PPL Corporation. A sandy boat ramp, day parking, trash disposal, picnic tables, and privies. A gate to the area is locked from 9:00 p.m. to 7:00 a.m. Camping and overnight parking are not permitted. No fee. Access from Martins Creek–Belvidere Highway (Pennsylvania 1004) to DePues Ferry Road near Martins Creek, Pennsylvania.

Oughoughton Creek enters, Pennsylvania side.

The final waves of Capush Rift, now a Class I rapids, continue 0.3 mile.

193.8 Begin a segment of the Lower Delaware Wild and Scenic River, extending from this point to Easton.

193.2 Water intakes for the Merrill Creek Reservoir, New Jersey side, constructed in 1988 to draw water for electric utilities. Buoys and signs advise *DANGER—submerged intake.* Stay to the right! The reservoir itself is about four miles from the river.

193.0 A Class I rapids, continuing 0.3 mile. Shallow ledges on the right.

192.6 Buckhorn Creek enters, New Jersey side. River turns sharply right.

Private docks and landings, both sides.

192.2 A brushy gravel island nestles against the Pennsylvania riverbank.

191.9 Keifer Island, extending 0.6 mile, begins in the middle of the river. Passage is good on both sides.

Smalleys Rift, a Class I rapids, begins in the left channel at the upstream end of the island. Standing waves to 1½ feet.

191.3 Keifer Island ends. The right-hand channel turns sharply left to rejoin the mainstream in a gravelly riffle. Smalleys Rift continues along the left, with a few boulders in right center.

191.0 Extensive gravel mining operations, New Jersey side.

190.4 Pass under a bridge constructed in 1885 to carry the Martins Creek branch of the old Pennsylvania Railroad line, now abandoned.

Martins Creek, a good-sized stream, joins the river on the Pennsylvania side immediately downstream from the bridge.

Stacks and silos of an old Alpha Portland Cement plant, now a ConAgra Foods storage facility, are visible on the Pennsylvania side. Cement made here was used in the construction of the Panama Canal. The water-filled quarry for limestone used at the plant is only yards from the river, but just out of view.

The community of Martins Creek Station is on the New Jersey side. No access from the river. Long ago, a ferry ran here.

190.3 A couple of small islets along the New Jersey (left) side, extending 0.3 mile.

190.2 Martins Rift, a Class I rapids. The flow moves from right to left at a constriction of the river, with shallows and gravel bars on the New Jersey side. This rapids was also known as Hog Rift, "so called from the many hogs which had died from eating distillery slops and been thrown into the river, and lodged against the shore, tainting the air with their putrid carcasses."[1] Thankfully, the hogs are long gone.

189.6 After a moderate riffle, the river slows into Sandts Eddy, continuing for the next 2.0 miles. This area is very popular with motorboaters and Jet-Skiers; canoeists should stay near the sides.

189.5 The giant silos of another ConAgra grain storage facility loom above the river, Pennsylvania side. This site was operated by Alpha Cement until 1962. In 1942, 20 tons of dynamite exploded prematurely at the quarry, killing 31 workers. The blast was felt 50 miles away.

189.3 **Access: Sandts Eddy, Pennsylvania.** Maintained by the Pennsylvania Fish and Boat Commission. A boat ramp to the river, with ample parking; no other facilities. Very popular with anglers using trailered powerboats. Access from U.S. Route 611, opposite ConAgra. All boats launched or landed here must bear a valid Pennsylvania boat registration or launch permit.

189.2 Mud Run enters, Pennsylvania side.

Private homes and cottages line both riverbanks for the next 0.4 mile.

Sandts Eddy continues, slowly. Canoeists and kayakers should try to hit the wakes of motorboats at an angle, not broadside.

187.8 Indian Rift, with a rocky ledge along the Pennsylvania side; mild riffles continue down the middle for about 0.5 mile. Very shallow.

The Weygadt, or Little Water Gap, just above Easton. *Weygadt* is an old Dutch word for "windy," and it often is. The rocky Class I+ rapids of Weygadt Rift lie ahead. (Photo by the author)

186.8   The river bends sharply to the right as Marble Mountain looms ahead. The current quickens.

186.6   Begin Weygadt Rift, a tricky Class I+ rapids. Wear your PFD; it's all too easy to get turned sideways and capsize.

      The rapids begin at an elongated boulder in the middle of the river, once known as Durham Boat Rock because it vaguely resembled an overturned Durham boat. Beware the submerged ledge to the left; best passage is to the right.

      One hundred yards farther, a second ledge reaches nearly across the river. There is clear passage around either end; or pick your way through gaps in the middle.

186.5   A gravel bar at the mouth of Frost Hollow Creek protrudes into the river at the right, while rocky ledges extend from the left. The final plunge of Weygadt Rift funnels between, offering clear passage with big standing waves.

186.4   **Access: Frost Hollow Park, Pennsylvania.** Maintained by the North Hampton County Division of Parks and Recreation. A scenic overlook with a few parking spaces at a turnout on Route 611. Hand-launch at the river down rough steps. No facilities, no fee. Difficult to find from the river, just at the confluence of Frost Hollow Creek.

186.3   The river passes through Weygadt Gap, also known as the Little Water

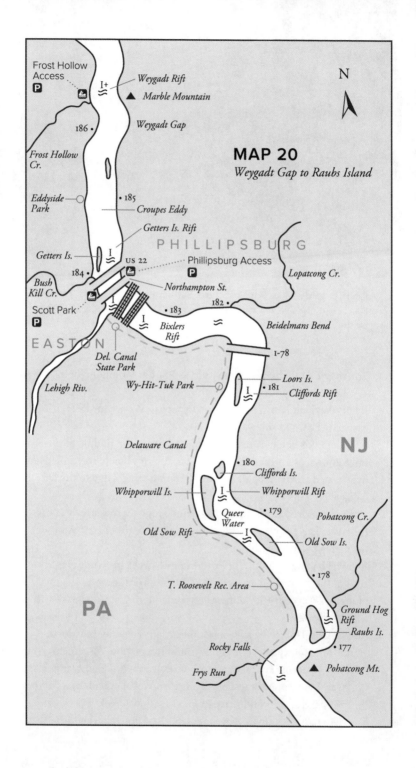

N

Frost Hollow
Access
P

Weygadt Rift

I+

▲ Marble Mountain

Weygadt Gap

186 •

MAP 20
Weygadt Gap to Raubs Island

Frost Hollow
Cr.

Eddyside
Park

• 185

Croupes Eddy

Getters Is. Rift

P H I L L I P S B U R G

Getters Is.

I

US 22

Phillipsburg Access

184 •

P

Bush
Kill Cr.

Northampton St.

Lopatcong Cr.

Scott Park
P

I

• 183

182 •

E A S T O N

I

Bixlers
Rift

Beidelmans Bend

Del. Canal
State Park

I-78

Lehigh Riv.

Wy-Hit-Tuk Park

Loors Is.

I

• 181

Cliffords Rift

Delaware Canal

N J

• 180

Cliffords Is.

Whipporwill Is.

I

Whipporwill Rift

Queer
Water

• 179

Pohatcong Cr.

Old Sow Rift

I

Old Sow Is.

• 178

T. Roosevelt Rec. Area

PA

Ground Hog
Rift

I

Rocky Falls

Raubs Is.

• 177

Frys Run

I

▲ Pohatcong Mt.

Gap, with high limestone bluffs on both sides. Chestnut Hill stands on the Pennsylvania (right) side, its rocky cliffs known as St. Anthony's Nose. Marble Mountain is on the New Jersey (left) side. Hiking trails lead to the tops of both peaks, where awesome views await.

Weygadt is an old Dutch term for "windy," and indeed, canoeists may be buffeted by gusts funneled between the mountains.

Map 20

186.0 Big rocks stick up in the middle of the river, a frequent perch for waterfowl.

185.6 A marshy gravel bar on the New Jersey side extends to the middle of the river. Passage to the right is clear.

185.5 This segment of the Lower Delaware Wild and Scenic River ends at the boundary of the City of Easton.

185.4 Pot Rock, a broad, bare ledge, lies at the Pennsylvania riverbank. According to legend, Lenape women came here to grind corn in natural mortars in the ledge, some of which can be discerned today.

185.3 The City of Easton water treatment plant intake, at an artificial spit on the Pennsylvania side. Stay clear to the left. Water from the Delaware River is treated for consumption by city residents.

Pass under power lines.

185.0 Eddyside Park, maintained by the City of Easton, on the right. The swimming pool and picnic area are available to city residents. The boat ramp is not open to public access.

This slow stretch of river was known as Croupes Eddy.

As paddlers approach the cities of Easton, Pennsylvania, and Phillipsburg, New Jersey, they will find the riverbanks increasingly urbanized.

184.4 Getters Island begins, extending 0.3 mile. Its slender upstream tip nearly touches the Pennsylvania riverbank. The island is named for Charles Getter, who in 1833 was publicly hanged here for the murder of his wife, the last public execution in Pennsylvania.

In 1860 the little stern-wheel steamboat *Alfred Thomas* exploded while beached at Getters Island, killing at least 10 passengers and ending the dream of steamboat commerce on the Delaware.

The narrow channel to the right of Getters Island is navigable, ending at the remnant of a low dam. A chute in the center of the dam makes an exciting quick drop into standing waves. The dam is submerged at above-average water level and should not be run; there is a dangerous "keeper" hydraulic.

Enter Class I rapids of Getters Island Rift in the main channel to the left of Getters Island. The best route is straight down the middle. Watch for boulders.

184.1   Bushkill Creek enters, Pennsylvania side, at the downstream tip of Getters Island. This is the third stream called Bushkill to join the Delaware River.

Look to the top of the hill above Easton to glimpse the brick edifices of Lafayette College.

184.0   Pass beneath the Easton-Phillipsburg toll bridge carrying U.S. Route 22, a single steel-truss span constructed in 1938.

Class I rapids continue; stay in the middle.

In 2005 the Delaware River Basin Commission installed a high-tech river gage on the downstream side of the bridge. A radar beam from the gage reflects from the river surface to give an accurate measure of elevation. The gage is in a glass-bottomed box fixed to the bridge structure. Base elevation is 157 feet above sea level; flood stage is 22 feet. The greatest flood was 43.7 feet in 1955.

183.9   **Access: Phillipsburg, New Jersey.** Maintained by the City of Phillipsburg. A boat ramp, large parking area, trash disposal, restrooms, and potable water. No fee. Access from South Main Street, Phillipsburg (near the entrance to the Northampton Street Bridge). From the river, just upstream from the Northampton Street Bridge.

Riverside Park sits atop a concrete abutment in Easton, Pennsylvania. It features a promenade, a little amphitheater, and a statue of Christopher Columbus. No access directly from the river.

183.8   Pass under the Northampton Street Bridge. Construction of a bridge here was chartered as early as 1795 and completed in 1806, the second bridge to span the Delaware. The covered wooden bridge afforded especially low clearance beneath and was the bane of timber raftsmen.

The present bridge, with new abutments and a unique cantilever-truss design, was completed in 1895. It survived battering by the great Pumpkin Flood of 1903 and Hurricanes Connie and Diane in 1955, earning the nickname "Gibraltar of the Delaware." It has been known locally as the "free bridge" since 1921, when tolls were abolished (not, some may think, to spite the U.S. 22 toll bridge just upstream).

Martins (or Bullmans) Ferry ran here before construction of the bridge.

The city of Easton, Pennsylvania, population 26,080 (est. 2008), the largest community on the Delaware River above Trenton, is on the right. Phillipsburg, New Jersey, population 14,528 (est. 2008), is on the left. There are plenty of restaurants and other services in both cities.

183.7 **Access: Scott Park, Pennsylvania.** Maintained by the City of Easton. A paved boat ramp, parking, trash disposal, and pay phone. No fee. From the river, immediately downstream from the Northampton Street Bridge and before the confluence of the Lehigh River. Access from U.S. Route 611 in Easton.

The Lehigh River enters, Pennsylvania side. The Lehigh, with a watershed of 1,360 square miles, is the largest tributary of the Delaware. The name Lehigh is derived from the Lenape *Lech-au-we-kink*, "place of forks." Early colonists called it the "West Branch of the Delaware," the main stem being the "East Branch." The Lehigh supports a busy whitewater rafting business through a spectacular gorge upstream. Portions of it have been designated the Lehigh River Water Trail.

The confluence of the Lehigh and Delaware Rivers is known as the "Forks of the Delaware," a strategic prize for centuries and a main objective of the infamous Walking Purchase of 1737, by which the area was acquired from the Lenape.

The Lehigh River falls over a 12-foot spillway just before entering the Delaware. This spillway was constructed to impound water for the Delaware Canal.

The flow of the Lehigh River into the Delaware causes shifting currents, boils, and whirlpools. Class I rapids continuing 0.2 mile; take care here.

183.6 The old Delaware Canal and Delaware Canal State Park begin on the bluff (Pennsylvania side) immediately downstream from the Forks. The canal parallels the river for 60 miles to tidewater at Bristol, Pennsylvania. The gate locks from the Lehigh River to the canal are here, along with two lift locks immediately below.

An elaborate fish ladder, overlooked by a public viewing area, allows fish to migrate into and out of the Lehigh.

Boats can be beached on the rocks just below the Lehigh confluence. It's a scramble up the riverbank to view the canal, fish ladder, spillway, and skylines of Easton and Phillipsburg. However, this is not a good access point to begin or end a trip. Use Scotts Park in Easton or the Phillipsburg access instead.

Pass under a three-span steel truss bridge that once carried the Lehigh and Hudson River Railway; today it's used by the Norfolk Southern Railroad.

The massive stone-arch gate lock to the Morris Canal stands at the

New Jersey riverbank just below the rail bridge. Completed in 1831, the Morris Canal ran across New Jersey to Newark. Canal barges were raised and lowered via inclined planes instead of lift locks. Only traces of the Morris Canal remain.

In the mid-nineteenth century three canals met here: the Lehigh Canal from the Pennsylvania coal fields, the Morris Canal across New Jersey; and the Delaware Canal along the Pennsylvania riverbank down to Bristol. Barges were ferried across the river at this point from one canal to the next.

183.5 Pass under twin railroad bridges, the first built for the Central New Jersey Railroad (now part of the Conrail network), the second for the now-defunct Lehigh Valley Railroad.

183.1 Begin Bixlers Rift, Class I rapids continuing about 0.7 mile; very shallow on the left, boulders and standing waves on the right.

182.8 City of Easton wastewater treatment plant is on the bluff, Pennsylvania side. The outfall from the plant can be seen as a gray, frothy discharge, quickly assimilated by the river. At one time, most communities along the Delaware discharged their untreated wastewater directly into the river; now, all discharges are treated to at least "secondary" (biological) treatment standards and subject to compliance with a discharge permit.

182.2 Beware Beidelmans Rocks—submerged ledges at the right and a couple of big limestone boulders sticking up in the middle.

Pass under power lines.

182.0 Lopatcong Creek enters, New Jersey side, at a grassy gravel bar.

The river curves sharply right into Beidelmans Bend. Members of the Beidelman family were among the early German settlers of Easton.

181.5 The massive concrete-and-steel bridge carrying Interstate 78, constructed in 1989, towers above the river.

181.1 Loors Island, a gravel bar extending 0.3 mile. Stay left; the slough to the right is too shallow.

Wy-Hit-Tuk Park, Pennsylvania side. Maintained by the Northampton County Parks and Recreation Division. Picnicking, nature trails, group camping by permit. Access to the Delaware Canal, but no good access to the river.

Cliffords Rift, a negligible riffle (Class I–), in the channel to the left (New Jersey side) of Loors Island.

A small stream enters, New Jersey side, midway along the island, at a gravel bar.

180.0 Cliffords Island on the left, then Whippoorwill Island on the right —brushy gravel bars at a sharp left turn of the river, extending 0.6 mile.

Go between the islands; the passages at extreme left and right are very shallow.

Begin Whippoorwill Rift, a strong Class I rapids between the islands, with a sharp drop and choppy waves.

179.6 Beware whirlpools and boils in the deep eddy at the tail of Whippoorwill Rift, aptly known as Queer Water.

178.8 Old Sow Island, with a narrow gravel bar extending 0.4 mile. Stay right.

Old Sow Rift, a Class I rapids, begins at a rocky ledge just below the head of the island, then continues with nice standing waves.

178.6 Water released from the Delaware Canal makes a pretty falls down the Pennsylvania riverbank.

178.4 Community of Raubsville, Pennsylvania side. This is the site of Raub's (Carpenters) Ferry, which plied the Delaware in the early nineteenth century.

Lunch. Raubsville, Pennsylvania: Raubsville Tavern, up a clear trail from the river.

178.0 A whitewashed stone building stands at the river's edge, Pennsylvania side. This was once a mini hydro-electric plant, powered by water diverted from the Delaware Canal. Some of the mechanism can be viewed from a walkway around the structure.

A rough trail just downstream from the old power plant leads up to the Theodore Roosevelt Recreation Area of the Delaware Canal State Park. Locks 22–23 of the old canal, restored to working condition, are here. There are picnic tables, barbeque grills, trash disposal, restrooms, and a water pump. This is a good place to check out the canal locks or to enjoy a picnic lunch; it is not a good boat launch/landing area.

177.8 Raubs (or Ground Hog) Island, extending 0.4 mile. Stay left (New Jersey side); the Pennsylvania side is very shallow.

Pass under power lines.

A concrete pylon on Raubs Island once supported a tramway used to haul goods from a factory on the Pennsylvania side to a railroad depot in New Jersey.

177.6 Begin Ground Hog Rift, a Class I rapids over a cobbly bottom.

177.5 Pohatcong Creek enters, New Jersey side, at a large gravel bar extending to the middle of the channel.

177.3 The river bends sharply right as it runs up against the hard rock of Pohatcong Mountain. Treacherous eddies and whirlpools boil up around the end of Raubs Island. At 35 feet, this is one of the deepest places on the river. The dark, angry water seems a little spooky. Take care here, wear your PFD, and do not attempt to swim.

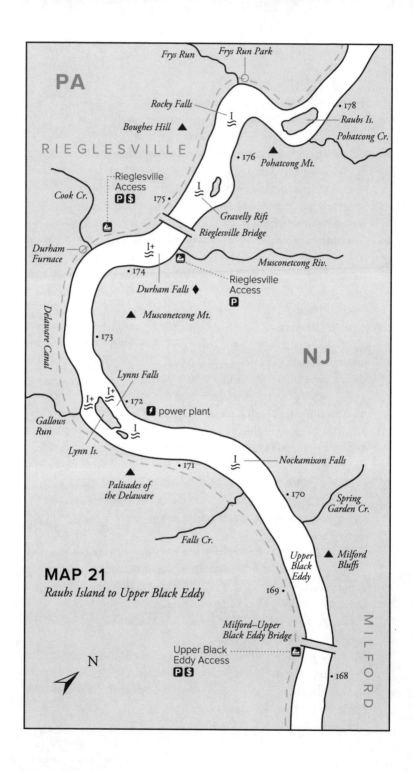

Frys Run   Frys Run Park

PA

Rocky Falls   • 178

Boughes Hill ▲   I   Raubs Is.

RIEGLESVILLE   Pohatcong Cr.

          Rieglesville   • 176
          Access   ▲
Cook Cr. P $ 175 •   Pohatcong Mt.

                    I
                         Gravelly Rift
          Rieglesville Bridge

Durham   I+   Musconetcong Riv.
Furnace

          • 174
     Delaware Canal   Durham Falls ◆   Rieglesville
                                          Access
          ▲ Musconetcong Mt.   P

          • 173

                              NJ

          Lynns Falls

     I+   I+ • 172   ⚡ power plant
Gallows
Run   I

Lynn Is.   I   Nockamixon Falls

          • 171
     ▲   • 170
Palisades of   Spring
the Delaware   Garden Cr.

          Falls Cr.

MAP 21   Upper   ▲ Milford
Raubs Island to Upper Black Eddy   Black   Bluffs
                              Eddy
                         169 •

          Milford–Upper
          Black Eddy Bridge

N   Upper Black   MILFORD
          Eddy Access
     ↑   P $ • 168

177.2　The current will try to push you into Heinemans Point, a prominent gneiss ledge protruding from the left (New Jersey) side. Passing it, you have run the Ground Hog!

Map 21

176.9　Frys Run Park, on U.S. Route 611, Pennsylvania side, operated by Northhampton County Parks. Paddlers will find only limited parking, rough trail access to the river, and no good place to launch a boat. A reconstructed historic stone arch bridge is the park's highlight.

　　　Frys Run enters, Pennsylvania side. The Delaware Canal crosses Frys Run over an aqueduct clearly visible from the river.

176.8　The river bends sharply to the left. A big, squarish boulder in the middle of the river is the "entering rock" for Rocky Falls, Class I rapids continuing about 0.7 mile.

　　　The sharp ledges and boulders of Rocky Falls were a hazard to early Durham boats and timber rafts, and over the years some of the worst were blasted away to clear the passage. Drill holes can still be seen in some of them. Pay attention: the sharp rocks can still grab your boat. Best passage is generally along the right.

176.6　Boughes Hill slopes steeply up on the right (Pennsylvania) side, Pohatcong Mountain on the left, a mini water gap.

176.5　A big, jagged rock at the right center was known as Calculation Rock; judging the river level against the rock determined safe passage below.

176.4　Limestone cliffs above the New Jersey riverbank are known as Pinchers Point.

175.7　Gravelly Rift, an easy Class I rapids, around a large gravel bar at a widening in the river.

174.9　There is a U.S. Geological Survey river gage at the New Jersey riverbank immediately upstream from the Riegelsville Bridge, housed in a tiny brown shack atop a concrete foundation. Base elevation is 124.3 feet above mean sea level. Good stage for boating is 3–6 feet; flood stage is 22 feet. The greatest flood was 38.85 feet in 1955.

　　　Pass under the Riegelsville Bridge. A wooden covered bridge was built here in 1835 and survived until the Pumpkin Flood of 1903. The present twin-cable suspension bridge, one of the most picturesque spans across the Delaware, was completed in 1904 by the Roebling Company.

　　　Shenks Ferry ran here before the bridge was built.

　　　The communities of Riegelsville, Pennsylvania, and Riegelsville, New Jersey, stand at opposite ends of the bridge.

Lunch. Just off the bridge on the Pennsylvania side stands the Riegelsville Inn, built by Benjamin Reigel in 1838 and serving as a hostelry ever since; other casual restaurants can be found on this side of the bridge.

174.8 Musconetcong River enters, New Jersey side. The upstream "Musky" is lined with historic mills, bridges, and farms, and is renowned for fly-fishing.

Access: Riegelsville, New Jersey. Maintained by the New Jersey Division of Fish and Wildlife. Steep asphalt boat ramp, parking. No fee. From the river, immediately below the Muscontecong River. Access from Old River Road/Riegelsville Road. This access has replaced the old Holland Church access downriver, now closed.

174.6 **CAUTION!** Durham Falls, a Class I+ rapids. A surprising rocky ledge about three feet high extends diagonally from the New Jersey side. A string of orange buoys may guard the approach to the ledge. This ledge is the remnant of a wing dam built long ago to divert water to a mill. At average water level you can sneak through gaps in the ledge; at higher water this is a severe and turbulent drop, stay to the right. Passage is clear, with choppy waves, near the Pennsylvania side.

174.0 **Access: Riegelsville, Pennsylvania.** Maintained by the Pennsylvania Fish and Boat Commission. Intended mainly for riverbank fishing access. A grassy path to the river (a carry of about 50 yards), ample parking, no other facilities. All boats must bear a valid Pennsylvania boat registration or launch permit. From the river, look for wide dirt trails up the riverbank. Access from U.S. 611.

173.9 Cook (or Durham) Creek enters, Pennsylvania side, with a gravel bar extending one-third of the way across the river. Lock 21 and the Durham Aqueduct of the Delaware Canal can be seen a short distance up Cook Creek. There are historic markers and a few picnic tables. Rough and steep access from the river at the mouth of the creek; it's worth a stop to scramble up and see the locks. This is not a good boat launch/landing point.

This was the site of Durham Furnace, which produced iron here from 1728 to 1908. The scene is bucolic today, but 150 years ago this was a busy industrial site. Flat-bottom scows known as Durham boats hauled iron from the furnace and other goods to market in the cities downriver.

A crossing called Parsley Ferry ran here in the nineteenth century. The river is slow for the next 1.6 miles.

Musconetcong Mountain rises on the New Jersey side.

173.5 A few boulders stick up on the right; the biggest is known as Old Fry Rock.

172.3 Lynn Island, extending 0.5 mile. The main channel runs to the left, but it's clear either way.

Begin Lynns Falls, Class I+ rapids, at the head of the island. Avoid the rocky ledges at the New Jersey riverbank. Lynns Falls drops 8.8 feet in 2,000 feet (23 ft/mi), making it one of the steeper drops on the river. Not many obstructions, big standing waves.

The channel to the right (Pennsylvania side) of Lynn Island is narrow but navigable, and is more interesting than the left channel. There is a good Class I+ rapids about halfway down, with maneuvers around boulders and an S-turn back into the main channel.

172.2 Gallows Run enters, Pennsylvania side, to the right of Lynn Island.

171.8 Lock 20 of the Delaware Canal, with a few picnic tables nearby, is on the Pennsylvania riverbank. A steep trail leads up from the river; not a launch/landing point.

Pass under power lines.

Spectacular red sandstone cliffs called the Palisades of the Delaware rise 500 feet above the river on the Pennsylvania side. Canal boatmen called this area the "Narrows of Nockamixen," as the Delaware Canal squeezed between the cliffs and the river.

171.7 The Gilbert Generating Station, with its giant smokestack and cooling tower, now (2010) operated by GenOn Energy, is on the New Jersey riverbank. Stay clear of the cooling-water intakes at the riverbank. Several high-tension lines cross the river in the vicinity.

Pennsylvania Route 32 and the Delaware Canal run very close to the river, Pennsylvania side.

171.5 Another segment of the Lower Delaware Wild and Scenic River begins.

171.0 If you have a vivid imagination, you might see the profile of an Indian in the rock formations atop the palisades.

More power lines.

170.8 Still more power lines.

170.7 A long, skinny island crowds the Pennsylvania riverbank; the slough to the right is not navigable.

170.6 Nockamixon Falls, a slalom through Class I rapids, continuing 0.6 mile. A series of ledges extends across the river. Look for passages through the ledges, at first near the right side, then to the left and center. The final ledge drops into standing waves to 2 feet.

The red sandstone cliffs of Milford Bluffs loom ahead on the left.

169.6 Spring Garden Creek enters, New Jersey side.

Falls Creek enters, Pennsylvania side. High Falls, a pretty but not-so-high waterfall (about 20 feet), tumbles over sandstone ledges about a mile from the river in Ringing Rocks County Park.

Ringing Rocks, a mile up Bridgeton Hill Road at Upper Black Eddy, is a field full of boulders that, when struck by a hammer, ring like bells. With some friends you can play a tune by banging on different rocks. Geologists are uncertain how the field came to be or why the boulders ring.

Enter Upper Black Eddy, slow water for the next mile. Watch out for speedboats, Jet Skis, and party boats.

169.4 Look for a rope swing at a little clearing on the New Jersey side. Rope swings tend to be ephemeral things, but this one has been here a long time, on a sturdy tree with a wooden jump-off. At your own risk!

168.3 Pass under the Milford–Upper Black Eddy Bridge. A wooden covered bridge was built here in 1842; the present three-span steel truss was completed in 1933. Lowreytown Ferry ran here before the bridge was constructed.

The hotel/tavern at Upper Black Eddy (Pennsylvania) was one of the favorite stopping places for timber raftsmen. Sometimes 100 or more rafts would be tied up for the night here.

The village of Milford, New Jersey, was at times known as Burnt Mills, Lowreytown, and Sunburn. The old Milford Mill stands empty, brooding over the river, just downstream from the bridge.

Lunch. Upper Black Eddy: café and general store. Milford: several casual restaurants.

Camping. Ringing Rocks Family Campground, about one mile from the river up the hill from the Upper Black Eddy access.

Access: Upper Black Eddy, Pennsylvania. Maintained by the Pennsylvania Fish and Boat Commission. A paved boat ramp, parking, no other facilities. All boats must bear a valid Pennsylvania boat registration or launch permit. From the river, about 100 yards downstream from the Milford–Upper Black Eddy Bridge. Access from Pennsylvania Route 32.

Features

The Walking Purchase

"He run, that not fair, he was to walk!" So said the Lenape chief when he learned that his people had been swindled out of their land by the sons of William Penn.

In 1681 King Charles II gave what would become Pennsylvania to William Penn in payment of a debt to Penn's father. A devout Quaker and honorable man, Penn forged a treaty with the great Lenape chief Tammany at Philadelphia. Peace between the peoples was to last "as long as the creeks and rivers run, and while the sun, moon, and stars endure."

Sadly, the peace did not last beyond Penn's lifetime. Penn's sons John and Thomas schemed to take possession of Lenape lands at the Forks of the Delaware and points north. In cahoots with the Iroquois, the Lenapes' archenemies, the Penn brothers produced a deed they said had been given to their father, which granted possession of land measured by a day-and-a-half walk west from Wrightstown. The Indians presumed a leisurely walk, as had been the practice in similar treaties, and that the distance would be about 25 miles. The Penns, however, had other ideas. Three runners set out along a path that had been cleared in advance, with horses carrying food and provisions. The athletes covered 65 miles in the time allotted, and the Penns took possession of the Delaware valley all the way up to the Minisink.

The Walking Purchase marked the end of peaceful relations with the Lenape. Many were squeezed from their homelands as settlers moved in, some evacuating to Ohio and points west. Others remained, fighting viciously against the settlers in the French and Indian War and the American Revolution. William Penn's peaceable kingdom was no more.

By way of postscript, the modern Delaware Nation filed a lawsuit against the state of Pennsylvania in 2004 to recover a tiny portion of the lands their forebears lost in the Walking Purchase. The court found that not only was the walk a scam, but the Penns' deed calling for the walk was a fake. Still, under the law of aboriginal title, the Lenape lands could be taken by the state for any reason, even by fraud. The Lenapes' claim was denied.

The Delaware Canal

The roads west were paved with water. In the early nineteenth century about 4,000 miles of towpath canals were built in eastern America, the tentacles of commerce penetrating the wilderness. There were 1,200 miles of canals in Pennsylvania alone, more than in any other state. The Delaware Canal—or, more formally, the Delaware Division of the Pennsylvania Canal—parallel to the river from Easton down to tidewater at Bristol, was completed in 1832. Coal mined in the mountains could be barged to Philadelphia in a few days.

Life on the canals was hard from the beginning. Irish immigrants, using only hand tools, dug the ditches and built the massive stone locks, bulkheads, and aqueducts. Barges were piloted by a crew of two, often husband and wife. They

Mule-drawn barges plied no fewer than five canals along or crossing the Delaware River, usually carrying Pennsylvania mountain coal to distant cities. This image depicts two barges passing on Pennsylvania's Delaware Canal, a tricky maneuver. (Photo courtesy of the National Canal Museum)

would stop only to rest their mules or exchange teams. Lock tenders were on call around the clock.

The canals could not survive competition from faster and cheaper railroads. Yet the Delaware Canal lived longer than any other. The last barge came down in 1931, marking the end of the towpath canal industry in America. Soon after the canal was abandoned for commerce, it was discovered for recreation. Fishing, canoeing, and party barges became popular, and still are. In 1940 the state of Pennsylvania established a park encompassing the entire length of the canal.

The Delaware Canal remains in great condition. Old locks and aqueducts have been restored. The towpath is an outstanding bicycle/hiking trail. Sections of the canal have been re-watered, once again attracting anglers and boaters. Excursions on mule-drawn barges run at New Hope and Easton.

The canal is never more than a few hundred yards from the Delaware River, and in places it is separated from the river by only a stone berm. Paddlers on the river often commune with cyclists and hikers walking the towpath. There are several places to scramble up the riverbank to check out the old locks and aqueducts, well worth the detour.

Easton and Phillipsburg

The first Christmas tree in America was set up right here along the river in 1816 by homesick German immigrants—so says the little plaque in Scott

Park. Strategically located at the Forks of the Delaware, Easton has always been a hub of transportation and industry. Three canals met here, then several railroads, carrying coal and steel. A lot of the old-time timber rafters ended their journeys here too, selling their lumber to the sawmills that lined the riverbanks.

Easton is the second-largest city along the non-tidal Delaware (Trenton is the largest), with a population of about 26,000 (est. 2008). The land was taken from the Lenape in the infamous Walking Purchase of 1737, and the city was founded by Thomas Penn a few years later. It is named for the English hometown of Penn's wife.

A self-guided walking tour around Centre Square takes visitors past more than 30 buildings remarkable for their historic interest or architecture, from a tavern built in 1754 to modern commercial buildings. Centre Square itself is anchored by a lovely Civil War memorial.

Easton offers restaurants from fast food to fancy fare, shopping centers, hotels, and the arts. Its Crayola Museum is a hands-on crayon playhouse for kids of all ages. The National Canal Museum, which shares the Crayola Building, tells the story of America's towpath canals, with exhibits, demonstrations, films, and artifacts. Take a ride on the *Josiah White II*, an authentic reproduction of an old canal barge now used for tourist excursions and cocktail parties. And, every April, Easton hosts the Forks of the Delaware Shad Festival, a weeklong celebration of what author John McPhee called the "founding fish."

Phillipsburg, New Jersey, with a population of about 15,000 (est. 2008), stands right across the river from Easton. The Phillipsburg area was sparsely settled until 1832, when the Morris Canal was opened, linking the Delaware River with the Passaic River at Newark. Phillipsburg became a seaport 60 miles from tidewater. The canal is long gone, yet Phillipsburg remains an important regional center. There are grocery stores, restaurants, a motel, and shops within walking distance from the river.

Mile 168.3 to 148.4 (19.9 miles)

A day's trip on this section is not a wilderness experience, yet the river offers a great getaway on summer weekends for thousands of canoeists, kayakers, and tubers. Long, slow pools are punctuated by exciting rapids at Tumble Falls and Bulls Falls. Several outfitters operate in this section, where tubing has become especially popular.

Busy roads—Pennsylvania Route 32 and New Jersey Route 29—run close to the river, and the hum of traffic is never far away. The historic villages of Milford, Frenchtown, Point Pleasant, Stockton, Lambertville, and New Hope are nestled along the riverbanks, offering convenient services to river users.

Canals parallel the river on both sides: the Delaware Canal in Pennsylvania and the Delaware & Raritan Canal in New Jersey. The old towpaths are now outstanding walking and bicycle trails.

Nine public access areas make it easy to get on the river in this section:

Upper Black Eddy, Pennsylvania, mile 168.3
Giving Pond, Pennsylvania, mile 166.0
Frenchtown, New Jersey, mile 165.0
Kingwood, New Jersey, mile 164.0
Tinicum County Park, Pennsylvania, mile 163.6
Byram, New Jersey, mile 156.6
Bulls Island, New Jersey, mile 155.7
Virginia Forrest, Pennsylvania, mile 153.7
Lambertville, New Jersey, mile 148.4

There are two camping areas right on the riverbanks: Tinicum County Park (Pennsylvania) and Bulls Island Recreation Area (New Jersey). Portions of this section are designated the Lower Delaware Wild and Scenic River. Most of the land along the river and on the river islands is privately owned—no trespassing.

Map 22

168.3 **Access: Upper Black Eddy, Pennsylvania.** Maintained by the Pennsylvania Fish and Boat Commission. A paved boat ramp and parking. All boats must bear a valid Pennsylvania boat registration or launch permit. From the river, just downstream from the Milford–Upper Black Eddy Bridge. Access from Pennsylvania Route 32.

This slow section of river is Upper Black Eddy, continuing another mile or so. A fellow named Black owned a tavern here, a favorite stopover for old-time river raftsmen. Rafts would be moored along the riverbanks for a mile or more.

Be alert for speedboats, Jet Skis, and party boats.

The communities of Upper Black Eddy, Pennsylvania, and Milford, New Jersey, stand on opposite sides of the river.

168.0 Bucks County Riverboat Company runs a 60-passenger party boat on Upper Black Eddy, offering dinner and sunset cruises. Its vessel *River Otter* is moored along the Pennsylvania riverbank.

167.8 Hakihokake Creek enters, New Jersey side. Gravel bars at the mouth of the stream extend about 20 yards into the river.

167.7 Pass under power lines.

167.6 The Lowreytown Bars, a series of narrow, brushy islands, dot the middle of the river for the next 0.7 mile.

The current quickens and the river becomes very shallow around and between the islands; not really a rapids. This area marks the end of Upper Black Eddy and was known to timber rafters as Fermans Falls.

The smokestacks, water tower, and abandoned structures of the Riegel Paper Corporation's Milford plant can be seen on the New Jersey side. The plant operated from 1907 to 2004.

167.4 A small unnamed creek enters, New Jersey side, with gravelly shallows near the mouth of the stream.

166.9 The cleared area at the New Jersey (left) riverbank, surrounded by a security fence and buttressed by boulders, is the Crown Vantage Landfill "Superfund" site. Wastes from nearby paper mills and other industries were dumped here for many years, leading to potential contamination of the soil and ultimately the Delaware River. The works seen today (2010) are designed to prevent erosion of contaminants into the river; further cleanup of the site is planned for the future.

166.4 Pass under power lines.

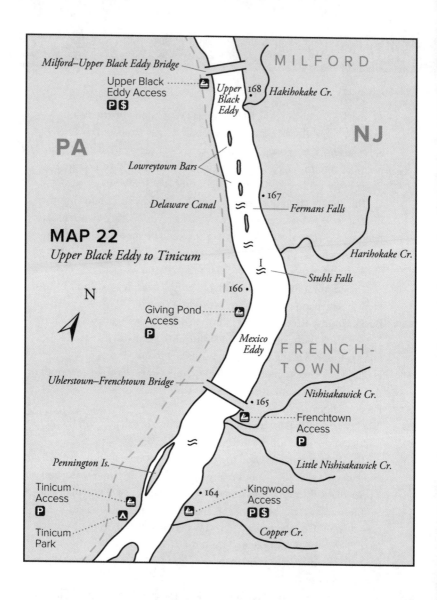

MAP 22
Upper Black Eddy to Tinicum

166.1 Harihokake Creek enters, New Jersey side, at a grassy gravel bar.

Stuhls Falls, a Class I rapids, begins with a submerged ledge extending diagonally across the river, then a second ledge about 40 yards downstream. The best passage is on the left: look for gaps in the ledge with standing waves below.

165.8 **Access: Giving Pond, Pennsylvania.** Maintained by Delaware Canal State Park for access to the Giving Pond Recreation Area. Access to the river is rough and awkward down a steep trail. Difficult to find from the river, immediately past the final ledge of Stuhls Falls. There is better boat access at Upper Black Eddy above and at Frenchtown below. No fee. Access from Pennsylvania 32 (River Road) at the Giving Pond Recreation Area.

Giving Pond itself—between the river and the Delaware Canal—is a water-filled quarry now protected as a natural area, full of waterfowl and other wildlife. There is access for canoes and kayaks.

The river bends slightly to the right.

Rocky ledges along the New Jersey side extend into and under the river for next 0.4 mile.

Slow water for the next mile, once known as Mexico Eddy.

165.0 Pass under the Uhlerstown-Frenchtown Bridge. A wooden bridge was built here in 1843; half of it washed away in the Pumpkin Flood of 1903. The present six-span steel truss was erected in 1931 on the original abutments and piers.

London Ferry ran here before the bridge was built.

The town of Frenchtown, New Jersey, originally called Alexandria, is on the left.

Uhlerstown, Pennsylvania, formerly known as Mexico, was a stop-over on the Delaware Canal. There are several old buildings dating from the canal's heyday and a beautiful historic covered bridge spanning the canal one mile from the river on Uhlerstown Road.

There is a U.S. Geological Survey river gage mounted on the upstream side of the bridge. Base elevation is 100 feet above sea level; flood stage is 16 feet. The maximum flood was 27.8 feet in 1955.

Access: Frenchtown, New Jersey. Maintained by the Village of French-town. Steep hand-launch area, limited parking, privies. No fee. From the river, immediately under the Frenchtown Bridge (New Jersey side). Access at Bridge Street in Frenchtown.

An outstanding hiker/biker trail on the right-of-way of the old Belvidere-Delaware Railroad and towpath of the Delaware & Raritan Canal begins at Frenchtown, continuing along the river all the way to Trenton.

164.8 Nishisakawick Creek enters, New Jersey side, with a large gravel bar extending nearly to the middle of the river.

Little Nishisakawick Creek enters, New Jersey side, just down-stream from its bigger brother.

The river is very shallow at the left; stay right.

164.4 Mile-long Pennington Island begins on the extreme right side of the

Rafting and tubing are popular on the slow stretches of the Delaware below Upper Black Eddy. (Photo by the author)

river at a very narrow slough. A footbridge crosses the little channel to New Life Island, a church camp.

164.0 **Access: Kingwood, New Jersey.** Operated by the New Jersey Division of Fish, Game and Wildlife. A concrete boat ramp, ample parking, privies. Access from New Jersey Route 29. As of 2010, a New Jersey fishing or hunting license, or boat ramp maintenance permit, may be required.

Outfitter. Delaware River Tubing, offering canoes, kayaks, rafts, and tubes, with shuttle, puts in at the Kingwood access.

163.6 **Access: Tinicum County Park, Pennsylvania.** Maintained by the Bucks County Department of Parks and Recreation. A concrete boat ramp, parking, trash disposal, telephone, water, and sanitary facilities. No fee. From the river, immediately at the downstream end of Pennington Island. Access from Pennsylvania Route 32.

Outfitter. Bucks County River Country, offering canoes, kayaks, rafts, and tubes, puts in at the Tinicum access.

Camping. Tinicum County Park, Pennsylvania, with picnic tables, fresh water, grills, and privies. Good tent sites, with easy access to the river

The historic Erwin-Stover House, open to the public, is located near the river in Tinicum County Park.

Map 23

163.5 Copper Creek enters, New Jersey side.

163.3 Easy riffles (Class I–) called Man-of-War Rift, at the head of Marshall Island.

163.2 Marshall Island, in the middle of the river. Marshall begins a maze of 11 islands that extends 2.5 miles. The passages both left and right of Marshall Island are good, and you will have to choose. To the right you will pass historic Stover Mill; to the left you will have better access to little channels among the islands.

Marshall Island was once known as Man-of-War Island because tall trees on the upstream end resembled the masts of a battleship. The tall trees are gone. The island is named for Edward Marshall, one of the runners who participated in the infamous Walking Purchase of 1737. The Lenape agreed to cede lands within a day's walk west of Wrightstown, Pennsylvania; Marshall, however, ran to cover more than twice the expected distance, cheating the Lenape of much of the land of eastern Pennsylvania and igniting generations of ill will.

Marshall Island and Treasure Island (immediately downstream) were long owned by the Cradle of Liberty (Philadelphia) Council of the Boy Scouts of America. A scout camp that started here in 1913 is today the oldest Boy Scout camp in the United States. The camp facilities were severely damaged in the floods of 2004, 2005, and 2006, and the camp has been open only intermittently since.

Marshall Island was sold to the state of Pennsylvania in 2010, to be open to public recreation and to serve as a wildlife sanctuary. The continued use of Treasure Island as a scout camp is uncertain.

RIGHT OF MARSHALL ISLAND

163.1 Fishing (or Stovers) Island, a low gravel bar, in the middle of the channel. Stay right for a better view of Stover Mill.

163.0 A diagonal rocky ledge connects the tip of Fishing Island to the Pennsylvania riverbank, making for a Class I rapids. Look for narrow gaps in the ledge to pass through. This ledge is the remnant of a wing dam built to divert water to Stover Mill.

162.9 The old Stover Mill, built in 1832 and one of the earliest turbine-wheel mills in the country, stands at the very edge of the Pennsylvania riverbank. The building is now maintained as a museum, library, and art gallery. It's a wonder this structure has withstood so many floods and ice jams.

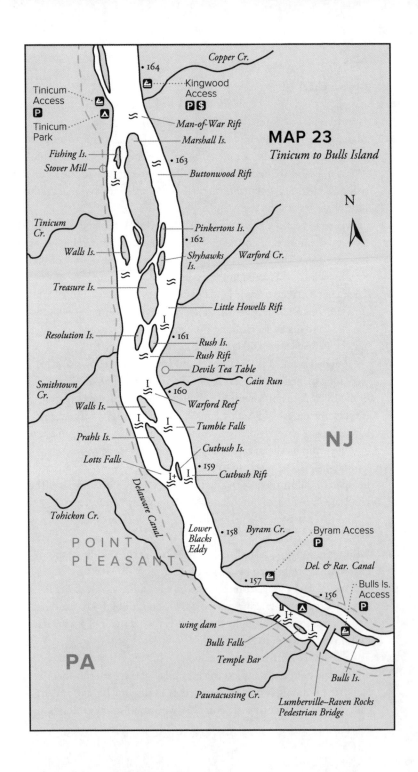

MAP 23
Tinicum to Bulls Island

Copper Cr.

• 164

Kingwood Access
P **$**

Tinicum Access
Tinicum Park

Man-of-War Rift

Marshall Is.

Fishing Is.
Stover Mill

• 163

Buttonwood Rift

N

Tinicum Cr.

Pinkertons Is.

• 162

Walls Is.

Shyhawks Is.

Warford Cr.

Treasure Is.

Little Howells Rift

Resolution Is.

• 161

Rush Is.

Rush Rift

Devils Tea Table

Cain Run

Smithtown Cr.

• 160

Walls Is.

Warford Reef

Tumble Falls

Prahls Is.

Cutbush Is.

Lotts Falls

• 159

Cutbush Rift

Tohickon Cr.

Lower Blacks Eddy

• 158

Byram Cr.

Byram Access
P

POINT PLEASANT

Del. & Rar. Canal

Delaware Canal

• 157

Bulls Is. Access
P

• 156

wing dam

Bulls Falls

Temple Bar

Bulls Is.

PA

NJ

Paunacussing Cr.

Lumberville–Raven Rocks Pedestrian Bridge

Historic Stover Mill at Erwinna, Pennsylvania, one of the earliest turbine-wheel mills in America, has survived many a flood. Today it is an art gallery and museum. (Photo by the author)

162.4   Pass under power lines.

162.1   An outfall from the Delaware Canal cascades down the riverbanks, Pennsylvania side.

162.2   Tinicum Creek enters at a large gravel bar extending into the river channel, Pennsylvania side. A high aqueduct of the Delaware Canal crosses Tinicum Creek about 50 yards from the river. All of Tinicum Creek is designated as part of the Lower Delaware Wild and Scenic River.

162.1   A shallow channel cuts into Marshall Island, rejoining the main channel in 0.3 mile. At average water level it's not navigable.

162.0   Walls Island, extending 0.5 mile, is nestled against the Pennsylvania riverbank. The narrow channel to the right is shallow but navigable.

161.5   Downstream tip of Marshall Island, marked by a shallow slough.

Treasure Island begins. There are Boy Scout camp facilities on both islands.

The boundary line between New Jersey and Pennsylvania passes down the narrow channel between Marshall Island (which is completely in Pennsylvania) and Treasure Island (completely in New Jersey).

161.4   Boy Scouts are ferried from a dock at the Pennsylvania riverbank to their camp on Treasure Island via canoes or a little ferry reminiscent of the scows used to cross the Delaware in the nineteenth century.

The Famous River Hot Dog Man runs a popular snack bar on, and in, the river on the banks of Resolution Island. (Photo by the author)

161.1 Resolution Island begins, extending 0.5 miles. Go to the left if you plan to stop at the Famous River Hot Dog Man.

160.9 Treasure Island ends. Fast water (Class I–).
Rush Island is now to your left. The state line here runs between Resolution and Rush Islands.

LEFT OF MARSHALL ISLAND

163.0 Easy rapids (Class I–) of Buttonwood Rift.

162.2 Pinkertons Island begins, nestled alongside Marshall Island. The main flow is to the left; the little passage to the right is shallow but navigable.

161.8 Shyhawks Island begins, left channel (New Jersey side).

161.6 End Marshall Island; begin Treasure Island (to the right of Shyhawks). The narrow channel separating the islands is spanned by a precarious wooden suspension bridge.

161.3 Very shallow; at low river levels gravel bars are exposed in the center of the main channel. Swift water (Class I–) of Little Howells Rift.

161.2 Warford Creek enters, New Jersey side, at a gravel bar.

161.1 Rush Island begins, extending 0.3 mile, near the downstream tip of Treasure Island. The main current is to the left, with the rocky Class I rapids of Rush Rift over a shallow diagonal ledge.

Go to the right of Rush Island if you plan to stop at the Famous River Hot Dog Man.

160.7 **Lunch.** The Famous River Hot Dog Man runs a grill and souvenir stand on a floating dock anchored between Resolution and Rush Islands, with picnic tables on the island. "The Man" is a favorite with river users.

160.5 Downstream tips of Rush and Resolution Islands.

LEFT AND RIGHT CHANNELS REJOIN

On clear days paddlers may see antique biplanes, gliders, ultralights, and other unusual aircraft flying over the Delaware. These originate from Van Sant Airport, a grass strip two miles from the river in Pennsylvania.

160.2 Smithtown Creek enters, Pennsylvania side.

160.3 The Devils Tea Table, a pedestal-shaped rock formation, can be seen high on the sandstone cliffs on the New Jersey side. A hike to the top is rewarded by spectacular views up and down the river.

159.9 Cain Run enters, New Jersey side.

The ledges of Warford Reef extend from the New Jersey side most of the way across the river. At average water level it's fun to maneuver through clefts in the ledges, although boats often get stuck on the flat rocks. In slightly higher water, the ledges are submerged and present a Class I+ rapids. There is always clear passage near the Pennsylvania side.

Swing way right if you want to go to the Pennsylvania side of Walls Island.

The community on the New Jersey side was once known as Tumble.

159.8 Begin Walls Island in the right middle of the river. The name is confusing, as there is another Walls Island only two miles upriver. The islands were evidently named for General Garrett D. Wall, a wealthy Hunterdon County landowner and U.S. senator of the early nineteenth century.

There is action on both sides of Walls Island: stay left for Tumble Falls, a series of intermittent ledges and Class I rapids; swing right for Lotts Falls, a shorter but more challenging Class I+ rapids where the channels rejoin 1.1 miles downstream.

RIGHT OF WALLS ISLAND

159.8 Class I rapids over a cobbly bottom begin at the head of the island.

159.5 End Walls Island, begin Prahls Island.

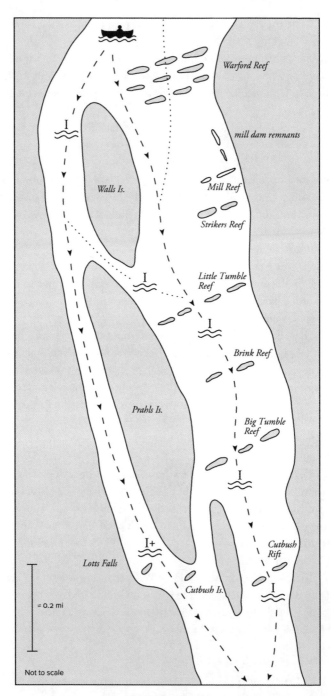

Warford Reef

mill dam remnants

Mill Reef

Strikers Reef

Walls Is.

Little Tumble
Reef

Brink Reef

Prahls Is.

Big Tumble
Reef

Cutbush
Rift

Lotts Falls

Cutbush Is.

≈ 0.2 mi

Not to scale

TUMBLE FALLS

A narrow slough leads diagonally left between the islands, Class I rapids with standing waves to 2 feet. This brings you back to the left channel, and there is no return. Do not take this inviting course if you want to run the more challenging Lotts Falls downstream; instead, continue to hug the Pennsylvania side.

Prahls Island and adjacent lands are now a Bucks County park; no facilities.

158.8   Lotts Falls, a nice little Class I+ rapids. Boulders and ledges protrude from the water and lurk just below the surface, requiring quick maneuvers to avoid upset. Beware the ledge on the left near the end of the rapids.

Zephaniah Lott was a local innkeeper and Revolutionary soldier.

A man named Solliday ran a mill here in the nineteenth century; the remnant of the mill dam marks the head of the rapids.

158.7   Downstream tip of Prahls Island; little Cutbush Island is now at your left.

158.6   Rejoin the main channel at the downstream tip of Cutbush Island.

LEFT OF WALLS ISLAND

159.7   Rocky ledges extend from the New Jersey riverbank. So begins Tumble Falls, a series of rocky "reefs" continuing almost a mile. Class I rapids. The reefs were a hazard to early Durham boats and timber rafts, and in some places they were blasted to make better passage.

A ledge parallel to the New Jersey riverbank is the remnant of a wing dam that diverted water to Kuglers Mill, at the former village of Tumble Station.

After a good rain several waterfalls plunge down the bluffs on the New Jersey side.

159.5   Downstream tip of Walls Island; Prahls Island is now to the right.

159.4   Little Tumble Reef, a ledge about one foot high, extends across the river. Look for gaps; the biggest is in the middle.

159.2   Brink Reef, a ledge in the middle right. Pass around either end or though gaps in the reef.

159.0   Big Tumble Reef, the last and most severe ledge of Tumble Falls. Rocks protrude from the water, especially at the left. Pass to the far right or look for gaps in the middle. It's a sudden drop of about two feet, with big standing waves.

158.9   Cutbush Island, a low gravel bar extending 0.3 mile, begins at the right.

158.7   Cutbush Rift, Class I rapids continuing 0.2 mile at the end of Cutbush Island. A few boulders, nice standing waves.

158.6 The left and right channels rejoin at the downstream tip of Cutbush Island.

157.7 Three piers of the old Point Pleasant–Byram Bridge stand in the river. The wooden covered bridge built here in 1855 was struck by lightning and burned in 1892. The steel bridge that replaced it was washed away forever in the floods of Hurricanes Connie and Diane in 1955.

Pearsons Ferry ran here until construction of the bridge.

Point Pleasant, Pennsylvania, was once an important stop on the Delaware Canal. It was originally known as Blacks or Pearsons Landing. Today, antique shops and galleries attract visitors.

Outfitters. Bucks County River Country's main base is on the Pennsylvania side at the bridge abutment.

The Delaware River Tubing landing is at the bridge pier on the New Jersey side. Although not an "official" access point, this area is public land and open to public use. Take care not to block the way of bicyclists.

Lunch. Point Pleasant Village Store.

157.6 Byram Creek enters, New Jersey side, at a little gravel bar.

157.5 Tohickon Creek enters, Pennsylvania side. Tohickon Creek is controlled by a dam at Lake Nockamixon; in the spring and at dam releases, it offers Class III and IV rapids for skilled kayakers and rafters. At other times Tohickon Creek is too shallow for any kind of boat. Gravel bars at the mouth of the creek extend almost to the middle of the river.

All of Tohickon Creek is designated as part of the Lower Delaware Wild and Scenic River.

Look up Tohickon Creek to see the beautiful red aqueduct carrying the Delaware Canal.

157.4 A gravel ramp at the Pennsylvania riverbank leads to a pump house for the Point Pleasant Diversion, constructed in 1989 to pump Delaware River water to the nuclear power plant at Limerick, Pennsylvania. This is not a boat access. The pump house looks like a big, sturdy barn, now well shrouded by maturing trees. The intake for the diversion is inconspicuously located under the river, sometimes marked by an orange buoy.

Many local residents were adamantly opposed to the diversion, fearing it would draw so much water that recreational and fishing use of the Delaware would be impaired. Citizens formed Del-Aware, a forerunner to today's Delaware Riverkeeper, to advocate alternatives to the diversion. Signs like Dump the Pump and Save the Delaware proliferated in nearby communities. Ultimately, the diversion was approved and construction completed; fortunately, water intakes are closely regulated by the Delaware River Basin Commission, and worst-case scenarios have not come to pass.

157.1 This stretch of slow water is Lower Blacks Eddy, continuing about 0.4 mile. It was another overnight stop for timber rafters. Today, boat docks and swimming rafts for summer homes in the community of Byram line the New Jersey riverbank. Cross the wakes of motorboats and Jet Skis at an angle, not broadside.

156.6 **Access: Byram, New Jersey.** Maintained by Delaware & Raritan Canal State Park. A concrete boat ramp, ample parking, picnic tables, and privies. Access from New Jersey Route 29. No fee. Put in here for a quick run through Bulls Falls, just downstream.

156.5 Bulls Island, New Jersey side, extending 1.2 miles. Stay right.

The channel to the left of Bulls Island leads 0.7 mile to the gate lock of the Delaware & Raritan Feeder Canal. There is a canoe launch/landing on the canal at the gate lock.

Canoes and kayaks can be beached at the head of Bulls Island for quick access to the Bulls Island Recreation Area and Campground.

156.3 **CAUTION!** The concrete wings of the Raritan (Lumberville) Dam extend from both riverbanks to a gap in the middle of the river. The river rushes through the narrow gap at the center of the dam in an exciting Class I+ rapids. There is a precipitous drop-off followed by standing waves up to 3 feet high. This rapids is known as Bulls Falls. Aim for the white water.

Water trickles over the wing dams at average river levels. When the river is high, there may be a dangerous "keeper" hydraulic below the dam. Do not go over the dam—go though the center chute.

Bulls Falls can be avoided by paddling down the channel to the left of Bulls Island to the Delaware & Raritan Canal gate lock, then carrying across the island back to the river. But unless the river level is too high, by all means go through the dam—it's a great ride!

There is a popular but unsupervised swimming/wading area just upstream from the wing dam on the New Jersey side in the Bulls Island Recreation Area.

The dam was constructed in 1834 to impound water for the Delaware & Raritan Feeder Canal, with renovations several times since.

The river below the wing dams is a favored fishing spot. Take care not to interfere with anglers.

Outfitter. Delaware River Tubing offers canoes and kayaks for use on the canal, via a concession at Bulls Island Recreation Area.

The beautiful Lumberville–Raven Rock Pedestrian Bridge at Bulls Island, built by the Roebling Company in 1947. Pennsylvania's Delaware Canal and towpath are in the foreground. (Photo by the author)

156.2 Temple Bar, a little gravel island on the right.

156.1 Bulls Falls continues, choppy Class I rapids with a few boulders and standing waves to 1½ feet.

156.0 Paunacussing Creek enters, Pennsylvania side, with large gravel bars extending to the center of the river. The Delaware Canal crosses the creek via an aqueduct.

155.9 A rough dirt trail leads up the Pennsylvania riverbank to lock 12 on the Delaware Canal; picnic tables and barbeque grills.

155.8 Pass under the Lumberville–Raven Rock Pedestrian Bridge, one of the most picturesque structures to span the Delaware. A wooden bridge was built at this site in 1853; it was condemned and closed in 1945. The present suspension bridge, for foot traffic only, was built by John A. Roebling and Sons Company in 1947 on the original piers and abutments.

The two-story stone house at the Pennsylvania end of the bridge, built in 1853, was used for many years by toll collectors. The famous Black Bass Hotel overlooks the canal and the river immediately downstream from the bridge.

Lunch. On the Pennsylvania side: Lumberville General Store, just off the pedestrian bridge.

155.7 **Access: Bulls Island, New Jersey.** Maintained by Delaware & Raritan

Canal State Park. A concrete boat ramp, ample parking, picnic areas, water, privies, and telephones. From the river, about 100 yards downstream from the Lumberville–Raven Rock Bridge. Access from New Jersey Route 29. No fee.

Bulls Island Recreation Area also provides access to the Delaware & Raritan Canal (canoe/kayak) and its towpath (hiking/bicycle).

Camping. Bulls Island Recreation Area, operated by the New Jersey State Park Service. Riverside tent sites, restrooms with showers, drinking water.

There are no public campgrounds along the river downstream from this point.

Slow water for the next 2.0 miles.

Map 24

155.3 A wide gravel bar extends from the downstream tip of Bulls Island.

154.8 Cuttalossa Creek enters, Pennsylvania side.

154.2 Lockatong Creek enters, New Jersey side. The Delaware & Raritan Canal towpath (and now, bikeway) crosses the creek via a high steel bridge.

153.8 Begin Eagle Island on the left, extending 0.4 mile. The best course is to the left of the island, through the Class I rapids of Eagle Rift. The channel to the right of Eagle Island, although fairly wide, is shallow.

153.7 **Access: Virginia Forrest, Pennsylvania.** Maintained by Delaware Canal State Park. Steep hand-launch, ample parking, privies. Intended mainly for access to the canal. No fee. From the river, immediately upstream from the head of Hendrick Island. Access from Pennsylvania Route 32 (River Road).

Begin Hendrick Island, to the right of Eagle Island, a broad, forested island extending about 1.0 mile. The narrow slough between the island and the Pennsylvania riverbank is very shallow, not navigable at average water level.

153.1 Arched stone floodgates, New Jersey side, allow release of excess water from the Delaware & Raritan Feeder Canal.

152.7 Wickecheoke Creek enters, New Jersey side, at extensive gravel bars.

Historic Prallsville Mills, with its scenic spillway, stands a short way up the creek. A typical nineteenth-century village industrial complex, the property is managed by Delaware & Raritan Canal State Park and used as a center for arts and music. Concerts sponsored by

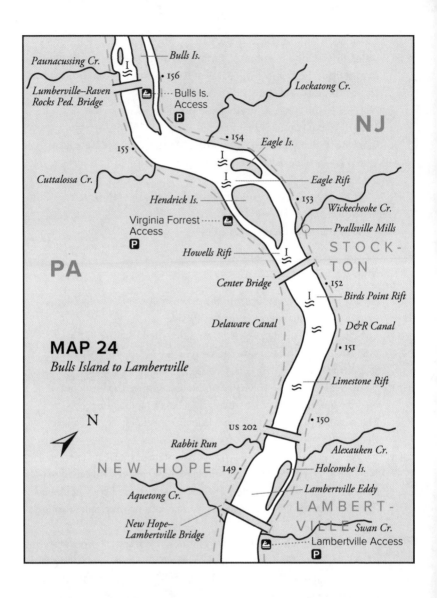

MAP 24
Bulls Island to Lambertville

the Delaware River Mill Society, the Delaware Riverkeeper, and other organizations are held at the gristmill on summer Saturdays.

The railbed of the Belvidere-Delaware Railroad crosses Wickecheoke Creek on a steel trestle; the canal towpath is a short way beyond.

Green Sergeants Bridge, the last remaining covered bridge in New Jersey, built in 1872, crosses Wickecheoke Creek about a mile from the Delaware.

Historic Prallsville Mills at Stockton, New Jersey, as seen from the river. Several buildings have been restored by the Delaware River Mill Society, a frequent host of music and arts events. Wickecheoke Creek falls over a little spillway. (Photo by the author)

Although canoes and kayaks can be beached on the gravel bars at Wickecheoke Creek, this is not a river access point.

152.6 End of Hendrick Island.

Howells (Galloping) Rift, a tricky Class I rapids continuing 0.3 mile. There are three submerged ledges with riffles between. Beware the Three Brothers, big rocks sticking up in the middle.

152.1 Pass under Center Bridge. This six-span crossing was constructed in 1926 on piers and abutments originally built in 1814. A wooden bridge built that year lasted until 1923, when it was destroyed by fire.

This is the site of Reading's Ferry, in 1711 the first commercial ferry across the Delaware.

The community of Stockton, New Jersey, stands at the east end of the bridge.

Fast water under the bridge.

Lunch. Dilly's Ice Cream Corner, Pennsylvania end of Center Bridge; several casual restaurants in Stockton. Access from the river is difficult, a scramble through the brush up the riverbank.

151.6 Birds Point Rift, a modest Class I rapids. Shallow ledges extend from both riverbanks.

150.4 Jagged rocks stick up in the middle of the river. This is Limestone Rift, not much of a rapids (Class I–), but do mind the rocks.

149.8 High-tension lines crackle overhead.

149.7 Pass under the U.S. 202 toll bridge, built in 1971.

149.5 Alexauken Creek enters, New Jersey side. Its large gravel bar extends well into the river.

Rabbit Run enters, Pennsylvania side.

Pass under more power lines.

Begin slow water of Lambertville Eddy, extending 1.5 miles to Wells Falls. Beware the powerboaters, Jet Skiers, and even float planes that use this eddy.

149.3 Holcombe (or Lewis) Island, New Jersey side, extending 0.5 mile, beginning at a little slough in the forest at the New Jersey side.

148.8 There is a concrete boat ramp at the downstream tip of Holcombe Island; public access is not permitted. This is the site of the Lewis Shad Fishery, where for more than 100 years the Lewis family has been licensed to seine-fish during the annual shad run. Lewis-caught shad, grilled on wooden planks, is a staple of Lambertville's annual shad festival, held every April

148.7 Pass under the New Hope–Lambertville Bridge. A wooden covered bridge was built at this site in 1814, rebuilt in 1842, and ultimately destroyed by the flood of 1903. The present six-span steel structure was built in 1904 on the original piers.

Ferries ran here as early as 1722, Wells Ferry from the Pennsylvania side and Coryells Ferry from New Jersey.

In 2007 the Delaware River Basin Commission installed a river gage on the downstream side of the bridge. A radar beam reflects from the river surface to give an accurate measure. The gage is in a glass-bottomed box fixed to the bridge structure. Base elevation is 49 feet above sea level; flood stage is 13 feet. The greatest flood was 24.3 feet in 1955.

The shops, galleries, and restaurants of New Hope are close to the water on the Pennsylvania side. Unfortunately, there is no easy access from the river.

Lunch. Many casual restaurants and other services may be found in both Lambertville and New Hope.

148.6 Aquetong Creek enters, Pennsylvania side, over a little waterfall at the famous Bucks County Playhouse in New Hope.

Swan Creek enters, New Jersey side.

148.4 **Access: Lambertville, New Jersey.** Maintained by Delaware & Raritan Canal State Park and the Delaware Valley Powerboat Association. A concrete boat ramp, parking, restrooms. The ramp is set up for trailered powerboats, but canoes and kayaks can be launched here as well. No fee or permit is necessary for unpowered boats. Access from Bridge Street, Lambertville, is a little tricky: go through the parking lot of the Lambertville Station restaurant, then follow a narrow paved road 0.2 mile to the boat launch.

Features

The Durham Boat

Durham boats were the workhorses of Delaware River commerce for about a hundred years. They carried iron, lumber, grain, and, on one momentous night, the most precious cargo of all: the very hope of an independent America.

The origin of the Durham boat is uncertain. Looking something like a big canoe, a Durham boat is flat-bottomed and double-ended, measures up to 60 feet long and can carry up to 20 tons. Legend has it that a man named Robert Durham, perhaps an ironworker at the Durham Furnace, invented the boat to haul finished iron to market. More likely, the craft had its origins with Swedish settlers of the lower Delaware, who used similar boats on the fast-moving rivers of their native Scandinavia. By the late eighteenth century, Rodmans Boat Works at Kingwood, New Jersey, was cranking out Durham boats by the score. Perhaps a thousand Durham boats plied the Delaware, many of them used to carry iron from Durham Furnace, at Riegelsville, down to Philadelphia. Durham boats became obsolete the day the Delaware Canal opened along the river, and they were completely gone by the mid-nineteenth century.

The trip downriver was an easy task, with rowers and a steersman navigating through the rapids much as they would in a modern canoe. But going upriver against the current was very difficult. Rowing, or even light sailing, sufficed in the eddies, but in the rapids the boatmen used 15-foot-long setting poles to walk the boat upriver. At Wells Falls and Foul Rift iron rings were driven into the rocks to anchor pulleys used to haul the heavy boats against the river's flow.

This brings us to the humble Durham boat's moment of glory. In the fall of 1776 George Washington's army retreated across the Delaware from New Jersey. Fearing the British would follow, the general ordered Captain Daniel Bray to sequester every boat—*especially the Durham boats*—to the Pennsylvania side, from Easton to Philadelphia. His army in tatters and with hope almost lost, Washington gambled on an all-or-nothing crossing of the river on Christmas night to attack the Hessian garrison at Trenton. Twenty-four hundred soldiers, together with their cannon, horses, and aspirations for a new nation, huddled in the Durham boats as they rowed and poled across the icy Delaware. Their

Durham boats were the workhorses of Delaware River commerce for more than 100 years. George Washington used them to cross the icy river on his way to surprise the Hessian garrison at Trenton in December 1776. Washington's crossing is reenacted every year on Christmas Day. (Photo by the author)

miraculous victory at Trenton the next morning breathed life into the spirit of the fledgling America.

Washington's crossing of the Delaware is re-enacted, complete with replica Durham boats, every Christmas Day.

The Delaware & Raritan Canal

There is a mass grave near Bulls Island. Laborers—mostly Irish immigrants—on the Delaware & Raritan (D&R) Canal succumbed to an epidemic and were buried where they fell. The canal, which has survived 180 years, remains their monument: the hand-laid rock walls that line the canal and the precision masonry of the locks and aqueducts testify to the quality of their workmanship.

None other than William Penn wanted to connect New York and Philadelphia via canal across New Jersey. Penn's vision was realized in 1834 when the D&R Canal was opened to traffic, a shortcut to the long and dangerous ocean passage around Cape May. There were locks to tidewater on the Raritan River at New Brunswick and to the Delaware River at Bordentown. A "feeder canal" along the Delaware from Bulls Island to Trenton provided water for the main link across New Jersey.

The feeder canal was not originally intended for navigation. Yet, where there is a market, there is a way, and for many years barges of coal, grain, and other goods plied the feeder canal through Stockton, Lambertville, and Titusville. The D&R Canal ultimately suffered the same fate as the other towpath canals in America, succumbing to competition from more efficient railroads. The Belvidere-Delaware Railroad was built parallel to the feeder canal in 1855 and for a while was operated under common ownership.

The last barge passed through the D&R Canal in 1932. But the canal still lives as a water supply conduit, carrying Delaware River drinking water to New Brunswick and other communities in central New Jersey. Most of the water control devices—locks, flumes, and gates—have been modified for the canal's modern use as an aqueduct. The D&R Canal continues to be maintained and is in excellent condition, perhaps the best of all of the old towpath canals in America.

The canal also lives as a state park, featuring camping areas, picnic grounds, and historic sites. It's popular with anglers (catfish and panfish are abundant), canoeists, and kayakers. The old towpath, once trod by mules, is today an outstanding bicycle/hiker trail, extended by the bed of the old Delaware-Belvidere Railroad up to Frenchtown.

New Hope and Lambertville

New Hope is a happening place. Tourists flock here year-round for the jazz clubs, art studios, boutiques, and restaurants. The village was founded in the early 1700s by John Wells, who owned the first ferry and tavern. It got its modern name in 1790, when Benjamin Parry's mills burned down; after rebuilding, Parry optimistically called them the New Hope Mills. The village flourished as an industrial community in the nineteenth century, its mills powered by the Delaware River. Today the old mills have been converted into shops, offices, and condominiums, standing close to the Pennsylvania riverbank above Wells Falls.

All of New Hope is squeezed onto four streets, two alleys, and a towpath. In addition to the clubs and boutiques, there are some special attractions: the historic Parry Mansion, regional theater at the Bucks County Playhouse, canal barge rides at the New Hope Canal Boat Company, party boats on the river at Wells Ferry Boat Rides, and steam train excursions on the New Hope & Ivyland Railroad.

Across the river, Lambertville began as a ferry town, grew as a canal port, and burgeoned as a regional industrial center. Most of Lambertville's industry is gone, and the village is enjoying a renaissance as a center of arts, culture, and historic renovation.

Emmanuel Coryell ran a tavern and started a ferry here in 1732, and the village became known as Coryells Ferry. The name changed to Lambertville in the early 1800s, after postmaster John Lambert. The Delaware & Raritan Canal in the 1830s and the Belvidere-Delaware Railroad in the 1850s brought prosperity, and Lambertville grew into an important regional commercial center. Mills for flour, paper, cotton, rubber, saw timber, and iron ran on the ample waterpower of the Delaware River. The Lambertville Pottery Works made toilets shipped across America.

The citizens of Lambertville are proud of their heritage and enthusiastically promote historic restoration. Many of the old brick row houses have been renovated into distinctive homes. The long-abandoned rail depot, built in 1880, has been reopened as Lambertville Station, a fine restaurant. A wide array of eateries, taverns, shops, and galleries attracts visitors from throughout the region.

Mile 148.4 to 131.8 (16.8 miles)

This last section begins with Wells Falls, the most severe rapids on the Delaware. It ends just below Trenton Falls, the boundary of tidewater. Although the lands along the river are increasingly urbanized, the riverbanks are lined with trees, and the scenery is pleasant most of the way. No river outfitters operate in this section, so paddlers must use their own craft and organize their own shuttles. Fishing is popular in season.

The river continues through the Piedmont geophysical province until Trenton Falls. Trenton Falls is on the *fall line*, where the solid rock of the Piedmont meets the soft sand and clay of the Coastal Plain. There are severe rapids on many eastern rivers where they cross this boundary: the Great Falls of the Potomac near Washington, D.C., is a striking example. Below Trenton Falls the Delaware estuary flows 133 miles to the Atlantic Ocean at Cape May.

Pennsylvania Route 32 and New Jersey Route 29 parallel the river closely on either side. The Delaware Canal continues along the riverbank in Pennsylvania, in places swerving away from the river, while the Delaware & Raritan Canal in New Jersey is very near the river for the first 10 miles. They offer the opportunity for a good circle trip by paddling down the river, then returning upstream on one or the other canal.

A turning point in American history took place on this section of the Delaware. On Christmas night of 1776 George Washington led his tired troops across the river at McConkeys Ferry for a surprise attack on the Hessian garrison at Trenton, a victory that revitalized the Revolutionary cause. Both New Jersey and Pennsylvania have established state parks to commemorate the event.

Below Trenton, the Delaware River is affected by the twice-daily surge of tides from the Atlantic Ocean. The river, now an estuary, becomes deeper and more polluted. Oil tankers, freight barges, and other heavy shipping ply the river to and from the industrial cities that line it. The estuary widens into Delaware Bay below Wilmington, Delaware, where saltwater fishing, sailing, and

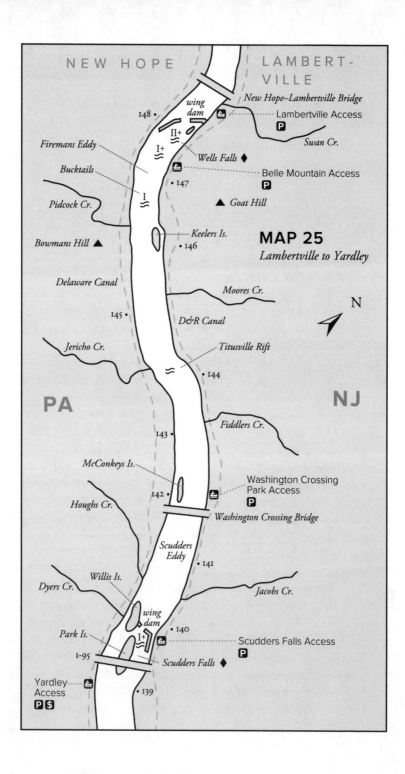

NEW HOPE

LAMBERT-
VILLE

New Hope–Lambertville Bridge

wing dam

148 •

Lambertville Access

II+

I+

Firemans Eddy

Wells Falls ◆

Swan Cr.

Bucktails

I

Belle Mountain Access

• 147

Pidcock Cr.

▲ *Goat Hill*

Keelers Is.

MAP 25

• 146

Lambertville to Yardley

Bowmans Hill ▲

Delaware Canal

Moores Cr.

145 •

D&R Canal

N

Jericho Cr.

Titusville Rift

• 144

PA

NJ

Fiddlers Cr.

143 •

McConkeys Is.

Washington Crossing
Park Access

142 •

Houghs Cr.

Washington Crossing Bridge

Scudders Eddy

• 141

Willis Is.

Dyers Cr.

Jacobs Cr.

wing dam

Park Is.

I+

• 140

Scudders Falls Access

I-95

Scudders Falls ◆

Yardley
Access

• 139

powerboating are popular. In recent years many people have enjoyed kayaking the edges and little creeks of the Delaware estuary, and portions of it (river miles 137–112) have been designated as the Tidal Delaware River Water Trail. As a rule, however, the Delaware downstream from Trenton is not well suited to open canoes.

There are eight public access areas in this section:

Lambertville, New Jersey, mile 148.4
Belle Mountain, New Jersey, mile 146.8
Scudders Falls, New Jersey, mile 139.6
Washington Crossing, New Jersey, mile 142.0
Yardley, Pennsylvania, mile 138.7
Ferry Road, Pennsylvania, mile 134.5
Morrisville (Pennsylvania), mile 133.4
Trenton waterfront, New Jersey, mile 131.8

Except for a group campsite at Washington Crossing State Park, New Jersey, there are no public campgrounds in this section. The riverbanks and islands are mostly privately owned; please do not trespass.

River Guide

Map 25

148.4 **Access: Lambertville, New Jersey.** Maintained by Delaware & Raritan Canal State Park and the Delaware Valley Powerboat Association. A concrete boat ramp, parking, and restrooms. The ramp is set up for trailered powerboats, but it's okay to launch canoes and kayaks. No fee or permit is necessary for unpowered boats. Access from Bridge Street, Lambertville, is a little tricky: go through the parking lot of the Lambertville Station restaurant, then follow a narrow paved road 0.2 mile to the boat launch.

This access is favored by canoeists and kayakers who want to tackle the rapids at Wells Falls a half mile downriver. Many people launch here, then take out at the Belle Mountain access just below the rapids.

The Swan Creek Rowing Club stores its rowing shells here, piled high on racks.

The river here is designated as the Lambertville Seaplane Base, although take-offs and landings on the river are rare.

The Lambertville wastewater treatment plant, surrounded by a security fence, stands adjacent to the boat ramp.

A lift lock on the Delaware & Raritan Canal can be found a few steps above the treatment works, as well as an overgrown gate lock to the river in the woods just below. Barges loaded with coal, lumber, and other goods were towed across the river from the Delaware Canal on the Pennsylvania side to enter the Delaware & Raritan Canal here, then make their way down to Trenton and across New Jersey.

148.2 The concrete gate lock for the Delaware Canal stands at the Pennsylvania side, mate to its counterpart across the river.

148.0 **DANGER!** Concrete wing dams extend from both sides to a 100-yard-wide chute in the center of the river, the entrance to Wells Falls (also known as Lambertville Rapids). The river drops 14 feet in 0.4 mile, most of it in the first half. Huge rocks are hard to avoid, and big waves can easily swamp an open boat. This is the most severe rapids on the Delaware.

Stop on the dam to reconnoiter and plan your route. Secure your gear. Wear your PFD! If the water is so high that it flows over the concrete wing dams, go home. Water flowing over the dams forms a deadly "keeper" hydraulic. Do not attempt to go though Wells Falls in high water conditions. Many people have drowned here, as recently as 2010.

Pass through the chute into Class II–III rapids. The flow is very powerful even at low water levels. Nasty ledges and rocks lurk in the maw of the chute, remnants of an earlier version of the wing dams. Standing waves rise to 3–4 feet.

The preferred course through Wells Falls is down the left middle, in Class II+ rapids, but even here hidden ledges can cause an upset. The right side of the rapids should be rated as Class III, with tortuous channels between boat-busting boulders, powerful flow, huge waves, and dangerous hydraulics.

Novice paddlers would be wise to avoid the most hazardous part of the rapids by lifting over the left-side wing dam, then sticking as close to the New Jersey (left) riverbank as possible. Or, carry the short distance to the Delaware & Raritan Canal at the Lambertville access area (put in just below the lock), and paddle safely down to the Belle Mountain access.

Wells Falls is especially favored by sport kayakers, who flock here to play the waves and eddies for hours on end. On summer weekends the concrete wing dams are often crowded with spectators watching the show.

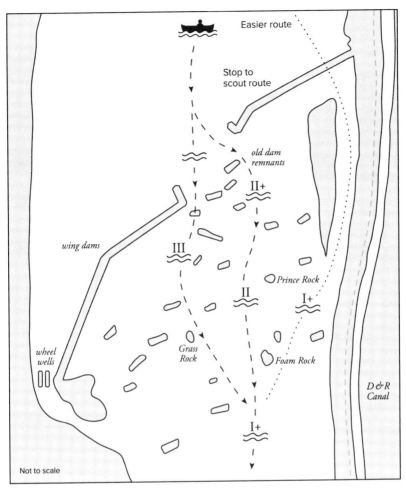

Easier route

Stop to
scout route

old dam
remnants

II+

wing dams

III

II

I+

Prince Rock

wheel
wells

Grass
Rock

Foam Rock

D & R
Canal

I+

Not to scale

WELLS FALLS

A wing dam from the Pennsylvania riverbank was built here in 1770 to power a mill. In 1835 it was expanded and raised to divert water into the Delaware Canal. The dams have been renovated and reconfigured several times over the years, most recently in 1968. The huge slots that once held water wheels for the mills of New Hope can still be seen at the extreme western (Pennsylvania) end of the wing dam.

Old-time Durham boaters and timber rafters would often hire experienced pilots to steer through Wells Falls. The pilots knew every rock by name: Foam, Rodmans, Buckwheat Ledge, Hundred Barrel,

A kayaker "surfs" a hole at the Class II+ rapids of Wells Falls, the most severe of all rapids on the Delaware. Novices would be wise to avoid this area; all paddlers should wear a PFD and scout their route. (Photo by the author)

and others marked navigation through the rapids. Reconfiguration of the wing dams and blasting of some of the worst ledges have made the exact locations of the named obstacles hard to find today, although a few can still be pinpointed.[1]

147.9   Wells Falls continues, diminished to Class I+ or II. Stay alert for boulders just beneath the surface.

The brushy flats at the right (Pennsylvania side) were once known as Malta Island. It was here that Washington's army sequestered Durham boats and other craft in preparation for the 1776 crossing of the Delaware.

147.6   The rapids peter out into Firemans Eddy. Watch for large rocks protruding from the water on the Pennsylvania side.

147.2   **Access: Belle Mountain (Firemans Eddy), New Jersey.** Maintained by Delaware & Raritan Canal State Park. Constructed by the Young Adult Conservation Corps in 1980. A paved boat ramp, limited day parking, privies. Mind the parking signs. No fee. Access from New Jersey Route 29, over a narrow wooden bridge just north of the Golden Nugget Flea Market.

This is a good place to end a run through the rapids at Wells Falls.

The Golden Nugget Market Flea Market, with more than 100

dealers of antiques and knick-knacks, is located a short walk down New Jersey Route 29 from the access area.

Goat Hill, elevation 440 feet, rises over the river, New Jersey side. Legend holds that George Washington stood on a rock at the top to survey the Delaware valley. An overlook at the summit, now within New Jersey's Washington Crossing State Park, provides magnificent views of New Hope and Wells Falls.

146.7 Class I rapids known as Bucktails; not much to it, watch for rocks.

146.4 Pidcock Creek enters, Pennsylvania side, at a sand bar.

Washington planned his 1776 assault on Trenton in the stone Thompson-Neely House near the mouth of Pidcock Creek, now part of Pennsylvania's Washington Crossing State Historic Park.

146.2 Keelers Island at the New Jersey side, extending 0.2 mile; the slough to its left is normally too shallow to navigate.

Bowman's Hill, elevation 310 feet, rises sharply on the Pennsylvania side. Bowman's Hill Tower, built in 1931 to commemorate George Washington and his army, stands atop, 125 feet high. The view from the tower is spectacular. Bowman's Hill Wildflower Preserve lies on the north flanks of the hill.

145.4 Moores Creek enters via twin concrete arches, New Jersey side.

144.3 Jericho Creek enters, Pennsylvania side. Sand bars extend into the river.

Enter Titusville Rift, an unobstructed riffle (Class I–) through a slight S turn. Very shallow on the right. Recently this little rift has become known as Fife and Drum rapids.

143.3 Fiddlers Creek enters via a stone arch, New Jersey side.

The David Library of the American Revolution, open to the public, is located on Pennsylvania Route 32.

143.2 The community of Titusville, New Jersey, stands on bluffs high above the river, New Jersey side. There are boat docks and swimming rafts along the riverbank for the next half mile.

142.8 The final segment of the Lower Delaware Wild and Scenic River ends here.

142.4 McConkeys Island, Pennsylvania side, extending 0.3 mile. The slough along the right (Pennsylvania) side is impassable at low water.

142.1 Washington Crossing State Historic Park, Pennsylvania. It was from here on Christmas night, 1776, that General George Washington led his tired troops across the river to a surprise victory over the Hessian garrison at Trenton. The event is re-enacted every Christmas day, with thousands of spectators watching from the bridge and riverbanks.

Washington Crossing State Park, New Jersey. The park features historic buildings and artifacts, recreation and picnic grounds, and summer theater productions.

Camping. Group camping in Washington Crossing State Park (New Jersey), by reservation. The camping area is over a mile from the river.

142.0 **Access: Washington Crossing, New Jersey.** Maintained by Washington Crossing State Park. Hand-launch only, a short but steep dirt path to the river, ample parking, restrooms, picnic tables. No fee. This is a good place to start a day run down to Yardley or Trenton. Access at the New Jersey end of Washington Crossing Bridge.

A reproduction of a nineteenth-century scow ferry like those once used to cross the Delaware here and at many other points can be seen just above the access area.

141.9 Pass under Washington Crossing Bridge, originally known as the Taylorsville-Delaware Bridge. A wooden bridge was built here in 1831, 55 years after Washington and his troops crossed in Durham boats. The present six-span steel truss bridge was completed in 1904 on the original masonry piers and abutments. There is barely room for two cars to pass.

McConkey's Ferry ran here before the bridge was built.

The stone house at the Pennsylvania end of the bridge is the historic McConkey's (later Old Ferry) Tavern, built in 1750. It was used as headquarters for Washington's army on the night of the 1776 crossing.

Lunch. Faherty's Deli at the New Jersey end of Washington Crossing Bridge; several shops and a convenience store at the Pennsylvania end.

Enter Scudders Eddy; slow water for the next mile.

140.5 Jacobs Creek enters, New Jersey side, at a gravel bar.

Houghs Creek enters, Pennsylvania side.

140.3 Willis Island, along the Pennsylvania side of the river, extending 0.5 mile. There is just a shallow slough between the island and the riverbank.

140.0 Dyers Creek enters, Pennsylvania side, behind Willis Island.

139.8 **CAUTION!** Enter Scudders Falls, a Class I+ rapids. Dilapidated concrete wing dams, covered with brush, extend from both sides to a chute at the center. Pass through the chute into standing waves to about 2½ feet. Great fun!

At average water level the river does not flow over the dams. If the water is high, *do not go over the dams*—there may be a dangerous hydraulic below, while brush on the dams can easily snag a boat.

Park Island, a narrow gravel bar extending 0.8 mile down the middle

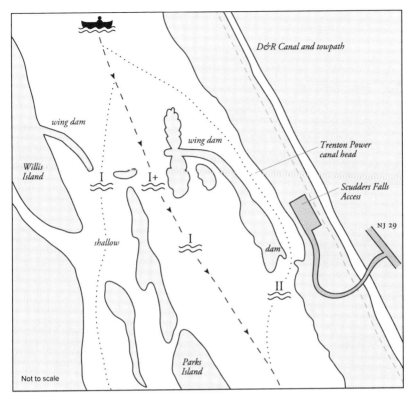

SCUDDERS FALLS

of the river, begins just below the dams. The channel to the right of the island is navigable, but the better ride is through the main chute down the middle.

Stay way left of the wing dam to reach a short but exciting Class II rapids. Passage along the dilapidated wall of the dam ends with a steep drop into big standing waves. This is a favored spot for sport kayakers, who perch nearly motionless as they "surf" the wave at the bottom of the chute. Open canoes will almost surely ship water while passing through the waves.

A wood-and-rock dam was built at Scudders Falls as early as 1819 to impound water for a long-gone mill. In 1835 the dam was expanded to divert river water into the Trenton Water Power Canal, feeding mills seven miles downstream at Trenton (the area now occupied by Waterfront Park); the long slough along the New Jersey riverbank is actually the head of the canal. The remainder of the waterpower canal was filled and paved over for New Jersey Route 29.

139.7 **Access: Scudders Falls, New Jersey.** Maintained by Delaware & Raritan Canal State Park. No boat ramp, day parking, privies, no other facilities. This access is intended mainly for people biking or hiking the canal towpath or fishing the canal. Narrow dirt trails lead from the parking area to the Class II chute at the end of the wing dams. Kayakers put in and take out here to play in the chute. No fee. Access from New Jersey 29 immediately north of the Interstate 95 interchange.

The area below the wing dams is very popular with anglers fishing for shad or striped bass, in season; canoeists must take care not to interfere.

The Delaware & Raritan Canal (New Jersey side) bends away from the river and is no longer easily accessible.

139.2 Pass under Scudders Falls Bridge, carrying Interstate 95, completed in 1959. Plans to improve and widen the bridge have recently (2009) been announced.

Park Island ends just under the bridge.

138.8 **Access: Yardley, Pennsylvania.** Maintained by the Pennsylvania Fish and Boat Commission. A wide paved ramp, ample parking, privies. All boats must bear a Pennsylvania registration or launch permit. Access from Pennsylvania Route 32. This area is busy during fishing seasons.

Map 26

138.1 Brock Creek enters, Pennsylvania side. The Delaware Canal crosses the creek in a high aqueduct a short distance from the river.

A brownstone abutment on the Pennsylvania side is all that remains of the Yardley-Wilburtha (or Four Mile Ferry) Bridge, built in 1835 and ultimately washed away in the great flood of 1955. Today a memorial to veterans stands on top of the bridge abutment.

Yardley's (Howell's or Four-mile) Ferry ran here before the bridge was built.

A rough trail leads along the bridge abutment up to the village of Yardley.

Lunch. Yardley, Pennsylvania: Casual restaurants, including Charcoal Steaks and Things. Started as a smoky hot dog stand for boaters in the 1940s, Charcoal Steaks has ever since been known to locals as "Dirty Bills." It was reconstructed, now more upscale, after near-destruction in the 2006 floods.

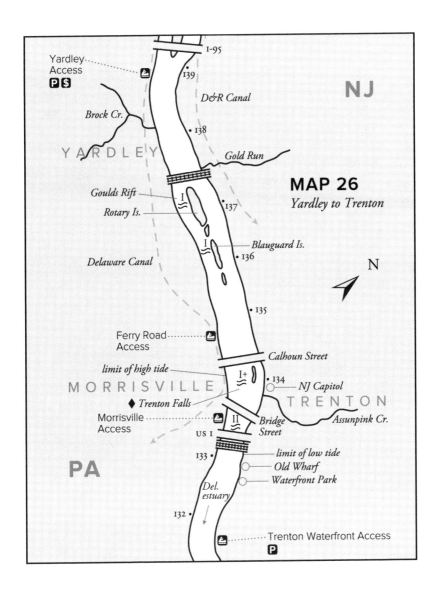

MAP 26
Yardley to Trenton

Yardley Access

Brock Cr.

YARDLEY

Goulds Rift

Rotary Is.

Delaware Canal

Ferry Road Access

limit of high tide

MORRISVILLE

Trenton Falls

Morrisville Access

PA

I-95

D&R Canal

Gold Run

Blauguard Is.

Calhoun Street

NJ Capitol

TRENTON

Assunpink Cr.

Bridge Street

limit of low tide

Old Wharf

Waterfront Park

Del. estuary

Trenton Waterfront Access

NJ

N

US 1

137.4 Pass under the multiple-arch concrete bridge carrying CSX Corporation's freight railway and SEPTA's West Trenton line. This spectacular bridge was built by the Philadelphia & Reading Railroad in 1911. The brownstone piers of the old bridge it replaced still stand in the river.

Gold Run enters, New Jersey side.

137.2 Rotary (Goulds) Island begins in the center of the river, extending

0.7 mile. The right channel is more interesting, with modest rapids. Rotary Island is public land, held by the New Jersey Park Service.

The upstream tip of Rotary Island marks the beginning of the Tidal Delaware Water Trail, continuing downstream to mile 112 at Rancocas Creek. Note that the tide does not affect the river until the Calhoun Street Bridge in Trenton at mile 134.3.

136.9 Moderate rapids (Class I), once known as Goulds Rift, begin just downstream from the point of Rotary Island.

136.6 A channel winds left to right through overhanging trees of Rotary Island, impassable at low water. The rope swing that hangs from a huge silver maple has been here for decades.

136.5 A Class I rapids immediately at the end of Rotary Island flows left to right.

136.4 Blauguard Island, long and slender, begins in the center of the river; the island is submerged at moderately high water. Long called Black-guard Island, it was once notorious as "a favored resort of indigent gentlemen of leisure."[2]

Stacy Park, New Jersey side, parallels the river for the next mile. Facilities include playgrounds, picnic tables, and a physical fitness course. The park originally extended all the way to tidewater, but the lower reaches were obliterated, amid some controversy, by improvements to New Jersey Route 29. There is no good access from the river.

134.6 **Access: Ferry Road, Pennsylvania.** Maintained by the City of Morrisville. A rough gravel ramp, very limited parking, no other facilities. No fee. This is the last public access before Trenton Falls and tidewater. Access from Pennsylvania Route 32 just north of the Calhoun Street Bridge.

A ferry run by George Beatty and others operated here from 1782 until construction of the Calhoun Street Bridge in 1861.

The City of Morrisville water treatment plant is located across Route 32 from the access point.

134.5 Stacy Park river rest stop, New Jersey. Just a clearing along the river-bank. No parking, no facilities. This is not a boat access.

Big rocks protrude from the river. Raftsmen called these Cocked Hat, Marble Roll, and Sunfish Ripple, guideposts to navigate Trenton Falls below. The rocks are favored perches for cormorants.

134.4 The concrete structure extending into the river from the New Jersey side is the intake for the City of Trenton water treatment plant; stay clear!

There is a U.S. Geological Survey river gage 250 feet downstream from the treatment plant intake, housed in a tiny brown shed on the

New Jersey riverbank. This is the last gage above tidewater. Base elevation is 0.00 ft., that is, right at sea level. Good stage for boating is 7–10 feet; flood stage is 20 feet. The maximum flood recorded here was 30.6 feet in a 1904 ice jam.

134.3 Pass under the Calhoun Street, or Upper Trenton, Bridge. A wooden covered bridge built here in 1861 was destroyed in a fire caused by a carelessly tossed cigar. The present seven-span steel truss was completed on the original piers and abutments in 1884, making it the second-oldest extant bridge across the Delaware (the Roebling Aqueduct at Lackawaxen, built in 1849, is the oldest). The bridge was given a major overhaul in 2010, and traffic is limited to automobiles and pedestrians.

Trenton, New Jersey, population 82,883 (est. 2008), the biggest city along the river as described in this book, and Morrisville, Pennsylvania, stand at opposite ends of the bridge.

134.2 CAUTION! Begin Trenton Falls, a Class I+ rapids extending nearly a mile. This marks the *fall line*—the demarcation between the hard bedrock of the Piedmont and the soft sand and clay of the Coastal Plain. The river drops 7.5 feet to the low tide mark, a steep pitch.

The first shallow ledge just below the bridge is known as Yellow Reef; a few yards beyond, the more imposing Blade Ledges nearly span the river.

Rocky little Yards (or Fishing) Island hugs the New Jersey riverbank. Stay in the main channel; an old mill dam in the slough to the left is potentially hazardous to boaters.

The river is very wide and shallow. The concrete-and-stone embankments on both sides, constructed in the 1950s, dramatically altered the shape of the channel and riverbanks.

134.0 Upper limit of tidewater; at high tide the river is flat from here on. The tide at Trenton rises 8–10 feet.

133.9 The gold dome of the New Jersey State House stands high over the riverbank.

The main channel slaloms down the middle of the river. Ledges on the right were called Woodpecker Lane by timber raftsmen, as the sharp rocks could chew a raft to pieces.

133.8 Assunpink Creek enters via a concrete channel, New Jersey side.

133.4 Pass under the Lower Trenton (Bridge Street) Bridge, commonly known as the "Trenton Makes" bridge. A south-facing sign proudly proclaims "Trenton Makes, The World Takes."

The first bridge to span the Delaware was built here 1803–1806 upon

The iconic "Trenton Makes, The World Takes" bridge harkens to the city's heyday as a manufacturing powerhouse. Tides from the Atlantic surge upriver as far as this bridge. At low tide, a tough Class II rapids churns beneath it. (Photo by the author)

the piers and abutments that support the present bridge, replacing a ferry operated by James Trent. The bridge structure was remodeled repeatedly, at one time carrying trains as well as vehicle traffic, until the present five-span steel truss was completed in 1930.

CAUTION! At low tide Trenton Falls is a tough Class II rapids between the Bridge Street Bridge and the U.S. Route 1 toll bridge. There are high standing waves through boulders and debris in the middle left of the river. Very shallow at the right.

At high tide the river is flat, and on a flow tide you are paddling against the current.

133.3 **Access: Morrisville, Pennsylvania.** Maintained by the City of Morrisville. A muddy landing area under the U.S. Route 1 toll bridge, limited parking, no facilities. No fee. Access via a gravel road off South Delmorr Avenue, Morrisville.

Pass under the U.S. Route 1 toll bridge, built in 1952.

The Route 1 bridge marks the limit of low tide. The Delaware is a tidal estuary from this point 133 miles to the Atlantic Ocean.

A ferry ran here as early as the mid-1600s. It was acquired by James Trent, namesake of the City of Trenton, in 1726.

133.2 Pass under the arched brownstone bridge carrying Amtrak's main line. This fine structure was built by the Pennsylvania Railroad in 1903.

133.1 Old Wharf fishing area, New Jersey side, maintained by the City of Trenton. At one time a marine pier; there is no boat access. Pilings rise 15 feet from the river.

132.9 Shops and offices of the Trenton waterfront complex are clustered on the New Jersey riverbanks. This area was once an industrial zone, its mills powered by the Trenton Water Power canal. A floating pier provides mooring for powerboats, but access for canoes and kayaks would be awkward.

132.8 Waterfront Park, home of the minor league (AA) Trenton Thunder baseball team, stands close to the river on the New Jersey side. Long home runs to right field splash into the river.

132.5 New Jersey Route 29 passes through a semi-open tunnel, hard against the river on the New Jersey side.

132.0 Trenton Marine Terminal, New Jersey side. Once a deepwater port to the City of Trenton, today it is a city park popular with anglers. No boat access.

131.6 **Access: Trenton waterfront, New Jersey.** Maintained by the City of Trenton. Concrete ramps, ample parking, trash disposal, telephone, and restrooms. Primarily intended for powerboat and sailboat access to the Delaware estuary. No fee or permit is necessary for unpowered boats. Access from Lamberton Street, off New Jersey 29 South, just beyond the tunnel.

Features

Washington's Crossing

You've seen Emanuel Leutze's iconic painting of *Washington Crossing the Delaware* (1851). Many historians argue that the American Revolution was saved here.

After heavy losses at Long Island and New York, and a ramshackle retreat across New Jersey, what was left of the American army camped in the cold forests of Bucks County, Pennsylvania. The soldiers were ready to give up and go home. Washington decided on a desperate gamble: attack the Hessian mercenaries quartered at Trenton. Stealth and secrecy were of the essence. A small armada of Durham boats and scow ferries was quietly commandeered, then hidden near Wells Ferry (New Hope).

Christmas night was cold and sleeting, the river choked with ice. For nine hours the Americans poled and rowed from Pennsylvania to New Jersey, then

General George Washington led his army across the icy Delaware on Christmas night, 1776, revitalizing the Revolutionary cause. The crossing is commemorated in state parks on both sides of the river. This statue is on the Pennsylvania side. (Photo by the author)

quick-marched eight miles down to Trenton. They'd had no sleep, and many had no shoes. But the Hessians were taken utterly by surprise and quickly captured with few American casualties. Word of Washington's astonishing victory quickly spread through the colonies and breathed new life into the "glorious cause."

State parks in both Pennsylvania and New Jersey commemorate the event. The parks feature historic buildings and museums, demonstrations, picnicking, and recreation areas. The crossing is re-enacted every Christmas afternoon, complete with Durham boats and troops in Revolutionary uniform. Thousands of spectators line the bridge and riverbanks to see if General Washington will once again make it across.

Bowman's Hill

Propagation of wild plants is a tricky business. Germination, soil, water, temperature, nutrients, and lighting must be just-so for wildflowers to prosper. Yet that is the business of Bowman's Hill Wildflower Preserve, where 134 acres are devoted to the cultivation of 800 species of wild plants. Visitors can walk 20 trails, including Marsh Marigold, The Barrens, Medicinal, and Azaleas at the Bridge, to see nature's miniature miracles up close. Birds and butterflies are naturally drawn to the preserve, and it's a fantastic place to spot a new one for your life list.

The Wildflower Preserve was founded in the 1930s when the Works Progress Administration cut trails, thinned undergrowth, drained swamps, and prepared soil to establish the range of habitats found here today. The preserve sponsors classes in wildflower horticulture, family hikes, and special events throughout the year. The little museum has hands-on exhibits about wildflowers and a surprising collection of bird nests, eggs, and mounted specimens. The admission fee for adults is $5 (2010). The entire experience is super family-friendly.

Bowman's Hill Tower stands at the summit, looming above the Wildflower Preserve. The tower was built in 1931 of native rocks gathered from nearby stone walls. Intended as a monument to commemorate General George Washington's 1776 crossing of the Delaware nearby, Bowman's Tower has been a tourist attraction for 80 years. Visitors can ride an elevator or climb the scary spiral staircase to the top. At 125 feet, the observation deck is higher than the trees, giving visitors an awesome view the Delaware valley and surrounding countryside.

The Wildflower Preserve and Bowman's Tower are within Pennsylvania's Washington Crossing State Historic Park.

Trenton, New Jersey

"Trenton Makes, The World Takes"—the huge neon sign on the Lower Trenton Bridge proudly proclaims Trenton's heritage. New Jersey's capital city has long been a hub of manufacturing. Your own home may well contain ceramic products made in Trenton: fine china by Lenox, or bathroom fixtures by American Standard. John Roebling's steel works arrived in 1848 and for over a century made wire rope for bridges and other specialty steel products. Other plants in Trenton made rubber goods, electrical parts, and cigars.

In 1679 Quaker Mahlon Stacy, escaping religious persecution in England, built a house and mill at "Ye Ffalles of Ye De La Warr." He sold some of his land to William Trent, and Trent's Town—at the head of the tidal Delaware River—began to thrive. Trent's 1719 stone home still stands, just off Market Street, and is open to visitors. By 1727, ferries at Trenton were carrying passengers en route between New York and Philadelphia, and the first bridge to span the Delaware was built here, in 1806, upon the stone piers that carry today's "Trenton Makes" bridge. George Washington's victory in the Battle of Trenton in 1776 brought international renown. The stone Old Barracks that housed the defeated Hessian garrison still stands. The U.S. Congress met at Trenton in 1784 and considered making the city the capital of the new nation.

The gold dome of the New Jersey State House rises proudly over the Delaware River, with other state buildings clustered nearby. The state museum features exhibits about the natural and human history of the Garden State. The best-surviving Lenape canoe, hand-hewn from a poplar tree, is on display at the museum; it looks pretty much like canoes today.

Trenton, population about 83,000, is the biggest city along the portion of the Delaware River covered in this book. All services are available, but not within walking distance for canoeists and kayakers. New Jersey Route 29 blocks the way to shops and restaurants, and there are no commercial districts nearby. The fishing piers and commercial areas are not paddler-friendly. Access to the river and services is better in Morrisville, on the Pennsylvania side.

The Delaware is a different river below Trenton. Twice-daily tides from the Atlantic surge to eight feet high. On a flow tide, boaters going downstream run against the current. At low tide, the riverbanks in some places are lined with mudflats. Salt water comes as far upriver as Philadelphia, bringing with it an entirely different ecosystem. The Delaware becomes wider and deeper, and a channel marked by red and green buoys has been dredged for heavy ships. Recreational boaters must contend with cargo vessels, tankers, tugboats, and other commercial traffic. And, with more urbanization comes more pollution.

Canoeists and kayakers participating in the 2009 Delaware River Sojourn paddle the Delaware estuary at Philadelphia. Portions of the estuary have been designated the Tidal Delaware Water Trail. (Photo by Jessica Anderson)

This is not to say that the tidal Delaware is unfit for paddling. In recent years more and more people have taken to kayaking on the estuary. The marshes, forests, and little tributaries along the way are great habitats for birds and other wildlife. Some areas are excellent for fishing striped bass and other game fish. The urban areas too have a certain appeal: paddling under the gigantic Ben Franklin Bridge, alongside the skyscrapers of Philadelphia, or even in the shadow of the great battleship *New Jersey* at Camden is an awesome experience. Indeed, the estuary has been designated as the Tidal Delaware Water Trail for 56 miles from Trenton to Marcus Hook, making it more user-friendly to all kinds of recreational boaters. The Delaware River Sojourn usually includes some paddling on the estuary in its annual excursion down the river.

Access to the Delaware estuary is mostly designed with trailered power-boats or sailboats in mind, but certainly can be used by kayakers. Many of the municipalities along the river, as well as private marinas, maintain river access areas. However, there are no commercial outfitters offering paddle craft for rent or shuttle on the tidal Delaware.

This book does not describe the Delaware estuary in detail. The Delaware River Basin Commission's recreational maps cover the river down to mile 104 at Philadelphia, indicating access points and other features. More information can be found via the Tidal Delaware Water Trail.

Appendixes

River Trip Checklist

It's easiest to travel light, but there are some essentials that should be carried on any river trip.

1. Personal Flotation Device (PFD, or life jacket). A PFD must be carried for each occupant of every boat, including canoes, kayaks, rafts, and tubes. On the upper Delaware, a PFD must be worn when the river stage measures above 6 feet on the Barryville gage, and by children 12 and under at all times.
2. Extra paddle, securely lashed to the canoe, to be used as a replacement when your primary paddles get washed away.
3. A bailer—cut the bottom off an empty milk jug or bleach bottle, then use the top part with the handle to bail. A large sponge will come in handy too.
4. Extra dry clothes, in a watertight bag or container, to change into when the day is done.
5. Sun protection, including lotion, hat, and sunglasses.
6. Fresh water—plan to drink plenty each day on the river. Do not drink untreated river water.
7. Garbage bags. Leave no trash in or on the river!
8. Insect repellent. Mosquitoes, black flies, deer flies, and their ilk can make an otherwise great trip miserable.
9. First aid kit, including items to treat cuts and scrapes, insect bites and stings, sore muscles, and sunburn.
10. Rope and/or bungee cords to secure gear into the boat. Assume you will capsize; invest in a "dry bag" that can be secured to be sure your possessions don't get washed away.

Additional gear depends on the length of the trip, the weather, accommodations if overnight, what and where you will be eating, and personal interests (wildlife? photography? fishing?) and preferences.

Note: cell phone service is unreliable in the Delaware valley upstream from the Delaware Water Gap.

River Conditions

River Information Line: 845-252-7100
(recorded report of river and weather conditions for the upper Delaware)

National Weather Service—real-time information on river flow and flood predictions

Middle Atlantic River Forecast Center
www.erh.noaa.gov/marfc

National Weather Service Advanced Hydrologic Prediction Service
http://water.weather.gov/ahps2/index.php?wfo=bgm

Delaware River Tides (Trenton and below)
www.saltwatertides.com/dynamic.dir/delawareriversites.html

National Park Service

Delaware Water Gap National Recreation Area

www.nps.gov/dewa/index.htm
24-hour emergency phone: 570-426-2435 / 800-543-HAWK

Park Headquarters
River Road off Route 209
Bushkill, PA 18324-9999
570-426-2451 (recording) / 570-426-2452

Visitor Centers
570-828-2253 / 908-496-4458

Upper Delaware Scenic and Recreational River

www.nps.gov/upde/index.htm
Emergencies: 911 / 570-426-2457
River Information Line: 845-252-7100

Park Headquarters
274 River Road
RR 2 Box 2428
Beach Lake, PA 18405-9737
570-729-7134

Visitor Information
570-685-4871

Lower Delaware Wild and Scenic River

www.nps.gov/lode/index.htm
c/o National Park Service
260 U.S. Custom House
2nd & Chestnut Streeıts
Philadelphia, PA 19106
215-597-6482

State of New York

New York Department of Environmental Conservation
(water quality, public lands, fish and game)
www.dec.ny.gov
50 Wolf Road
Albany, NY 12233-4790
518-457-3521

NY-DEC Regional Office, Reg. 3 (Sullivan and Orange Counties)
21 South Putt Corners Road
New Paltz, NY 12561-1696
845-256-3018

NY-DEC Regional Office, Reg. 4 (Delaware County)
65561 State Highway 10, Suite 1
Stamford, NY 12167
518-357-2068

State of New Jersey

New Jersey Department of Environmental Protection
(water quality, public lands, fish and game)
www.state.nj.us/dep
PO Box 402
Trenton, NJ 08625–0402
800-843-6420

Division of Parks and Forestry
www.state.nj.us/dep/parksandforests

Delaware and Raritan Canal State Park
http://www.dandrcanal.com/
145 Mapleton Road
Princeton, NJ 08540
609-924-5705

Bulls Island Recreation Area (camping)
2185 Daniel Bray Highway
Stockton, NJ 08559
609-397-2949

High Point State Park (camping)
1480 Route 23
Sussex, NJ 07461
973-875-4800

Stokes State Forest (camping)
1 Coursen Road
Branchville, NJ 07826
973-948-3820

Washington Crossing State Park
355 Washington Crossing Road
Titusville, NJ 08560
609-737-0623

Worthington State Forest (camping)
HC 62 Box 2
Columbia, NJ 07832
908-841-9575

Commonwealth of Pennsylvania

Pennsylvania Fish and Boat Commission
Permits for use of PA F&B access points
http://fishandboat.com/registration.htm
Fishing regulations, licences, information
http://fishandboat.com/regs_fish.htm

Northeast Region Office
5566 Main Road / PO Box 88
Sweet Valley, PA 18656
570-477-5717

Delaware Canal State Park
www.dcnr.state.pa.us/stateparks/parks/delawarecanal.aspx
11 Lodi Hill Road
Upper Black Eddy, PA 18972
610-982-5560

Washington Crossing State Historic Park
www.ushistory.org/washingtoncrossing/
PO Box 107
Washington Crossing, PA 18977
215-493-4076

River, Outdoors, and Community

American Rivers
www.americanrivers.org
Protects and restores America's rivers for the benefit of people, wildlife, and nature
1101 14th Street NW, Suite 1400
Washington, DC 20005

American Whitewater
www.americanwhitewater.org/
Conservation of white-water resources and opportunities to enjoy them
PO Box 1540
Cullowhee, NC 28723
828-586-1930

Appalachian Trail Conservancy
www.appalachiantrail.org
Advocacy and management of the Appalachian Trail
PO Box 807
Harpers Ferry, WV 25425
304-535-6331

Delaware River Basin Commission
www.state.nj.us/drbc/
Administration of river resources in four-state area; river recreation maps
PO Box 7360
West Trenton, NJ 08628
609-883-9500

Delaware River Greenway Partnership
www.delrivgreenway.org
A public/private consortium for Lower Delaware Wild and Scenic River; Delaware
    River Water Trail; Delaware River Sojourn
PO Box 54
Erwinna, PA 18920
609-239-0444

Delaware River Heritage Trail
www.delrivgreenway.org/heritagetrail
Driving tour Trenton and points south

Delaware Riverkeeper Network
www.delawareriverkeeper.org
Advocate for protection of the Delaware River and estuary
300 Pond Street, Second Floor
Bristol, PA 19007
215-369-1188
800-8-DELAWARE (pollution hotline)

Delaware River Sojourn
www.riversojourn.com
www.state.nj.us/drbc/sojourn.htm
Annual canoe/kayak trip highlighting environmental and cultural aspects of the
    river
c/o Delaware River Basin Commission
PO Box 7360
West Trenton, NJ 08628
609-883-9500

Delaware River Water Trail
http://www.delrivgreenway.org/pdf/Water%20Trail%20Guide%202007-01-22.pdf
Water Trail map and information
c/o Delaware River Greenway Partnership
PO Box 54
Erwinna, PA 18920
609-239-0444

Delaware Valley Eagle Alliance
www.dveaglealliance.org
Promotes awareness and conservation of bald eagles and other wildlife in the upper
    Delaware valley.
PO Box 498
Narrowsburg, NY 12764
845-252-6509

Eagle Institute
www.eagleinstitute.org
Non-profit organization dedicated to the protection of bald eagles and other birds
    of prey; field office at Roebling Bridge, Lackwaxen, PA.
PO Box 182
Barryville, NY 12719
845-557-6162

Friends of Delaware Water Gap National Recreation Area
www.friendsofdewa.org
Civic boosters of the DWGNRA
River Road
Bushkill, PA 18324
570-426–2435 x2510

Friends of Washington Crossing Park
www.friendsofwashingtoncrossingpark.com
Civic boosters of Washington Crossing State Historic Park, PA; annual
    re-enactment of Washington's crossing
PO Box 1776
Washington Crossing, PA 18977

Lenape Nation Tribal Community
www.lenapenation.org
The Lenape Nation of Pennsylvania
PO Box 362
Gilbert, PA 18331

Mohawk Canoe Club
http://www.mohawkcanoeclub.org/
Canoeing/kayaking club for the Delaware River basin

National Canoe Safety Patrol
Upper Delaware
www.nationalcanoesafetypatrol.com/
Lower Delaware
www.ncspldc.org/
Volunteer group providing river safety and rescue

Tidal Delaware Water Trail
http://www.tidaltrail.org/
Informal paddlers' guide to the Delaware River estuary

Upper Delaware Council
www.upperdelawarecouncil.org/
Consortium of government agencies for management of Upper Delaware Wild and
    Scenic River
211 Bridge Street
PO Box 192
Narrowsburg, NY 12764
845-252-3022

Upper Delaware Preservation Coalition
www.udpc.net
Citizens advocating protection of the upper Delaware
PO Box 252
Narrowsburg, NY 12764

Upper Delaware Scenic Byway
www.upperdelawarescenicbyway.org
Driving tour, Port Jervis to Hancock
PO Box 127
Narrowsburg, NY 12764
866-511-8372

Bowman's Hill Wildflower Preserve
www.bhwp.org
PO Box 685 / 1635 River Road
New Hope, PA 18938–0685
215-862-2924

Bucks County Riverboat Co.
www.kellerslanding.com
Party boats at Upper Black Eddy
1469 River Road
Upper Black Eddy, PA 18972
610-982-5252

Delaware & Hudson Canal Historical Society and Museum
www.canalmuseum.org
23 Mohonk Road / PO Box 23
High Falls, NY 12440-0023
845-687-9311

Dingmans Choice and Delaware Bridge Company
www.dingmansbridge.com

Fishing Guide Services (Compiled by Upper Delaware Scenic and Recreational
    River)
http://www.nps.gov/upde/planyourvisit/fishingguides.htm

Fort Delaware Museum
http://co.sullivan.ny.us/Default.aspx?TabId=3192
6615 Route 97
Narrowsburg, New York
845-807-0261

Grey Towers National Historic Site
www.fs.fed.us/na/gt/
151 Grey Towers Drive
PO Box 188
Milford, PA 18337
570-296-9630

National Canal Museum/Hugh Moore Park
www.canals.org
200 North Delaware Drive
PO Box 877
Easton, PA 18044-0877
610-250-6700

New Hope & Ivyland Railroad
www.newhoperailroad.com
Steam train excursions from New Hope, PA
32 West Bridge Street
New Hope, PA 18938
215-862-2332

New Hope Canal Boat Company
Mule-drawn canal boat rides on the Delaware Canal
149 South Main Street
New Hope, PA 18938
215-862-0758

Wells Ferry Boat Rides
www.newhopeboatrides.com
Party boats in New Hope, PA
22 North Main Street
New Hope, PA 18938
215-205-1140

Outfitters and Campgrounds

River Outfitters/River Trips/Rentals/Liveries

Upper Delaware (Hancock to Port Jervis)

Cedar Rapids Kayak and Canoe
http://cedarrapidsny.com/
PO Box 219
Barryville, NY 12719
845-557-6158

Indian Head Canoes
www.indianheadcanoes.com
Route 97
Barryville, NY 12719
845-557-8777 / 800-874-2628

Jerry's Three River Campground
www.jerrys3rivercampground.com
PO Box 7 / 2333 Route 97
Pond Eddy, New York 12770
845-557-6078

Kittatinny Canoes
www.kittatinny.com
PO Box 95, Route 97
Barryville, NY 12719
845-557-8611 / 800-356-2852

Landers River Trips
www.landersrivertrips.com
PO Box 500, 5961 State Route 97
Narrowsburg, NY 12764
800-252-3925

Lou's Tubes at Skinners Falls
PO Box 11 / Skinners Falls Road
Milanville, PA 18843
845-252-3593

Silver Canoe and Raft Rentals
www.silvercanoe.com
37 South Maple Avenue
Port Jervis, NY 12771
800-724-8342

Soaring Eagle Campground
www.soaringeaglecampground.com
RD 1, Box 300
River Road
Equinunk, PA 18417
570-224-4666

Two River Junction
www.tworiverjunction.com
106 Scenic Drive
Lackawaxen, PA 18435
570-685-2010

Whitewater Willie's
www.whitewaterwillies.com
37 South Maple Avenue
Port Jervis, NY 12771
800-724-8342 / 845-856-7055

Wild and Scenic River Tours
www.landersrivertrips.com/wildscenic/index.htm
166 Route 97
Barryville, NY 12719
845-557-8723 / 800-836-0366

Middle Delaware (Port Jervis to Delaware Water Gap)

Adventure Sports
www.adventuresports.com
PO Box 175 / Route 209
Marshalls Creek, PA 18335
800-487-2628

Chamberlains Canoes
www.chamberlaincanoes.com
PO Box 555 / River Road
Minisink Hills, PA 18341
800-422-6631

Delaware River Family Campground
www.njcamping.com/delaware/
100 Route 46 / PO Box 142
Delaware, New Jersey 07833
908-475-4517 / 800-543-0271

Dingmans Campground
www.dingmanscampground.com
1006 Route 209
Dingmans Ferry, PA 18328
877-828-1551

Indian Head Canoes and Rafts
www.indianheadcanoes.com
PO Box 293 / 3883 Route 97
Barryville, NY 12719
570-874-2628

Jerry's Three River Campground & Canoes
www.jerrys3rivercampground.com
Box 7 / 2333 Route 97
Pond Eddy, NY 12770
845-557-6078

Kittatinny Canoes
www.kittatinny.com
PO Box 95, Route 97
Barryville, NY 12719
800-356-2852 / 845-557-8611

Pack Shack Adventures
www.packshack.com
PO Box 127 / 88 Broad Street
Delaware Water Gap, PA 18327
800-424-0955

Shawnee River Trips
www.ShawneeRiverTrips.com
Minisink Hills, PA 18341
800-SHAWNEE (742–9633)

Silver Canoe Rentals
www.silvercanoe.com
37 South Maple Avenue
Port Jervis, NY 12771
800-724-8342

Lower Delaware (Delaware Water Gap to Trenton)

Bucks County River Country
www.rivercountry.net
2 Walters Lane
Point Pleasant, PA
215-297-5000

Delaware River Family Campground
www.njcamping.com/delaware/
PO Box 142 / 100 Route 46
Delaware, NJ 07833
908-475-4517 / 800-543-0271

Delaware River Tubing
www.delawarerivertubing.com
PO Box 97 / 2998 Daniel Bray Highway (NJ Route 29)
Frenchtown, NJ 08825
908-996-5386

Driftstone on the Delaware
www.driftstone.com/index.html
2731 River Road
Mt. Bethel, PA 18343
570-897-6859 or 888-355-6859

Paddle Creek
www.paddlecreekfrenchtown.com
26 Race St.
Frenchtown, NJ 08825
908-996-0000 / 888-794-4459

Campgrounds

Upper Delaware (Hancock to Port Jervis)

Ascalona Campground
http://ascalonacampgrounds.com
4499 Route 97
Minisink Ford, NY 12719
845-557-6554

Cedar Rapids Kayak and Canoe
http://cedarrapidsny.com/
PO Box 219
Barryville, NY 12719
845-557-6158

Delaware State Forest / Buckhorn Natural Area
Permits available at: Upper Delaware Scenic and Recreational River
274 River Road
Beach Lake, PA 18405
570-685-4871

Indian Head Canoes
www.indianheadcanoes.com
Route 97
Barryville, NY 12719
845-557-8777 / 800-874-2628

Jerry's Three River Campground
www.jerrys3rivercampground.com
PO Box 7 / 2333 Route 97
Pond Eddy, New York 12770
845-557-6078

Kittatinny Canoes
www.kittatinny.com
PO Box 95, Route 97
Barryville, NY 12719
800-356-2852 / 845-557-8611

Landers River Trips
www.landersrivertrips.com
PO Box 500, 5961 State Route 97
Narrowsburg, NY 12764
800-252-3925 / 845-252-3925

Red Barn Campground
Hankins, NY 12741
845-887-4995

Soaring Eagle Campground
www.soaringeaglecampground.com
RD 1, Box 300
River Road
Equinunk, PA 18417
570-224-4666

Upper Delaware Campgrounds
PO Box 331
36 Upper Delaware Camp Road
Callicoon, NY 12723
845-887-5344

Wild and Scenic River Tours
www.landersrivertrips.com/wildsenic/index.htm
166 Route 97
Barryville, NY 12719
845-557-8723 / 800-836-0366

Middle Delaware (Port Jervis to Delaware Water Gap)

Delaware Water Gap National Recreation Area
(Valley View and Rivers Bend Group Campsites)
www.nps.gov/dewa/planyourvisit/group-campsites.htm
Group Campsite Reservations
Delaware Water Gap National Recreation Area
Headquarters, River Road off Route 209
Bushkill, PA 18324
570-296-8757
Primitive campsites provided by the National Park Service are first-come, first-served; no fee and no reservations. For persons on river trips only.

Dingmans Campground
www.dingmanscampground.com
1006 Route 209
Dingmans Ferry, PA 18328
570-828-1551

River Beach Campground (Kittatinny Canoes)
www.kittatinny.com
PO Box 95, Route 97
Barryville, NY 12719
800-356-2852 / 845-557-8611

Worthington State Forest
www.stateparks.com/worthington.html
HC 62, Box 2
Columbia, NJ 07832
908-841-9575

Lower Delaware (Delaware Water Gap to Trenton)

Bulls Island Recreation Area and Campground
www.dandrcanal.com/camping.html
2185 Daniel Bray Highway
Stockton, NJ 08559
609-397-2949

Delaware River Family Campground
http://www.njcamping.com/delaware/
100 Route 46 / PO Box 142
Delaware, NJ 07833
908-475-4517 / 800-543-0271

Driftstone on the Delaware
http://www.driftstone.com/index.html
2731 River Road
Mt. Bethel, PA 18343
570-897-6859 or 888-355-6859

Ringing Rocks Family Campground
www.ringingrocksfamilycampground.com/
75 Woodland Drive
Upper Black Eddy, PA 18972
610-982-5552

Tinicum County Park
www.buckscounty.org/government/departments/parksandrec/Parks/Tinicum.aspx
Parks and Recreation
901 East Bridgetown Pike
Langhorne, PA 19047–1597
215-348-6114 or 215-757-0571

River Stage at Barryville

Recreational Boating Guidelines

The National Park Service provides the following table of river levels. (Remember, river stage is not the depth of the river, but the elevation of the water surface.) The numbers at Barryville do *not* represent river stage at other gaging points:

< 2½ feet	**Low**	Many exposed rocks, especially in rapids. Narrow channels make rapids difficult to navigate. Expect to scrape rocks and/or river bottom. Slow river trip. Shorter trips recommended. Limit weight in vessel.
2½–4 feet	**Average**	Some rocks exposed in rapids. Some waves up to 3 feet. Average river level for recreational boating. River current 2 MPH. Good water level for boating.
4–6 feet	**Moderate**	*Rafting suggested for less skilled paddlers.* Waves up to 4–5 feet. Swift river currents. Only the larger rocks exposed in rapids. Open and wide channels. River current 2.5+ MPH. Increased canoe/kayak skills required.
6–8 feet	**High**	*Not suited to open canoes.* Waves up to 6 feet. Hydraulics (undercurrents) noticeable. Very swift river current, 3 MPH. Higher skill level recommended for open boat use. Rafts recommended for less experienced paddlers.
8–12 feet	**Very high**	*Properly equipped rafts and/or closed boats only.* Waves up to 8 feet. Floating debris hazard. Very swift currents of 4+ MPH. Water temperature decreased. Increased hydraulics (undercurrents) in rapids. Hazards/obstructions along shoreline may be present. Wet/dry suit recommended. Highest skill level.

12–17 feet	**Near flood**	Many waves above 8 feet. Violent currents, hydraulics (undercurrents), and whirlpools. Extreme current speed, 6–7 MPH. Maneuvering and rescue extremely difficult. Floating debris very hazardous. Hazards/obstructions along shore. *Boating is not recommended at this level!*
> 17 feet	**Flood**	Do not even think about boating. The highest stage recorded at Barryville was 28.97 feet, in 2006.

International Scale of River Difficulty

Class I: Moving water with a few riffles and small waves. Few or no obstructions.

Class II: Easy rapids with waves up to three feet and wide, clear channels that are obvious without scouting. Some maneuvering required.

Class III: Rapids with high, irregular waves capable of swamping an open canoe. Narrow passages that often require complex maneuvering. May require scouting from shore.

Note: There are no rapids on the Delaware ordinarily greater than Class III. Under normal conditions, only Wells Falls is rated Class II+.

Class IV: Long, difficult rapids with constricted passages that require precise maneuvering in very turbulent waters. Scouting from shore necessary; conditions make rescue difficult. Boaters in covered canoes and kayaks should have ability to eskimo roll. *Generally not possible in an open canoe.*

Class V: Extremely difficult, long, and very violent rapids with highly congested routes, which should always be scouted from shore. Rescue conditions difficult. Significant hazard to life in the event of a mishap. Ability to eskimo roll essential for boaters in kayaks and decked canoes.

Class VI: Very dangerous, nearly impossible to navigate. For teams of experts only, after a close study has been made and all precautions taken.

Notes

Overview

1. American Whitewater, the main advocate for white-water canoeing and kayaking in the United States, uses an expanded and more detailed scale of difficulty. The principles are the same: Class I = easy, Class VI = virtually impossible.
2. Louis C. Senger, "The Passing of a Picturesque Industry," *The Quaker* 6, no. 3 (October 1899).
3. *New Jersey v. New York, et al.*, 51 S. Ct. 478, 283 U.S. 336 (1931).

Hancock to Long Eddy

1. These islands offer a good example of the difficulty of fixing place-names on the Delaware. There is no "official" U.S. Geological Survey name for these islands. Joshua Pine called them the Murray Islands, "standing sentry over the union of the two rivers." Pine, *The Bygone Era: Rafting on the Delaware, 1883* (Andes, NY: Pepacton Press, 1995), 22. Max Schrabisch found aboriginal artifacts here and called them Read's Island. Schrabisch, *Archaeology of Delaware River Valley Between Hancock and Dingmans Ferry* (Harrisburg: Pennsylvania Historical Commission, 1930), 2. In 1976 R. Cella called them Reeds and Doyles Islands. Cella, *Recreation Map of the Upper Delaware River* (Barryville, NY: Upper Delaware Publications, 1976). These names likely came from the landowners. Paul Weamer calls them the Swan Islands, reported by long-time anglers of the upper Delaware. Weamer, *Fly Fishing Guide to the Upper Delaware River* (Mechanicsburg, PA: Stackpole Books, 2007), 109. Swans have indeed been seen nesting near these islands. In most cases, where "official" names are not available, the most recent historical or colloquial name is used.

Long Eddy to Narrowsburg

1. J. Wallace Hoff, *Two Hundred Miles on the Delaware* (Trenton: Brandt Press, 1893).

Narrowsburg to Barryville

1. Zane Grey, "A Day on the Delaware," *Recreation* 26, no. 5 (May 1902), 339.

Barryville to Port Jervis

1. Hoff, *Two Hundred Miles on the Delaware*, 76.
2. This was a verse of "The Raftsman's Song," or "Shore Around the Grog," sung for many years in the Delaware valley. Norman Cazden, *Folk Songs of the Catskills* (Albany: State University of New York Press, 1982), 631.
3. Hoff, *Two Hundred Miles on the Delaware*, 76.
4. Horace Townsend, "Animals and Their Trainers," *Frank Leslie's Popular Monthly* 26 (December 1888), 730.

Port Jervis to Dingmans Ferry

1. Joel Sayre, "A Pennsylvania Inn," *Atlantic* 208, no. 1 (July 1961), 118.

Dingmans Ferry to Smithfield Beach

1. Charles Hine, *The Old Mine Road* (New Brunswick: Rutgers University Press, 1963), 153.
2. Senger, "Passing of a Picturesque Industry," 512
3. Herbert C. Kraft, *The Archaeology of the Tocks Island Area* (South Orange, NJ: Seton Hall University Museum, 1975).

Smithfield Beach to Martins Creek

1. G. F. Swain, *Report on the Water-Power of the Middle Atlantic Watershed*, in Census Reports, Tenth Census, June 1, 1880 (Washington, DC: Government Printing Office, 1885), 97. Swain cites an 1847 survey. The author was unable to find a more recent survey or obtain an accurate reading by GPS to verify this measurement. A fall of 22.8 feet over 1.75 miles averages to 13 ft/mi. The drops at Skinners Falls and Wells Falls are steeper, but over much shorter distances.
2. John B. O'Reilly, "Down the Delaware River in a Canoe," in O'Reilly, *Athletics and Manly Sport* (Boston: Pilot Pub. Co., 1890).

Martins Creek to Upper Black Eddy

1. Pine, *Bygone Era*, 48.

Lambertville to Trenton

1. The wing dams at Wells Falls as configured in 1872 and the named rocks, including Entering, Hundred Barrel, Prince, Grass, Foam, Dram, Rodmans, Bake Iron, Buckwheat Ledge, Corneel's, Dollar Roll, and Fish Rocks, are described, and depicted on accompanying maps, in *Report of the Chief of Engineers: Survey of the Delaware River between Trenton, New Jersey, and Easton, Pennsylvania* (Washington, DC: Government Printing Office, 1873). See also J. A. Anderson, *Navigation of the Upper Delaware* (Trenton: MacCrellish & Quigley, 1913), 5–6.
2. *Survey of the Delaware River between Trenton and Easton*, 916.

Bibliography

Adams, Richard C. *A Brief History of the Delaware Indians*. Reprinted at 59th Congress, 1st Sess., Doc. no. 501. Washington, DC: Government Printing Office, 1906.

Albert, Richard C. *Damming the Delaware: The Rise and Fall of Tocks Island Dam*. University Park, PA: Pennsylvania State University Press, 1998.

Albert, Richard C., and Carrie Albert. *Along the Delaware*. Portsmouth, NH: Arcadia Publishing, 2002.

Anderson, J.A. *Navigation of the Upper Delaware*. Trenton: MacCrellish & Quigley, 1913.

Backes, William J. "Transportation." In *A History of Trenton, 1697–1929*, vol. 1. Trenton: Trenton Historical Society, 1929.

Beck, Henry Charlton. *Tales and Towns of Northern New Jersey*. New Brunswick: Rutgers University Press, 1964.

Bertland, Denns N. *The Minisink: A Chronicle of One of America's First and Last Frontiers*. N.p.: Four-County Task Force on the Tocks Island Dam Project, 1975.

Board of Engineers for Rivers and Harbors. *The Delaware River from Trenton, N.J., to Easton, PA*. Reported in House of Representatives, 65th Cong., 1st Sess. Washington, DC: Government Printing Office, 1917.

Bowman's Hill Wildflower Preserve Association. *Ways with Wild Flowers*. New Hope, PA: Bowman's Hill Wildflower Preserve Association, 1983.

Brodhead, L.W. *The Delaware Water Gap: Its Scenery, Its Legends and Early History*. Philadelphia: Sherman & Company, 1870.

Burbank, James W. *Tom Quick Trail: A Chronicle of the Delaware Valley*. N.p.: Xlibris, 2006.

Burmeister, Walter F. *The Delaware and Its Tributaries*. His Appalachian Waters, 1. Oakton, VA: Appalachian Books, 1974.

Carluccio, Tracy. "Will We Sacrifice Our Water for Gas?" *Outdoor America* (Spring 2010), 27–33.

Cazden, Norman. *Folk Songs of the Catskills*. Albany: State University of New York Press, 1982.

Cella, R. *Recreation Map of the Upper Delaware River*. Barryville, NY: Upper Delaware Publications, 1976.

Cohen, David Steven. *The Folklore and Folklife of New Jersey*. New Brunswick: Rutgers University Press, 1983.

Conklin, Robert. *Pioneer'n the Delaware*. N.p.: Robert Conklin, 2001

Conference of Upper Delaware Townships. *Final River Management Plan*, Upper Delaware Scenic and Recreational River, 1986. Available at www.nps.gov/upde/parkmgmt/planning.htm.

Corbett, Roger, and Kathleen Fulcomer. *The Delaware River: A Resource and Guidebook to the River and the Valley*. Springfield, VA: Seneca Press, 1981.

Cunningham, John T. *New Jersey, America's Main Road* Garden City, NY: Doubleday, 1966.

Curtis, Charles T. *Stories of the Raftsmen*. Callicoon, NY: Town of Delaware Bicentennial Commission, 1976.

Curtis, Mary. *Rafting Tales*. Narrowsburg, NY: Delaware Valley Arts Alliance, 1983.

Dale, Frank. *Bridges over the Delaware River: A History of Crossings*. New Brunswick: Rutgers University Press 2003.

———. *Delaware Diary: Episodes in the Life of a River*. New Brunswick: Rutgers University Press, 1996.

———. *The Ferry Boat Business on our Delaware River*. N.p.: Xlibris, 2008.

Delaware and Raritan Canal Commission. *Delaware and Raritan Canal State Park Master Plan*. 2nd ed. Trenton, 1977. Available at http://www.dandrcanal.com/pdf/DRCC_MasterPlan_2ndEd_1989.pdf.

DeNio, Pierre. *The Winding Delaware: Written Between the Years 1955–1960*. 2nd. ed. Equinunk, PA: Equinunk Historical Society, 1999.

Douglas, D. B. "Canal Documents: Report and Estimate on the Survey of a Canal Line from Easton to Carpenter's Point." In Samuel Hazard, *The Register of Pennsylvania*, 3, no. 7 (February 1829), 101.

Equinunk Historical Society. *Once Upon a Memory: The Upper Delaware*. 3 vols. Equinunk, PA: Equinunk Historical Society, 1987.

Fisher, Ronald M. *The Appalachian Trail*. Washington, DC: National Geographic Society, 1972.

Fluhr, George J. *A Generation of Suffering on the Upper Delaware Frontier, 1742–1782*. Reprinted from the *News-Eagle*, Hawley, PA. Shohola, PA, 1976.

———. *Quarries, Kilgour, and Pike County, PA*. Milford, PA: Pike County Historical Society, 1984.

Grey, Zane. "A Day on the Delaware." *Recreation* 21, no. 5 (May 1902).

Grove, Ed, et al. *Appalachian Whitewater: The Central Mountains*. Dallas: Taylor Publishing, 1994.

Henn, William F. *The Story of the River Road: Life Along the Delaware from Bushkill to Milford*. Milford, PA: Pike County Historical Society, 1975.

———. *Westfall Township, Gateway to the West*. Milford, PA: Pike County Historical Society, 1978.

Hine, Charles Gilbert. *The Old Mine Road*. Orig. pub. 1909. New Brunswick: Rutgers University Press, 1963.

Hoff, J. Wallace. *Two Hundred Miles on the Delaware: A Canoe Cruise from Its Head-waters to the Falls at Trenton*. Trenton: Brandt Press, 1893.

Hungerford, Edward. *Men of Erie: A Story of Human Effort*. New York: Random House, 1946.

Hunter, Richard. *Power to the City: The Trenton Water Power*. Trenton: New Jersey Department of Transportation, 2005. Available at http://www.state.nj.us/counties/mercer/commissions/pdfs/ch_trentonwaterpower.pdf.

Hunter, William A. *The Walking Purchase*, Historic Pennsylvania Leaflet no. 24. Harrisburg: Pennsylvania Historical and Museum Commission, 1972. Available at http://www.portal.state.pa.us/portal/server.pt/community/things/4280/walking_purchase/478692.

Kraft, Herbert C. *The Archaeology of the Tocks Island Area*. South Orange, NJ: Seton Hall University Museum, 1975.

———. *The Lenape: Archaeology, History, and Ethnography*. Trenton: New Jersey Historical Society, 1987.

Letcher, Gary R. *Waterfalls of the Mid-Atlantic States*. Woodstock, VT: Countryman Press, 2004.

Macha, Rich. "Canoe or Kayak? That is the Question." *Adirondac* 74, no. 2 (March–April 2010), 12–14.

MacLeod, William, and John Benson. *Harpers New York and Erie Rail-road Guide Book*. New York: Harpers and Brothers, 1851.

Mathews, Alfred. *History of Wayne, Pike and Monroe Counties, Pennsylvania*. Philadelphia: R. T. Peck & Co., 1886

McPhee, John. *The Founding Fish*. New York: Farrar, Strauss, Giroux, 2002.

———. *In Suspect Terrain*. New York: Farrar, Strauss, Giroux, 1982.

Menzies, Elizabeth. *Before the Waters: The Upper Delaware Valley*. New Brunswick: Rutgers University Press, 1966

Munsell, William W. *The History of Delaware County 1797–1880*. New York: W. W. Munsell, 1880.

New York–New Jersey Trail Conference. *New Jersey Walk Book*. 2nd. ed. New York: New York–New Jersey Trail Conference, 2004.

Obiso, Laura. *Delaware Water Gap National Recreation Area*. Charleston, SC: Arcadia Publishing, 2008.

O'Reilly, John B. "Down the Delaware River in a Canoe." In O'Reilly, *Athletics and Manly Sport*. Boston: Pilot Pub. Co. 1890.

Pine, Joshua. *The Bygone Era: Rafting on the Delaware, 1883*. Andes, NY: Pepacton Press, 1995.

Punola, John A. *Canoeing and Fishing the Upper Delaware River*. Madison, NJ: Pathfinder Publications, 1979.

Quinlan, James. E. *History of Sullivan County*. Liberty, NY: G. M. Beebe Co., 1873

———. *Tom Quick, the Indian Slayer*. Monticello, NY: DeVoe & Quinlan, 1851.

Riviere, Bill. *Pole, Paddle, and Portage*. New York: Van Nostrand Reinhold Co., 1969.

Rivinus, Willis M. *Guide to the Delaware Canal: Along the Delaware River between Bristol and Easton, Pennsylvania.* [New Hope:] Willis M. Rivinus, 2004.

Schoonmaker, Theodore D. "Tom Quick—Indian Slayer." Read before the Historical Society of Newburgh Bay and the Highlands, March 7, 1904. http://www.jrbooks online.com/HTML-docs/tom_quick_schoonmaker.htm.

Schrabisch, Max. *Archaeology of Delaware River Valley between Hancock and Dingmans Ferry.* Harrisburg: Pennsylvania Historical Commission, 1930.

Senger, Louis C. "The Passing of a Picturesque Industry." *The Quaker* 6, no. 3 (October 1899).

Shafer, Mary A. *Devastation on the Delaware: Stories and Images of the Deadly Flood of 1955.* Ferndale, PA: Word Forge Books, 2005.

Stutz, Bruce. *Natural Lives, Modern Times: People and Places of the Delaware River.* Orig. pub. 1992. Philadelphia: University of Pennsylvania Press, 1998.

Swain, G. F. *Report on the Water-Power of the Middle Atlantic Watershed.* In Census Reports, Tenth Census, June 1, 1880. Washington, DC: Government Printing Office, 1885.

U.S. Department of the Interior, National Park Service. *Spanning the Gap.* Newsletter of the Delaware Water Gap National Recreation Area, 1983–2007. Some issues are available online at http://www.nps.gov/DEWA/parknews/newspaper.htm.

U.S. House of Representatives. *Report of the Chief of Engineers: Survey of the Delaware River between Trenton, New Jersey, and Easton, Pennsylvania.* 43rd Cong., 1st sess. Washington, DC: Government Printing Office, 1873.

Wakefield, Manville B. *Coal Boats to Tidewater: The Story of the Delaware and Hudson Canal.* Orig. pub. 1965.Fleischmanns, NY: Purple Mountain Press, 1992.

Weamer, Paul. *Fly Fishing Guide to the Upper Delaware River.* Mechanicsburg, PA: Stackpole Books, 2007.

Weiss, Harry B, and Grace Weiss. *Rafting on the Delaware River.* Trenton: New Jersey Agricultural Society, 1967.

Wenning, Scott H. *Handbook of the Delaware Indian Language.* Williamsport, PA: Wennawoods Pub., 2000.

Weslager, Clinton Alfred. *The Delaware Indians: A History.* Orig. pub. 1972. New Brunswick: Rutgers University Press, 1990.

Widmer, Kemble. *The Geology and Geography of New Jersey.* Princeton: Van Nostrand, 1964.

Wood, Leslie C. *Holt! T'other Way!* Orig. pub. 1950. 2nd. ed. Equinunk, PA: L. C. Wood, 1991.

Wray, Henry Russell. "Canoeing on the Upper Delaware." *Outing* 20 (April 1892), 31–32.

Index

Eddyside Park, Easton, 143
eels and eel weirs, 23, 50, 52–54, 53, 59, 78
estuary. *See* Delaware estuary
Equinunk, Pennsylvania, 30, 31
Erie Railroad, 43, 55, 74, 75, 82, 84–85, 86

fall line, 179, 191
Famous River Hot Dog Man, 164, *164*, 165
ferries, historic
    Beatty, 190
    Bullman, 144
    Carpenter, 90; (Raub's), 147
    Coryell, 174
    Decker, 121
    Dill, 123
    Dimmick, 109
    Dingman, 96
    Fisher, 109
    Foul Rift, 132
    Four-mile, 188
    Hartzell, 125
    Howell, 188
    Kellam, 40
    London, 159
    Mapes, 83, 89
    Martin, 144
    McKonkey, 186
    Meyer, 125, *125*
    Parsley, 150
    Pearson, 168
    Raub's, 147
    Reading, 173
    Rosenkranz, 106
    Shenk, 149
    Shoemaker, 109
    Skinner, 47
    Stockport, 30
    Trent, 192
    Walker, 117
    Walpack, 107
    Wells, 93, 174
    Westfall, 89
    Yardley, 188
fish and fishing, 21–23
    guides, 22 (*see also appendix*)
Flatbrookville, New Jersey, 107
    floods and flooding, 11

Hurricanes Connie and Diane (1955), 11,
    17, 115, 119, 123, 133, 144, 168, 188
    Pumpkin Flood (1903), 11, 33, 76, 123, 128,
    144, 149, 159
    2004–2006, 11, 89, 102, 109, 120, 161
forks of the Delaware, 137, 145, 153, 155
Fort Namanock, 96
fracking (hydraulic fracturing), 36
French and Indian War, 52, 98, 153
Frenchtown, New Jersey, 159
Frisbie, Dr. Frank, 30
Frys Run Park, Pennsylvania, 149

gage, river stage
    Barryville, 6, 11, 63
    Belvidere, 129
    Callicoon, 44
    Easton, 144
    Frenchtown, 159
    Lambertville, 174
    Matamoras (PA), 90
    Milford (PA), 94
    Riegelsville, 149
    Tocks Island, 117
    Trenton, 3, 190
Marcellus shale, 36
GenOn Energy, power plant, 124, 151
geophysical provinces
    Appalachian Plateau, 26, 37, 56, 71, 87
    Coastal Plain, 179, 191
    Piedmont, 137, 179, 191
    Ridge and Valley, 87, 137
Getter, Charles, 143
Giardia, 20
Giving Pond Recreation Area, 158, 159
glacial features, 87, 112, 127
Golden Nugget Flea Market, 184
Grey Towers (Pinchot estate), 93, 98, 99
Grey, Zane, 16, 57, 61, 63, 68–69, 69
Grumman Aircraft company, canoes, 2

Hancock, New York, 26, 27
Hankins, John, 40
Hankins, New York, 40
Hialeah Picnic Area, 117
High Point, New Jersey, 83
High Point State Park, New Jersey, 112

Gary Letcher has been paddling the Delaware River for more than forty years. As director of youth programs with the New Jersey State Park Service, he led many a trip down the river. He has also served on the Board of Advisors of the Delaware Riverkeeper Network. Although he now lives in Maryland with his family, Mr. Letcher can often be found in his blue canoe on the beautiful Delaware River.